classic
Chinese
recipes

classic
Chinese
recipes

Carol Bowen

Carole Handslip

Kathryn Hawkins

Deh-Ta Hsiung

Wendy Lee

Jenny Stacey

Rosemary Wadey

SIENA

A Siena Book
Siena is an imprint of Parragon

First published in Great Britain in 1998 by
Parragon
13 Whiteladies Road
Clifton
Bristol BS8 1PB

ISBN: 0-75252-745-2

Printed in Italy

Edited, designed and produced by Haldane Mason, London

Acknowledgements
Editor: Linda Doeser
Design: dap ltd
Photography: Karl Adamson, Martin Brigdale, Amanda Heywood,
Joff Lee, Andrew Sydenham
Home Economists: Carol Bowen, Carole Handslip, Kathryn Hawkins,
Deh-Ta Hsiung, Wendy Lee, Jenny Stacey, Rosemary Wadey

Note
Cup measurements in this book are for American cups.
Tablespoons are assumed to be 15 ml. Unless otherwise stated, milk is assumed to be
full-fat, eggs are medium and pepper is freshly ground black pepper.

Contents

Introduction 8

Appetizers 20

Crispy Wontons with Piquant Dipping Sauce **22**
Crispy Seaweed. **23**
Spinach Meatballs. **24**
Spring Rolls. **25**
Pork Pancake Rolls **26**
Lettuce-Wrapped Minced (Ground) Meat . . . **27**
Steamed Cabbage Rolls. **28**
Rice Paper Parcels **29**
Chinese Ravioli. **30**
Deep-Fried Prawns (Shrimp) **31**
Butterfly Prawns (Shrimp) **32**

Sesame Prawn (Shrimp) Toasts. **33**
Deep-Fried Spare Ribs. **34**
Pork with Chilli & Garlic Sauce **35**
Pork Dim Sum **36**
Barbecue Spare Ribs **37**
Spicy Spare Ribs **38**
Barbecue Pork (Char Siu) **39**
Pot Sticker Dumplings **40**
Steamed Duck Buns **41**
Chinese Omelette. **42**
Honeyed Chicken Wings **43**

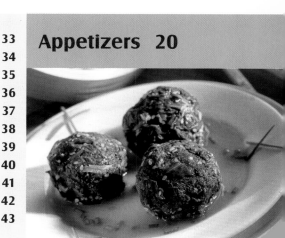

Salads & Pickles 44

Sweet & Sour Tofu
  (Bean Curd) Salad **46**
Sweet & Sour Cucumber **47**
Chinese Hot Salad **48**
Oriental Salad. **49**
Pickled Vegetables. **50**
Hot & Sour Duck Salad **51**
Cucumber & Beansprout Salad **52**
Broccoli, (Bell) Pepper &
  Almond Salad **53**

Soups 54

Mixed Vegetable Soup **56**
Hot & Sour Soup **57**
Vegetarian Hot & Sour Soup **58**
Chinese Cabbage Soup **59**
Wonton Soup **60**
Spinach & Tofu (Bean Curd) Soup. **61**
Beef & Vegetable Noodle Soup **62**
Noodles in Soup **63**
Mushroom & Cucumber Noodle Soup **64**
Fish Soup with Wontons **65**
Seafood & Tofu (Bean Curd) Soup. **66**
(Small) Shrimp & Dumpling Soup. **67**
Fish & Vegetable Soup. **68**

Crab & Ginger Soup. **69**
Three-Flavour Soup **70**
Curried Chicken & Sweetcorn (Corn) Soup. . **71**
Prawn (Shrimp) Soup **72**
Sweetcorn (Corn) & Crabmeat Soup **73**
Peking Duck Soup. **74**
Chicken & Sweetcorn (Corn) Soup **75**
Clear Chicken & Egg Soup. **76**
Chicken Soup with Almonds **77**
Lamb & Rice Soup. **78**
Pork & Szechuan Vegetable Soup **79**

Fish & Seafood 80

Trout with Pineapple 82
Fish with Black Bean Sauce. 83
Crispy Fish with Chillies 84
Braised Fish Fillets 85
Mullet with Ginger 86
Fish in Szechuan Hot Sauce 87
Steamed Snapper with
    Fruit & Ginger Stuffing 88
Scallops in Ginger Sauce. 89
Spiced Scallops 90
Stir-fried Prawns (Shrimp) & Vegetables 91
Stir-fried Prawns (Shrimp) 92
Seafood Combination 93

Szechuan Prawns (Shrimp) 94
Sizzled Chilli Prawns (Shrimp) 95
Prawn (Shrimp) Stir-fry with Lemon Grass . 96
(Small) Shrimp Fu Yong. 97
Sweet & Sour Prawns (Shrimp)
    with Chilli 98
Cantonese Prawns (Shrimp) 99
Sweet & Sour Prawns (Shrimp) 100
Fried Prawns (Shrimp) with Cashews 101
Baked Crab with Ginger 102
Squid in Oyster Sauce & Vegetables 103
Fried Squid Flowers 104
Fish & Ginger Stir-fry 105

Poultry Dishes 106

Chinese Chicken Salad 108
Chicken with Beansprouts 109
Kung Po Chicken with Cashew Nuts. 110
Chicken with Cashew Nuts & Vegetables . . 111
Lemon Chicken. 112
Chicken with Yellow Bean Sauce. 113
Peanut Sesame Chicken 114
Braised Chicken. 115
Chicken with (Bell) Pepper 116
Spicy Peanut Chicken 117
Chicken Fu Yong 118
Bang-Bang Chicken 119

Chilli Chicken. 120
Szechuan Chilli Chicken 121
Chicken Chop Suey. 122
Chicken with Mushrooms 123
Crispy Chicken 124
Chicken with Celery & Cashew Nuts 125
Stir-fried Duck with Broccoli & (Bell) Peppers 126
Aromatic & Crispy Duck 127
Duck in Spicy Sauce 128
Honey & Soy Glazed Duck. 129
Duck with Pineapple 130
Duck with Mangoes 131

Meat Dishes 132

Lamb Meatballs in Soy Sauce 134
Hot Lamb 135
Lamb & Ginger Stir-Fry 136
Stir-fried Lamb with Sesame Seeds. 137
Five-Spiced Lamb 138
Lamb in Mushroom Sauce 139
Lamb in Garlic Sauce 140
Oyster Sauce Beef 141
Beef & Pak Choi. 142
Spicy Beef & Broccoli Stir-Fry 143
Beef & Chilli Black Bean Sauce 144
Beef & Green Beans. 145
(Bell) Peppered Beef Cashew. 146

Chinese Beef 147
Crispy Shredded Beef 148
Sweet & Sour Pork. 149
Spare Ribs with Chilli 150
Deep-Fried Pork with a Soy
    Dipping Sauce 151
Fish-flavoured Shredded Pork. 152
Red Spiced Beef 153
Pork with Plum Sauce 154
Stir-fried Pork with Vegetables 155
Braised Pork & Tofu (Bean Curd). 156
Fish, Aubergine (Eggplant) & Pork. 157

Vegetable Dishes 158

Vegetable Chop Suey. 160
Sweet & Sour Vegetables 161
Vegetable Casserole. 162
Stir-fried Mixed Vegetables. 163
Braised Bamboo Shoots. 164
Golden Needles with Bamboo Shoots. 165
Bamboo Shoots with Green Vegetables. . . . 166
Chinese Braised Vegetables. 167
Stir-fried Cucumber with Ginger & Chilli . . 168
Stir-fried Beansprouts. 169
Beansprouts with (Bell) Peppers 170
Stir-fried Seasonal Vegetables 171
Vegetables in Black Bean Sauce. 172
Vegetable & Nut Stir-fry. 173
Chinese Green Bean Stir-fry 174

Stir-fried Greens 175
Ma-Po Tofu (Bean Curd) 176
Tofu (Bean Curd) & Vegetables with
    Black Bean Sauce 177
Sweet & Sour Tofu (Bean curd) with
    Vegetables 178
Vegetable & Tofu (Bean Curd) Casserole . . . 179
Vegetable Stir-fry with Tofu (Bean Curd) . . 180
Stir-fried Mushrooms, Cucumber &
    Smoked Tofu (Bean Curd) 181
Deep-fried Tofu (Bean Curd) with
    Chinese Five Spice 182
Braised Vegetables with Tofu (Bean Curd) . 183
Aubergine (Eggplant) in Chilli Sauce 184
Spicy Aubergines (Eggplants) 185

Aubergine (Eggplant) in Black Bean Sauce . **186**
Spicy Mushrooms **187**
Money Bags. **188**
Steamed Vegetable Cabbage Rolls **189**
Braised Chinese Leaves. **190**
Creamy Cabbage & Leeks **191**
Lemon Chinese Leaves. **192**
Chinese Leaves Stir-fried in Soy & Honey. . **193**

Lentil Balls with Sweet & Sour Sauce **194**
Crisp Fried Pak Choi with Almonds **195**
Broccoli with Ginger & Orange **196**
Gingered Broccoli **197**
Broccoli in Oyster Sauce **198**
Garlic Spinach. **199**
Spinach with Straw Mushrooms **200**
Chinese Potato Chips **201**

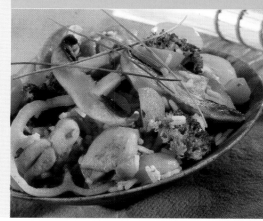

Vegetable Dishes continued

Chinese Fried Rice **204**
Vegetable Fried Rice **205**
Fragrant Steamed Rice
   in Lotus Leaves **206**
Green Fried Rice with Spinach **207**
Egg Fried Rice with Chilli **208**
Egg Fried Rice **209**
Egg Fu Yong with Rice **210**
Special Fried Rice **211**
Fried Rice with Prawns (Shrimp) **212**
Special Fried Rice with Prawns (Shrimp) . . **213**
Chicken & Rice Casserole **214**
Special Fried Rice with Cashew Nuts **215**

Fried Rice & Prawns (Shrimp) **216**
Crab Fried Rice **217**
Rice with Crab & Mussels **218**
Fried Rice with Pork, Tomatoes,
   Peas & Mushrooms **219**

Rice Dishes 202

Chow Mein. **222**
Fried Vegetable Noodles **223**
Mixed Vegetable Chow Mein **224**
Transparent (Cellophane) Noodles with
   Yellow Bean Sauce. **225**
Homemade Noodles with
   Stir-fried Vegetables. **226**
Transparent (Cellophane) Noodles with
   Prawns (Shrimps) **227**
Seafood Chow Mein **228**
Curried Prawn (Shrimp) Noodles **229**
Noodles with Prawns (Shrimp). **230**
Singapore-Style Rice Noodles **231**

Cantonese Fried Noodles **232**
Chicken Noodles **233**
Chicken on Crispy Noodles **234**
Pork Chow Mein. **235**
Chilli Pork Noodles. **236**
Beef Chow Mein **237**
Fried Noodles with Mushrooms
   & Pork **238**
Lamb with Transparent (Cellophane)
   Noodles. **239**

Noodle Dishes 220

Sweet Fruit Wontons **242**
Banana Pastries. **243**
Mango Dumplings **244**
Sweet Rice. **245**
Honeyed Rice Puddings **246**
Mango Mousse **247**
Poached Allspice Pears **248**
Chinese Custard Tarts **249**
Ginger Lychees with
   Orange Sorbet **250**
Chinese Fruit Salad. **251**

Desserts 240

Index 252

Introduction

Chinese cuisine was known to and appreciated by a small elite of westerners privileged to travel to the East, but for a long time it was virtually unknown outside China. Chinese settlers in San Francisco first introduced America to the pleasures of their cuisine, especially during the years of the Gold Rush and the building of the Pacific Railroad. However, it was not until much later in the twentieth century that Chinese cuisine found its way to Britain and other parts of Europe. Once it had found a foothold, however, there was no turning back, as its popularity rocketed across the world. Even then, it remained very much in the realm of restaurants and professionals and it is only comparatively recently that western cooks have started preparing Chinese dishes at home.

CHINESE CUISINE

The nature of Chinese cuisine has been shaped by two very different elements – one practical and the other philosophical and religious. For the majority of Chinese peasants, life was bitterly harsh. They were at the mercy of

natural disasters, from floods to failed harvests. Not only was food often in short supply, but fuel with which to cook it was always a scarce commodity. That a cuisine of international renown should have developed from such an unpromising and uncompromising situation is a remarkable example of ingenuity and imagination.

The perennial shortage of fuel brought about the development of fast-cooking techniques, the best known of which is stir-frying. Slicing, chopping, dicing and shredding food into very small pieces meant that it could be cooked more quickly and required less wood for the fire. Filling foods, such as rice and wheat products, depending on what grew best locally, were used to satisfy the appetite or sometimes just to appease hunger. Even when they were available, meat, fish and fresh vegetables had to be used sparingly. Consequently, if only a small portion of a savoury sauce was all there was to flavour a bland bowl of rice, it needed to be packed full of delicious tastes. A careful use of herbs and spices and the development of flavourings, such as soy, hoi-sin and fermented bean sauces, was the practical – and happy – solution to this problem.

Of course, not everyone in China was poor and the influence of the wealthy and aristocratic is also reflected in modern Chinese cooking. One of the first and certainly one of the most important appointments made by a new Emperor of China was the court chef. No mere cook, he was an exalted person with the heavy responsibility of ensuring that food served in the royal household kept its members physically and spiritually fit and healthy. There was also a natural sense of rivalry with his predecessors and each new chef worked to outdo the skills of previous ones and constantly sought new flavours, ingredients and recipes. Consequently, a kind of haute cuisine grew up in Peking, China's one-thousand-year-old capital, and in other parts of the North.

The second major influence on Chinese cuisine is connected with the philosophical and religious belief that everything in the universe is balanced and harmonious. As Yin balances Yang, day balances night and man

balances woman, so with food, the textures, colours and flavours should balance each other to create a harmonious whole. Harmony is achieved through contrast, so a crispy dish is served with one that has a creamy texture, and a spicy dish is accompanied by a mild, sweet-tasting one. Balance of the four basic flavours – sweet, sour, bitter and salty – may even be encompassed in a single dish.

REGIONAL COOKING

China is a huge country, covering an area of over 9,500 million square kilometres (about the same size as the United States). The terrain varies widely from the high Tibetan Plateau to the flat flood plain of the Yangtze River. Climate varies accordingly, too, so it is hardly surprising that there are many distinctive regional styles of cooking.

Northern China – Shantung and Honan

This region, stretching to the borders of Inner Mongolia, is dry and quite arid. Wheat, rather than rice, is the staple ingredient, giving rise to all kinds of noodles, breads, pancakes, steamed buns and dumplings. Cooking methods tend to be simple, mainly roasting and boiling, and strong-tasting dipping sauces are characteristic. Sesame seeds, now widely used throughout China, were first introduced in the North by invading Tartars and the seeds and oil still feature prominently there. An abundant supply of seafood is to be found on the coast, and the Yellow River is a source of excellent freshwater fish. Sweet-and-sour carp is a speciality. Fine grapes and peaches are grown in Shantung, which is also the homeland of pak choi.

China's capital is now more accurately written as Beijing in English characters, but in cookery terms will probably remain Peking for decades. Its style of cooking is elegant and light, rather than rich. From time to time the city was invaded by Tartars and the Moslem traditions of Central Asia have had their effect on Peking cuisine, not least in that this is one place in China where pork is not the most commonly-eaten meat.

Southern China – Canton

Cantonese cuisine is the best known in the West because the first immigrants to America and Europe came from there. The province of Kwangtung has an excellent climate for agriculture, producing a plentiful supply of fresh vegetables throughout the year. These feature in Cantonese dishes, usually quickly stir-fried and served with a little additional sauce. Sugar cane, tangerines, mandarins, orange and loquats grow in the semi-tropical valleys and these are often combined with meat and poultry in a sweet-and-sour sauce.

Fish and seafood are abundantly available and Cantonese dishes feature prawns (shrimp), crab, abalone or scallops. Crab or lobster and ginger is a classic combination. Steaming is a favourite method of cooking, although the region is also famous for char siu roasting, a process in which the meat, often pork, is marinated for a long period and then roasted very quickly. Dim sum, small steamed parcels, which in China are usually served as an afternoon snack in tea houses, originated in Canton. Fish-flavoured meat, that is using oyster sauce and other flavourings normally associated with cooking fish to prepare meat, is also a speciality of the region. Spices tend to be aromatic rather than hot, and light soy sauce is preferred to dark because it affects the colour of other ingredients less. Other popular Cantonese sauces are plum, hoi-sin, oyster and black bean. Cantonese cuisine is very sophisticated and varied. This results partly from an influx of chefs from the royal household in 1644, when the Ming Dynasty was overthrown, and partly from Canton's role as the first major Chinese trading port open to foreign influences.

Western China – Szechuan and Yunnan

A fertile mountain-ringed basin, Szechuan is a prosperous region famous for producing robustly spiced dishes which feature chillies, hot pepper oil, sesame paste and Szechuan peppercorns. Pungent vegetables, such as onions and spring onions (scallions), are extensively used.

Not all Szechuan food is hotly spiced, however. The region is also known for a method of cooking meat and vegetables in a clear broth, flavoured with wine and spices, until it has reduced to a thick, rich sauce, and for prolonged dry-frying, which results in crisp, well-coloured dishes.

Both Szechuan and its southern neighbour Yunnan are well known for food preservation techniques, which include salting, smoking, drying and pickling. Szechuan hot pickle and Yunnan cured, smoked ham are local specialities.

Eastern China – Fukien, Kiangsu and Chekiang

This region is rich in fruit and vegetables for, lying on the Yangtze delta, it is one of the most fertile in China. Wheat and rice are both grown, as well as corn, potatoes, peanuts and soya beans. Freshwater fish are widely available and Kiangsu and Chekiang are well known for seafood. Kiangsu, north of the river is famous for dumplings, noodles and pork dishes, too.

South of the river lies Chekiang and the style of cooking here is known as Kiangche, a combination of the two provinces' names. Food is sophisticated and has absorbed many influences from other parts of China, not least because both Hangchow and Nanking have been the capitals of China in the past. Duck dishes and spare ribs are specialities. This region also produces the best rice wine in China, in Shaoxing.

The huge port of Shanghai has a culinary style all of its own which is characterized by richness and elegance. As a major trade port in the nineteenth century, it absorbed many foreign influences, which can be seen in the use of ingredients such as butter, milk and lard. To the south, Fukien makes good use of its agricultural land and abundant seafood in a style strongly influenced by its Cantonese neighbour.

THE CHINESE MEAL

Family meals also observe the Chinese approach to a life of harmony and balance. Three or even four generations gather peacefully together to share the food, with everyone taking only what they need from the communal selection of dishes placed on the table. To select an especially delicious piece of food with the chopsticks and offer it to someone else is a mark of both respect and affection. All the savoury dishes, including soup, are placed on the table at once. Individual portions are never served. Family meals do not usually include a dessert; these are usually served only at banquets and on very special occasions. Fresh fruit may be eaten at the end of the meal and sweet snacks are often eaten between meals.

The choice of dishes for any meal should reflect balance through contrast. The same main ingredients are to be avoided and a hot and spicy dish should be served with a sweet-and-sour dish, for example. The number of dishes served at a family meal depends on the number of people. An easy rule of thumb is to serve one dish per person although, of course, everyone will share all the dishes, plus soup and rice or noodles. It is always wiser to increase the number of dishes, rather than to increase the size of individual dishes, as this produces far greater variety. It is sensible to avoid too many dishes that require last-minute attention.

A formal dinner has more strictly-observed rules. The number of guests is usually twelve or fourteen, always an even number, and the same number of dishes as people are served. Appetizers, perhaps one cold and three hot dishes, are served first, followed by soup. A main course of, say, six dishes follows, with rice or noodles. Finally, two desserts complete the meal. Balance and harmony are, again, essential to the Chinese meal and dishes are always garnished in different ways.

The Chinese Store-cupboard

Many Chinese dishes can be prepared with ingredients commonly used in the West – spring onions (scallions), garlic, (bell) peppers, peanut oil, many herbs, fish and meat. Some more unfamiliar and exotic ingredients may need an explanation. They will usually be available from Chinese foodstores, some health-food shops and some supermarkets.

Baby Corn Cobs have a sweet flavour and a crunchy texture. They are available fresh, frozen and canned.

Bamboo Shoots are mild-flavoured and widely available in cans. Drain and rinse thoroughly before use. Fresh shoots can sometimes be found in Chinese foodstores. They can be stored in fresh water in a covered jar in the refrigerator for up to 1 week.

Basil is a popular herb in Asian cooking and a number of different varieties are used.

Bean Sauce may be black or yellow and is made from crushed, salted soya beans mixed with flour and spices, such as ginger and chilli, to make a thick paste. It is used both as a flavouring during cooking and as a condiment. It is sold in cans and jars and once opened, should be stored in the refrigerator.

Beansprouts from mung or soya beans are widely available from supermarkets. Canned and frozen sprouts are also sold, but these are not usually so crisp as fresh. You can sprout your own beans very easily.

Black Beans are salted fermented soya beans, available in packets or cans.

Cardamom is an aromatic spice, available in two forms – small green pods and large black pods. Use the green variety for Chinese cooking.

Cashews are often used to provide extra flavour and texture, particularly in chicken dishes.

Chilli Bean Paste is a fermented bean paste mixed with hot chillies and other seasonings. It can vary from mild to fiery hot.

Chilli Oil is a hot, red oil flavoured with chillies and sometimes containing chilli flakes. Use it sparingly. You can make your own by infusing a few dried chillies in a small bottle of oil for several days.

Chilli Sauce is widely used as a dipping sauce and a flavouring in cooking. Made from chillies, vinegar, sugar and salt, it is extremely hot.

Chillies may be red or green and vary in size, shape and spiciness. As a rule, dark green chillies are hotter than pale green or red ones, but this is not invariably the case. Thin, pointed chillies tend to be hotter than short, blunt ones. Dried chillies are usually hotter than fresh. Take care when handling chillies, as the juice stings, and always wash your hands thoroughly afterwards. For a milder taste, remove and discard the seeds before using the chilli.

Chinese Five-Spice Powder is a distinctive mixture of star anise, fennel seeds, cloves, cinnamon and Szechuan pepper. It is very pungent and should be used sparingly. It is different from Indian five-spice powder.

Chinese Leaves (Cabbage) are widely available in two different varieties. One has a pale green, tightly wrapped elongated head, rather like a Cos (romaine) lettuce, and the other is shorter and fatter with yellow or green leaves.

Chinese Pancakes are made from flour and water, with no added seasoning. They are available fresh and frozen. Thaw frozen pancakes before use.

Coriander (Cilantro) is also known as Chinese parsley. It has a distinctive flavour and also makes an attractive garnish. Tearing rather than chopping the leaves results in a more subtle flavour.

Garlic is a primary seasoning in Chinese food. It may be chopped, crushed or pickled, depending on how strong you wish the flavour to be. Store in a cool, dry place, but not in the refrigerator.

Ginger has an unmistakable, sharp, pungent taste. Fresh ginger root is widely used in savoury dishes and stem (preserved) ginger in sweet ones. Ground dried ginger is not an adequate substitute. Look for plump, unwrinkled roots, then peel and grate, shred, slice or chop before using.

Hoi-sin Sauce is made from soy beans, sugar, flour, vinegar, salt, garlic, chillies and sesame seed oil. Available in cans or bottles, it will keep in the refrigerator for several months.

Lemon Grass is an aromatic herb with a strong, lemon flavour. It is available fresh, bottled or dried as a powder. Chop or slice the lower part of the stem to use.

Lily Buds are also known as golden needles. They are available dried from Chinese foodstores and should be soaked before use.

Lotus Leaves are usually sold dried and should be soaked in hot water before use. They are very large and often used as a wrapping for other ingredients when steaming.

Mangetout (Snow Peas) are tender pea pods with flat peas. They are sweet with a crisp texture. The whole pod is cooked and eaten.

Mushrooms, both fresh and dried, are widely used in Chinese cookery, very often for their texture rather than their flavour. Straw mushrooms are slippery. Dried mushrooms must be soaked in warm water for 25–30 minutes. The soaking liquid may be used as stock. Cut the hard stems of the mushrooms and use the caps.

Noodles may be made from a variety of ingredients, including rice, wheat and pulses, and most types are available both fresh and dried. Follow the packet instructions for cooking.

Oyster Sauce is a thick, soy-based sauce used as a flavouring in Cantonese cooking. It is available in bottles and will keep in the refrigerator for several months.

Pak Choi is an elongated dark green vegetable with smooth white stems. It is available from Chinese foodstores and some large supermarkets.

Plum Sauce has a sweet-and-sour fruity flavour.

Rice comes in many forms. White long-grain is the type most widely used in savoury dishes, while glutinous rice is used for desserts.

Rice Vinegar is available as red or white. Red rice vinegar is made from fermented rice and has a distinctive dark colour and depth of flavour. White rice vinegar is distilled from rice wine and has a strong flavour. It is available from Chinese supermarkets, but you can substitute cider vinegar, if necessary.

Rice Wine is usually made from glutinous rice and is available from Chinese foodstores. It is different from sake or Japanese rice wine and a better substitute, if it is unavailable, is dry sherry.

Sesame Oil is an aromatic oil made from toasted sesame seeds. It is not usually used for cooking, but for flavouring and is generally added to a dish shortly before serving.

Sesame Seeds add texture and a nutty flavour to dishes. Dry-frying them adds colour and accentuates the flavour.

Shallots are members of the onion family, but smaller and milder in taste.

Soy Sauce is an important Chinese seasoning and is made from fermented soy beans, yeast, salt and sugar. It may be light or dark. It is best used with other ingredients, such as wine or stock, for cooking, and mixed with other sauces, vinegar and strong flavourings, such as garlic and ginger, for dipping sauces.

Spring Onions (Scallions) are slender onions with small bulbs. Sometimes a recipe specifies separating the white and green parts – the white part is the main part of the onion, the green part is essentially the leaves.

Spring Roll Skins are thin wrappers made from wheat or rice flour and water. Wheat skins are usually sold frozen and must be thawed before use. Rice skins are dried and need gentle soaking before use. Both are available in a range of sizes from Chinese foodstores.

Szechuan Peppercorns are aromatic, hot red peppercorns. They are best used roasted and ground.

Szechuan Preserved Vegetable is a speciality from western China. It is the root of a variety of mustard green pickled in salt and chillies. It should be rinsed thoroughly before use. Other Chinese pickles include winter pickle and snow pickle.

Tofu (Bean Curd) is a soy product that is sold in blocks. Firm tofu (bean curd) is most suitable for stir-frying, but other types, including marinated and smoked, are available. It has a fairly bland flavour, but readily absorbs the flavours of other ingredients.

Water Chestnuts are the bulbs of an Asian water-plant and not related to the edible chestnut. They are sometimes available fresh from Chinese foodstores and easily obtained canned, whole or sliced.

Wonton Wrappers are readily available from Chinese foodstores. They are paper-thin squares of dough.

Wood (Cloud) Ears are a dried black fungus, sold in plastic bags in Chinese supermarkets. Soak them in a bowl of warm water for 20 minutes, drain and rinse in cold water before use.

Equipment

Traditional Chinese equipment, especially if you buy it from Chinese stores, is usually inexpensive. 'New improved' western versions may prove to be more expensive and less satisfactory.

Chinese Cleaver is a very finely balanced tool with an extremely sharp blade. Good, strong, sharp kitchen knives are adequate, but it is worth learning how to use a cleaver. Heavy cleavers can be used for chopping through bones, such as spare ribs, while lighter ones are perfect for thinly slicing vegetables. The point can be used for precision work, such as deveining prawns (shrimp).

Chopsticks are not difficult to use. Place one chopstick in the hollow between the thumb and index finger of your right hand if right-handed or left hand if left-handed. Keeping that chopstick completely still, hold the other between the tips of the index and middle finger, steady its upper half against the base of the index finger and use the tip of the thumb to keep it in place. To pick up food, move the upper chopstick with index and middle fingers. When eating rice and other difficult-to-hold foods, it is better to lift the bowl to the chin and 'shovel' the food into the mouth with the chopsticks, as the Chinese do. It is worth learning to use chopsticks as, after all, Chinese food is designed to be eaten this way.

A pair of long chopsticks is a wonderful, multi-purpose cooking tool. Chopsticks can be used for stirring, whipping and beating, lifting food in and out of a wok, fluffing up rice and separating noodles. They are available from most cookware shops, Chinese foodstores and restaurants.

Steamers may be as simple as a plate placed on a rack over boiling water in a covered saucepan. A wok with a well-fitting lid is ideal. Traditional Chinese steamers are made of bamboo, a material which allows excess steam to escape. They are designed to stand one on top of the other, so that several dishes can be steamed simultaneously. They come in a wide range of sizes and are available in Chinese supermarkets and good cookware shops.

Strainer made of metal with a long bamboo handle makes lifting foods from hot oil easier. A long-handled slotted spoon will do as well.

Wok is a round-based utensil, traditionally made of cast-iron. Its design means that it conducts heat more evenly than other types of cooking utensils, such as a frying pan (skillet). Because of its shape, the ingredients always return to the centre, where the heat is most intense, however vigorously you stir. The wok is also ideal for deep-frying – its conical shape requires far less oil than a flat-based deep-fryer. It has more depth, which means more heat, and more cooking surface, which, in turn, means a larger quantity of food can be cooked at the same time. Besides being ideal for stir-frying and deep-frying, the wok is also used for braising, steaming, boiling and poaching – in other words, the whole spectrum of Chinese cooking methods can be executed in a single utensil. For safety, however, you should always use a wok stand when deep-frying, steaming or braising.

All new woks, other than non-stick ones, must be seasoned before use. Wash thoroughly in hot water and detergent to remove the manufacturer's protective coating of oil. Dry the wok well and set it over a low heat. When the metal heats up, wipe the inside with a pad of kitchen paper (paper towels) that has been dipped in oil. Be careful not to burn your fingers. Repeat this process with fresh oiled paper until it remains clean. The wok is now seasoned. After use, it should be wiped out and rinsed in hot water without detergent. A wok brush may help remove any stubborn food. Dry the wok thoroughly. If you do not use the wok frequently, coat it with a little vegetable oil to prevent rusting. If the wok does rust, scour the rust off and then repeat the seasoning process.

Wok Brush is a bundle of stiff, split bamboo used for cleaning the wok. An ordinary kitchen brush is just as good.

Wok Lid is a dome-shaped cover, usually made of aluminium. Lids are sometimes supplied with the wok, but can also be bought separately. It is important that it fits snugly.

Wok Scoop and Spatula are often supplied with a wok. If they are not, it is worth investing in them, especially a scoop. This is a flat, slotted implement for adding ingredients and seasonings to a wok and for tossing the food around during stir-frying.

Wok Stand provides a secure base for the wok during deep-frying, braising and steaming. It is made of metal and may be a simple, open-sided frame or a solid metal ring with holes punched around the sides.

Wok Trivet is used as a stand when steaming on a plate. Trivets may be made of wood or metal.

Cooking Techniques

Chinese food generally takes longer to prepare than it does to cook, so it is important to start the preparation of each dish as far in advance as possible. Ensure that all of the vegetables are chopped and the sauces are blended before you start cooking.

Chopping

Cut the ingredients into small, uniform pieces to ensure that the food cooks evenly. Shredding vegetables thinly and slicing them diagonally ensures fast cooking, as it increases the area in contact with the hot oil.

Stir-frying

This is the method of cooking most commonly associated with Chinese cuisine. The correct piece of equipment for this is a wok, as it gives the best results. However, any large frying pan (skillet) or heavy saucepan will do.

Stir-frying in a wok is very healthy way to cook, as it uses very little oil and preserves the nutrients in the food. It is very important that the wok is pre-heated to very hot before you begin to cook. This can be tested by holding your hand flat about 7.5 cm/3 inches above the base of the interior, when you should be able to feel the heat radiating from it. The success in stir-frying lies in having the wok at just the right temperature and in ensuring correct timing when cooking the food.

Before you begin cooking, make sure that all the required ingredients have been prepared, so that they are ready to be added to the wok the instant the oil is the right heat. Cooking at too low a temperature or for too long will produce inferior results.

Add a small amount of oil to the hot wok and heat it, then add, in stages, the various ingredients to be cooked. Those requiring longer cooking go in first, while those that require only very little cooking go in last.

Using a wok scoop or long-handled metal or wooden spoon, constantly stir the ingredients for a very short time. This ensures that all the ingredients come into contact with the hot oil, so the natural juices of the food are sealed in, leaving it crisp and colourful. The technique also ensures that all the ingredients are evenly cooked. Stir-fry dishes look and taste best when served immediately.

Deep-frying

Use a wok, deep-fryer or heavy-based saucepan. When deep-frying in a wok, use enough oil to give a depth of about 5 cm/2 inches. Heat it over a moderate heat until you can see a faint haze of smoke rising before gently lowering in the food to be fried. Make sure the oil is up to temperature before adding the food, so that the hot oil cooks the food quickly on the outside, forming a protective seal. If the oil is not hot enough, the food will act like a sponge and become soggy and greasy. Before frying the food, make sure that is thoroughly dry to prevent the oil from splattering. If the food has been marinated, let it drain well. If it is in batter, wait for it to stop dripping.

Cook the food in small batches to avoid overcrowding the wok, as this can reduce the temperature of the oil and lead to unevenly cooked food. Always remove the food from the oil with a long-handled bamboo strainer or slotted spoon and drain thoroughly on kitchen paper (paper towels) to absorb any excess oil. Once it has been strained, cooking oil can be used up to three times, but only for the same type of food. Always use a wok stand to ensure that the wok is steady when deep-frying.

Steaming

This is a very popular method of cooking. There are two basic methods. In the first, food is arranged on a plate or in a bowl, which is then put inside a steamer on a perforated rack and placed over a large pan of boiling water. The plate or bowl can also be put inside a wok. The steam passes through the steamer and cooks the food. Larger items of food, such as dumplings, can be placed straight on to the rack or laid on cabbage leaves or soaked lotus leaves. The leaves not only prevent the food from falling through, but also add extra flavour.

In the second method, the bowl of ingredients is partially immersed in boiling water. The food is cooked partly by the boiling water and partly by the steam it produces.

Braising

This is a similar technique to that used in the West and is generally used for cooking tougher cuts of meat and firm varieties of vegetables. The ingredients are stir-fried until lightly browned, then stock is added and brought to the boil. The heat is reduced to simmering until cooking is complete. Red braising uses the same method, but the food is braised in a reddish-brown liquid, such as soy sauce. This sauce can be re-used.

Roasting

This method is used much less in China than it is in the West because most domestic kitchens do not have an oven. It is popular in restaurant kitchens, particularly in Canton and Peking. It usually involves hanging the meat or poultry on a hook in the oven or cooking it on a rotisserie.

Basic Recipes

Common to many recipes are standard preparations, such as stock, plain boiled rice and cornflour (cornstarch) paste. Dipping sauces are also served with many dishes.

Chinese Stock

This basic stock is used not only for soup-making, but also for general use in Chinese cooking. It will keep for 4–5 days in the refrigerator. Alternatively, it can be frozen in small containers and thawed as required. These quantities make 2.5 litres/4½ pints/11 cups.

750 g/1 lb 10 oz chicken pieces
750 g/1 lb 10 oz pork spare ribs
3.75 litres/6 pints/15 cups cold water
3–4 pieces fresh ginger root, crushed
3–4 spring onions (scallions), each tied into a knot
3–4 tbsp Chinese rice wine or dry sherry

Trim off any excess fat from the chicken and spare ribs, then chop them into large pieces. Put the chicken and ribs into a large pan with the water, ginger and spring onion (scallion) knots, bring to the boil and skim off the scum. Reduce the heat and simmer, uncovered, for at least 2–3 hours. Strain the stock, discarding the chicken, pork, ginger and spring onions (scallions). Pour the liquid back into the pan and add the Chinese rice wine or sherry. Bring to the boil, then simmer for 2–3 minutes. Leave to cool, then store in the refrigerator.

Plain Rice

Use long-grain or patna rice or, better still, try Thai fragrant rice. If using Thai fragrant rice, do not add salt during cooking. This amount serves 4.

225 g/8 oz/1¼ cups long-grain rice
about 200 ml/7 fl oz/1 cup cold water
pinch of salt
½ tsp oil (optional)

Rinse the rice once. Place the rice in a saucepan and add just enough water so that there is no more than 1 cm/½ inch above the surface of the rice. Bring to the boil, add salt and oil, if using, and stir once to prevent the grains sticking to the base of the pan. Reduce the heat to very, very low, cover and cook for 15–20 minutes. Remove from the heat and let stand, covered, for about 10 minutes. Fluff up the rice with chopsticks or a fork before serving.

Cornflour (Cornstarch) Paste

This is made by mixing 1 part cornflour (cornstarch) with about 1½ parts cold water. Stir until smooth and use to thicken sauces.

Dipping Sauces

Traditional sauces for Chinese food
include the following.

Sweet & Sour Sauce

A tasty sweet-and-sour sauce which goes well with
many deep-fried foods. Store in a well-sealed
container in the refrigerator.

2 tbsp ginger marmalade
2 tbsp orange marmalade
1/4 tsp salt
1 tbsp white rice vinegar or cider vinegar
1 tbsp hot water

Combine all the ingredients in a small bowl, mixing
well.

Salt & Pepper Sauce

This dry-fried salt and pepper mixture made with
Szechuan peppercorns is found throughout China as a
dip for deep-fried foods. The dry-frying method brings
out all the flavour of the peppercorns.

4 tbsp Szechuan peppercorns
1/3 cup coarse sea salt

Preheat a wok or heavy-based frying pan (skillet) over
a medium heat. Add the peppercorns and salt and stir-
fry until the mixture begins to brown. Remove the
wok or pan from the heat and cool. Grind the mixture
in a grinder or in a mortar with a pestle.

Spring Onion (Scallion) Sauce

Heated oil poured over the seasonings brings out their
full flavour. The sauce goes well with meat and
poultry dishes.

3 tbsp finely chopped spring onions (scallions)
3 tbsp finely grated fresh ginger root
2 tsp salt
1 tsp light soy sauce
3 tbsp peanut or sunflower oil

Place the spring onions (scallions), ginger root, salt
and soy sauce in a small, heatproof bowl. Put the oil
into a small pan and cook over a moderate heat until
it begins to smoke. Remove the pan from the heat and
pour the oil over the seasonings. Let stand for at least
2–3 hours before using to allow the flavours to blend.

Garnishes

Chinese food should always please the eye as well as
the palate. Dishes are often intricately garnished with
delicately cut vegetables, adding colour as well as a
finishing touch. It is traditional to garnish each dish
differently. Garnishes may be as simple or elaborate
as you wish. The simplest would just be sprigs of
fresh herbs, such as coriander (cilantro), chervil or
chives, shreds of spring onion (scallion), chilli, lemon
zest or radish, or twists of lime or lemon. Some
elaborate garnishes are described below.

Cucumber Fans can be made by cutting a piece of
cucumber about 7.5 cm/3 inches long and dividing it
in half lengthways. Lay a piece of cucumber, cut side
down, and using a small, sharp knife, cut thin slices
along the length to within 1 cm/1/2 inch of the end.
Carefully turn alternate slices over, in half and tuck in.
Place in iced water until required.

Carrot Flowers are made from a peeled carrot.
Using a sharp knife, make about five or six tiny V-
shaped cuts along the length. then cut into slices: the
V-shapes will ensure that each slice looks like a flower.

Fresh Chilli Flowers are made from unpeeled,
trimmed chillies. Make four cuts lengthways from the
stem of the chilli to the tip to make four sections.
Remove and discard the seeds. Soak the chillies in cold
water; they will 'flower' in the water.

Prawn (Shrimp) Crackers are compressed slivers
of prawn (shrimp) and flour paste, which expand into
large, translucent crisps (chips) when deep-fried.

Radish Flowers are made from trimmed radishes.
Using a sharp knife, make V-shaped cuts around the
top and remove the cut parts to expose the white of
the radish.

Radish Roses require trimmed radishes. Then,
holding the knife flat to the radish skin, make short,
vertical cuts around the sides, as if you were shaving
off the outer skin, but without detaching each 'petal'.
Plunge straight into iced water.

Tomato Roses are made by peeling off the skin of
the tomato in one long strip, using a sharp knife. Curl
the skin into a circle.

Chinese Tea

Tea grows in almost every part of China, but was not used as a beverage until the sixth century and was not commonly drunk for a further 200 years. It is undoubtedly the most popular beverage in the country today and, together with fuel, oil, rice, soy sauce and vinegar, is regarded as one of the seven essentials for any household.

Tea is served throughout the day in China and is always offered to visitors. Not to offer tea is a mark of extreme discourtesy. In times when people were too poverty-stricken to afford tea, they would offer boiled water, calling it white tea, rather than be inhospitable to a visitor. However, tea is never drunk with food, except in a few places in the south. Even in tea houses, where people go for snacks and dim sum, tea is drunk before and after eating, but not with the food. This is because most food contains oil and this detracts from the flavour of the tea, spoiling its taste. Tea may be served before a meal and is a popular choice afterwards, as it is so refreshing.

There are hundreds of varieties of Chinese tea, the best coming from the south, where the climate is well suited to its cultivation. However, tea can be divided into two main categories: green, unfermented tea and black, fermented tea. To make green tea, the leaves are withered in the sun, during which about 60 per cent of the water content is lost. The leaves are then heat-treated to prevent fermentation, before being dried. This results in a very delicate-tasting, pale-coloured brew and is the most popular kind of tea in China. For black tea, the leaves are also withered after picking. They are then broken up to release enzymes and during the oxidation process, they turn brown. They are then dried, which turns them black.

The best green tea is said to be lung ching from Hanchow in the East of the country. Perhaps gunpowder tea is the best-known green tea in the West. It is so called because the leaves are tightly rolled into small balls and expand almost explosively when hot water is added. The best black tea is said to come from a mountainous region on the borders of Fukien. It is known as 'cliff' tea because of the precipitous heights at which it grows. One of the best-known varieties of this tea is called Ti Kuan Yin – Iron Goddess of Mercy. Chinese black teas are more popular than green ones in the West and varieties, such as Pouchong, also known as Congou and Keemum, are widely available.

Much of the tea exported by China is blended and known by a blend name rather than the name of the plantation. Most of it is large-leaf, requiring a longer brewing time than small- or broken-leaf teas. There are other types of Chinese tea available in the West, the best-known probably being jasmine tea. This may be either black or green leaves mixed with dried white jasmine flowers. It is very fragrant and slightly sweet. Chrysanthemum tea is similar, in that black or green tea leaves are mixed with dried white or yellow flower heads. However it is not so powerfully fragrant as jasmine tea. Smoked teas are fermented black teas that have been smoke-dried to produce a characteristic tarry flavour. Probably the best known is lapsang souchong. Finally, brick tea is something of a novelty, nowadays brought back from China by tourists as a souvenir. Before modern transportation, black teas were steamed and compressed into bricks to make transporting them easier. The required amount could then be broken off or grated. The tea usually incorporated a mixture of coarse leaves, stems and tea dust and was not of very high quality. The bricks are still produced and embossed with attractive symbols and designs.

Tea-making is regarded as an art in China. The choice of utensils and water is as important as the variety of leaves. Kettles are earthenware and teapots and cups are porcelain or earthenware. Tea-making utensils should always be washed separately to avoid contamination from greasy dishes. Spring water, melted snow, river water and rainwater – all pollution-free – are highly prized. Water must be freshly boiled, as re-boiled water loses its oxygen content and spoils the flavour of the tea. The teapot must be rinsed with boiling water to warm it thoroughly before the tea is added. Once made, the tea should be allowed to infuse for 3 minutes before being poured. It is always drunk very hot without milk or sugar.

Alcoholic Drinks

Wine is an essential part of a formal meal. In fact, wine is never drunk on its own, but always as an accompaniment to food. Hardly surprisingly, rice wine is the most popular alcoholic drink in China. It is golden in colour and so is also known as yellow wine. The best is said to come from Shaoxing, its quality being attributed to the waters of the nearby lake and to a special type of yeast. The fact that it may be matured for as long as forty years probably also contributes to its fine flavour. Generally, however, it goes on sale when it has been matured for ten years. It is made from a mixture of rice, glutinous rice and millet. Another high-quality, slightly sweet rice wine, Chen Gang, comes from Fukien. Home-made glutinous rice wines are also popular.

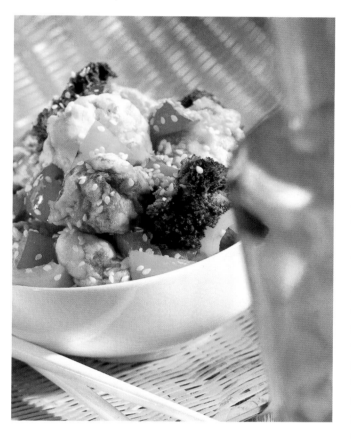

Another popular drink is not really a wine at all. Made from sorghum, a kind of millet, Mao Tai is actually stronger than pure vodka. In the eighteenth century a salt merchant from north China was so mesmerized by the beauty of the village of Mao Tai and the surrounding countryside in South-West China that he decided to settle there. He started to make 'wine', using water from the river flowing through a nearby gorge. It rapidly became very popular throughout the whole of China and, following its introduction to the West at an international exposition in 1919, it achieved worldwide fame.

A number of other, highly potent spirits are produced in various regions of China. Some are considered to have medicinal properties and others are served as after-dinner liqueurs. Many Chinese people regard it as perfectly normal to drink spirits such as these throughout a meal, but this has little appeal to Western palates. In general, rice wine is served in regions south of the Yangtze river, where rice grows abundantly and the climate is warmer, while more powerful spirits are served in the north, where sorghum and millet grow and the climate is colder.

It may be something of a surprise to learn that the art of making wine with grapes has been known in China since the seventh century. However, it is only comparatively recently that the production of table wines has become of any importance. Cabernet and Muscat wines are produced in Shantung and both red and white wines are made in Manchuria. While drinkable, they are not yet of major interest, not even to the people of China.

If you are not going to serve rice wine throughout the meal, as the Chinese people do themselves, a minimum of one red and one white wine is essential for a formal occasion. Choose a light white wine to accompany appetizers and stir-fries and a full-bodied red wine for more robust dishes. If you are going to serve only one type of wine, a full-bodied red, such as Burgundy, is the better choice. If the occasion is a special one, you can extend the wine list to include sherry or even Champagne to begin with. Brandy, liqueurs or even whisky may be served at the end of the meal, if you are not making tea.

The Chinese never drink wine or other alcoholic drinks with the rice dish that is served at the end of a formal meal. This is because it is thought to be inappropriate, even sacrilegious to eat this valuable grain while drinking a beverage made from grain.

Drinking in China is a social activity and a solitary drinker is a very rare sight. The Chinese do not follow the western custom of individuals sipping their wine throughout the meal as desired, but drink with formal toasts. Given that a formal meal usually involves at least ten people and everyone needs to toast everyone else and return the toasts, copious quantities of wine may be consumed.

The toasting ritual begins with the host toasting the guest of honour and then both the host and guest drain their wine cups, turning them upside down afterwards. Everyone else also toast the host and guest. This process continues throughout the meal.

Appetizers

A formal Chinese meal is likely to start with a selection of at least three different appetizers. These may range from robust and spicy to delicate and fragrant. As with all Chinese cuisine, harmony and balance are central, so the colour, aroma, texture and flavour of the dishes should complement and contrast. To be authentic, do not serve more than one dish of the same type.

The recipes in this chapter include many dishes that are popular in the West, such as Crispy Seaweed, Spring Rolls, Sesame Prawn (Shrimp) Toasts and Spicy Spare Ribs. Some may, perhaps, be less familiar. Try Rice Paper Parcels, Pork with Chilli and Garlic Sauce or Pot Sticker Dumplings, for example. They are so delicious that they will soon become family favourites, too.

Crispy Wontons with Piquant Dipping Sauce

Mushroom-filled crispy wontons are served on skewers
with a chilli-flavoured dipping sauce.

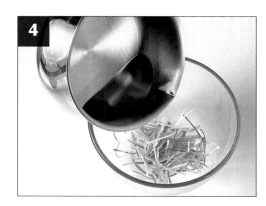

Serves 4
1 tbsp vegetable oil
1 tbsp chopped onion
1 small garlic clove, chopped
$^{1}/_{2}$ tsp chopped fresh ginger root
50 g/1$^{3}/_{4}$ oz/$^{1}/_{2}$ cup chopped flat mushrooms
16 wonton skins
vegetable oil, for deep-frying
salt

SAUCE
2 tbsp vegetable oil
2 spring onions (scallions), thinly shredded
1 red and 1 green chilli, seeded and thinly shredded
3 tbsp light soy sauce
1 tbsp vinegar
1 tbsp dry sherry
pinch of sugar

1 Heat the oil in a preheated wok or
frying pan (skillet). Add the onion,
garlic and ginger root, and stir-fry for
2 minutes. Stir in the mushrooms and
fry for a further 2 minutes. Season
well with salt and let cool.

2 Place 1 teaspoon of the cooled
mushroom filling in the centre of
each wonton skin. Bring two opposite
corners together to cover the mixture
and pinch together to seal. Repeat
with the remaining corners.

3 Thread the wontons on to
8 wooden skewers. Heat enough oil in
a large saucepan to deep-fry the
wontons in batches until golden and

crisp. Remove with a slotted spoon
and drain on kitchen paper (paper
towels).

4 To make the sauce, heat the oil in a
small saucepan until a small cube of

bread browns in a few seconds. Put
the spring onions (scallions) and
chillies in a bowl and pour the hot oil
slowly on top. Then mix in the
remaining ingredients and serve with
the crispy wontons.

Crispy Seaweed

Popular in many Chinese restaurants, this dish is served as a starter.
This 'seaweed' is in fact deep-fried spring (collard) greens.

Serves 4
225 g/8 oz spring (collard) greens
vegetable oil, for deep-frying
1$\frac{1}{2}$ tsp caster (superfine) sugar
1 tsp salt
25 g/1 oz/$\frac{1}{4}$ cup flaked (slivered) almonds

1 Wash the spring (collard) greens thoroughly. Trim off the excess tough stalks. Place on kitchen paper (paper towels) or a dry tea towel (dish cloth) and let drain thoroughly.

2 Using a sharp knife, shred the spring (collard) greens very finely then spread out the shreds on kitchen paper (paper towels) for about 30 minutes to dry.

3 Heat the oil in a wok or deep-fat fryer. Remove the pan from the heat and add the spring (collard) greens in batches. Return the pan to the heat and deep-fry until the greens begin to float to the surface and become translucent and crinkled. Remove with a slotted spoon, and drain on kitchen paper (paper towels). Keep each batch warm while you are deep-frying the next.

4 Mix the sugar and salt together, sprinkle the mixture over the 'seaweed' and toss together thoroughly to mix well.

5 Add the flaked (slivered) almonds to the hot oil and fry until golden. Remove the almonds with a slotted spoon and drain on kitchen paper (paper towels).

6 Serve the crispy 'seaweed' with the flaked (slivered) almonds.

COOK'S TIP

The greens must be completely dry or they will not crispen when fried.

Spinach Meatballs

These are somewhat of a surprise. Balls of pork mixture are coated in spinach and steamed to be served with a sesame and soy sauce dip.

Serves 4
125 g/4¹/₂ oz pork
1 small egg
1-cm/¹/₂-inch piece fresh ginger root, chopped
1 small onion, finely chopped
1 tbsp boiling water
25 g/1 oz canned bamboo shoots, drained and chopped
2 slices smoked ham, chopped
2 tsp cornflour (cornstarch)
450 g/1 lb fresh spinach
2 tsp sesame seeds
SAUCE
150 ml/¹/₄ pint/²/₃ cup vegetable stock
¹/₂ tsp cornflour (cornstarch)
1 tsp cold water
1 tsp light soy sauce
¹/₂ tsp sesame oil
1 tbsp chopped chives

1 Mince (grind) the pork very finely in a food processor or meat mincer (grinder). Beat the egg in a bowl and stir into the pork.

2 Put the ginger, onion and bamboo shoots in a separate bowl, add the boiling water and let stand for 5 minutes. Drain and add to the pork, together with the ham and cornflour (cornstarch). Mix well and roll into 12 balls with your hands.

3 Wash the spinach and remove the stalks. Blanch in boiling water for 10 seconds, drain, rinse in cold water and drain again. Slice the spinach into thin strips, then mix with the sesame seeds. Spread out the mixture in a shallow baking tin (pan) and roll the meatballs in it to coat on all sides.

4 Place the meatballs on a heatproof plate in the base of a steamer, cover and steam for about 8–10 minutes, until cooked through.

5 Meanwhile, heat the sauce ingredients in a saucepan. Transfer the cooked meatballs to a warm plate and serve with the sauce.

Spring Rolls

Thin slices of vegetables are wrapped in pastry and deep-fried until crisp. Spring roll wrappers are available from Chinese foodstores and some supermarkets.

Makes 12
5 Chinese dried mushrooms (or open-cup mushrooms)
1 large carrot
50 g/1¾ oz/1 cup canned bamboo shoots, drained
2 spring onions (scallions)
50 g/1¾ oz Chinese leaves (cabbage)
2 tbsp vegetable oil
225 g/8 oz/1 cup beansprouts
1 tbsp soy sauce
12 spring roll wrappers
1 egg, beaten
vegetable oil for deep-frying
salt

1 Place the dried mushrooms in a small bowl and cover with warm water. Soak for 20–25 minutes. Drain the mushrooms and squeeze out the excess water. Remove the tough centres and slice the mushrooms fairly thinly.

2 Cut the carrot and bamboo shoots into very thin julienne strips. Chop the spring onions (scallions) and shred the Chinese leaves (cabbage).

3 Heat the oil in a preheated wok or frying pan (skillet). Add the mushrooms, carrot and bamboo shoots, and stir-fry for 2 minutes. Add the spring onions (scallions), Chinese leaves (cabbage), beansprouts and soy sauce. Season with salt and stir-fry for 2 minutes. Set aside to cool.

4 Divide the mixture into 12 equal portions and place one portion on the edge of each spring roll wrapper. Fold in the sides and roll each one up, brushing the join with a little beaten egg to seal.

5 Heat the oil for deep-frying in a wok or large saucepan. Add the spring rolls, in batches, and deep-fry for 4–5 minutes, or until golden and crispy. Take care that the oil is not too hot or the spring rolls will brown on the outside before cooking on the inside. Remove and drain on kitchen paper (paper towels). Keep each batch of spring rolls warm while the others are being cooked. Serve at once.

Pork Pancake Rolls

This is another classic Dim Sum dish which is adaptable to almost any filling of your choice. Here the traditional mixture of pork and cabbage is used.

Serves 4
4 tsp vegetable oil
1–2 garlic cloves, crushed
225 g/8 oz minced (ground) pork
225/8 oz Chinese cabbage, thinly shredded
4$^{1}/_{2}$ tsp light soy sauce
$^{1}/_{2}$ tsp sesame oil
8 spring roll skins, 25 cm/10 inches square, thawed if frozen
oil, for deep-frying
chilli sauce, to serve

COOK'S VARIATION

You could substitute minced (ground) chicken or prawns (shrimp) for the pork.

COOK'S TIP

Allow the pancake rolls to stand for a little while after rolling to allow them to seal firmly.

1 Heat the vegetable oil in a preheated wok and fry the garlic for 30 seconds. Add the pork and stir-fry for 2–3 minutes, until sealed.

2 Add the cabbage, soy sauce and sesame oil and stir-fry for 2–3 minutes. Set aside to cool.

3 Spread out the spring roll skins on a work surface (counter) and spoon 2 tbsp of the pork mixture along one edge of each. Roll the skin over once and fold in the sides. Roll again to make a sausage shape, brushing the edges with a little water to seal.

4 Heat the oil for deep-frying in a wok until it is almost smoking. Reduce the heat slightly and fry the pancake rolls for 3–4 minutes, until golden brown. Remove from the oil with a slotted spoon and drain. Transfer to a warm serving plate and serve with chilli sauce.

Lettuce-Wrapped Minced (Ground) Meat

Serve the minced (ground) meat and lettuce leaves on separate dishes:
the guests then wrap their own parcels.

Serves 4
225 g/8 oz minced (ground) pork or chicken
1 tbsp finely chopped Chinese mushrooms
1 tbsp finely chopped water chestnuts
pinch of sugar
1 tsp light soy sauce
1 tsp Chinese rice wine or dry sherry
1 tsp cornflour (cornstarch)
2–3 tbsp vegetable oil
$^{1}/_{2}$ tsp finely chopped ginger root
1 tsp finely chopped spring onions (scallions)
1 tbsp finely chopped Szechuan preserved vegetables (optional)
1 tbsp oyster sauce
a few drops of sesame oil
salt and pepper
8 crisp lettuce leaves, to serve

1 Mix the minced (ground) meat with the mushrooms, water chestnuts, sugar, soy sauce, wine, cornflour (cornstarch), and salt and pepper.

2 Heat the oil in a preheated wok or frying pan (skillet) and add the ginger and spring onions (scallions) followed by the meat. Stir-fry for 1 minute.

3 Add the Szechuan preserved vegetables and continue stirring for 1 more minute. Add the oyster sauce and sesame oil, blend well and cook for 1 more minute. Transfer to a warm serving dish.

4 To serve, place about 2–3 tablespoons of the mixture on a lettuce leaf, tuck in the sides and roll it up tightly to form a small parcel. Eat with your fingers.

COOK'S VARIATION

You can use Chinese leaves instead of lettuce for the wrappers.

Steamed Cabbage Rolls

These small cabbage parcels are quick and easy to prepare and cook and are ideal for a speedy starter.

Serves 4
8 cabbage leaves, trimmed
225 g/8 oz minced (ground) chicken
175 g/6 oz minced (ground) prawns (shrimp)
1 tsp cornflour (cornstarch)
$\frac{1}{2}$ tsp chilli powder
1 egg, lightly beaten
1 tbsp vegetable oil
1 leek, sliced
1 garlic clove, thinly sliced
sliced fresh red chilli, to garnish

1 Bring a large pan of water to the boil. Blanch the cabbage leaves for 2 minutes. Drain, rinse under cold water and drain again. Spread the leaves out on work surface (counter).

2 Mix the chicken, prawns (shrimp), cornflour (cornstarch), chilli powder and egg together in a bowl. Place 2 tbsp of the mixture towards one end of each cabbage leaf.

3 Fold the sides of the cabbage around the filling and roll up to form a firm parcel.

4 Place the parcels, seam side down, on a heatproof plate and cook in a steamer for 10 minutes, or until cooked through.

5 Meanwhile, heat the oil in a preheated wok and sauté the leek and garlic for 1–2 minutes.

6 Transfer the cabbage parcels to warm serving plates.

7 Serve the cabbage parcels with the leek and garlic sauté and garnish with fresh red chilli slices.

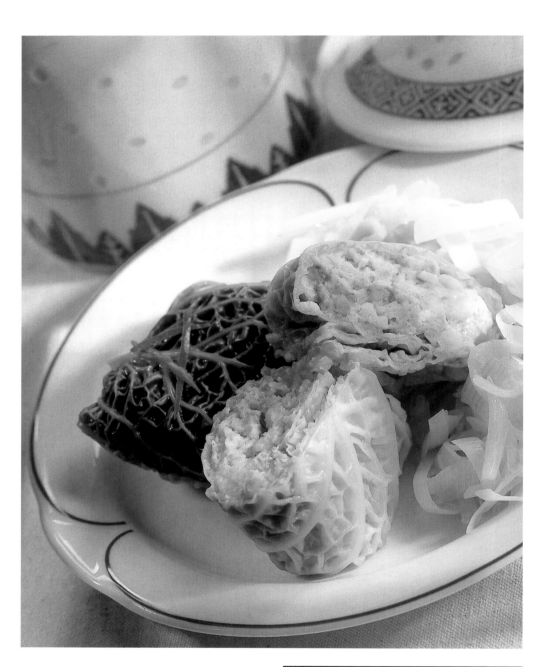

COOK'S TIP

Use Chinese cabbage or Savoy for this recipe, choosing leaves of a similar size for the parcels.

Rice Paper Parcels

These special rice paper wrappers are available in Chinese supermarkets and health-food shops. Do not use the rice paper sold for making cakes.

Serves 4

1 egg white, lightly beaten

2 tsp cornflour (cornstarch)

2 tsp Chinese rice wine or dry sherry

1 tsp caster (superfine) sugar

2 tsp hoi-sin sauce

225 g/8 oz peeled, cooked prawns (shrimp)

4 spring onions (scallions), thinly sliced

25 g/1 oz water chestnuts, chopped

8 Chinese rice paper wrappers

vegetable oil, for deep-frying

hoi-sin sauce, for serving

COOK'S VARIATION

For a spicier flavour, serve the parcels with a hot chilli sauce instead of hoi-sin sauce.

COOK'S TIP

Use this filling inside steamed dumplings (see page 36) if the rice papers are unavailable.

1 Mix together the egg white, cornflour (cornstarch), Chinese rice wine or sherry, sugar and hoisin sauce. Add the prawns (shrimp), spring onions (scallions) and water chestnuts, mixing well.

2 Soften the rice papers by dipping in water. Spoon a little of the prawn (shrimp) mixture into the centre of each paper and wrap the paper around the filling to make a secure parcel.

3 Heat the oil in a wok until almost smoking. Reduce the heat slightly and deep-fry the parcels for 4–5 minutes, until crisp. Remove from the oil with a slotted spoon and drain on absorbent kitchen paper (paper towels). Transfer to a warm serving dish, spoon a little hoisin sauce on top and serve immediately.

Chinese Ravioli

These small parcels are made from wonton wrappers, filled with mixed vegetables and crabmeat, and cooked to perfection for a superb starter.

Serves 4
450 g/1 lb crabmeat (fresh or canned and drained)
¹/₂ red (bell) pepper, seeded and finely diced
125 g/4¹/₂ oz Chinese leaves (cabbage), shredded
2 tbsp roughly chopped beansprouts
1 tbsp light soy sauce
1 tsp lime juice
16 wonton wrappers
1 small egg, beaten
2 tbsp peanut oil
1 tsp sesame oil
salt and pepper

1 Mix together the crabmeat, (bell) pepper, Chinese leaves (cabbage), beansprouts, soy sauce and lime juice in a bowl. Season and let stand for 15 minutes, stirring occasionally.

2 Take a wonton wrapper and place a little of the mixture in the centre. Repeat with the remaining wrappers and stuffing; reserve any extra stuffing.

3 Brush the edges of the wrappers with the beaten egg and fold in half to make triangles, pushing out any air. Press the edges together with your fingers to seal tightly.

4 Heat the peanut oil in a preheated wok or frying pan (skillet) and fry the ravioli, in batches, for 3–4 minutes, turning frequently, until browned all over. Remove with a slotted spoon and keep warm.

5 Heat the reserved stuffing in the frying pan (skillet) over a gentle heat until hot.

6 Transfer the ravioli to a serving dish and sprinkle with the sesame oil. Serve with the hot stuffing.

COOK'S TIP

Make sure that the edges of the ravioli are sealed well and that all the air is pressed out to prevent them from opening during cooking.

Deep-Fried Prawns (Shrimp)

Use raw tiger prawns (jumbo shrimp) in their shells. They are 7–10 cm (3–4 inches) long, and you should get 18–20 prawns (shrimp) per 450 g (1 lb).

Serves 4

250–300 g/9–10$\frac{1}{2}$ oz raw tiger prawns (jumbo shrimp) in their shells, thawed if frozen

1 tbsp light soy sauce

1 tsp Chinese rice wine
or dry sherry

2 tsp cornflour (cornstarch)

vegetable oil, for deep-frying

2–3 spring onions (scallions),
to garnish

SPICY SALT & PEPPER

1 tbsp salt

1 tsp ground Szechuan peppercorns

1 tsp Chinese five-spice powder

1 Pull the legs off the prawns (shrimp), but leave the shells intact. Dry on kitchen paper (paper towels).

2 Place the prawns (shrimp) in a bowl with the soy sauce, wine and cornflour (cornstarch). Turn to coat thoroughly and marinate for about 25–30 minutes.

3 To make the spicy salt and pepper, mix the salt, pepper and five-spice powder together. Place in a frying pan (skillet) and dry-fry, stirring constantly, for about 3–4 minutes over a low heat. Remove from the heat and set aside to cool.

4 Heat the oil in a preheated wok until smoking. Deep-fry the prawns (shrimp) in batches until golden brown. Remove with a slotted spoon and drain on kitchen paper (paper towels).

5 Place the spring onions (scallions) in a bowl, pour on 1 tablespoon of the hot oil and leave for 30 seconds. Transfer the prawns (shrimp) to a serving dish, garnish with the spring onions (scallions), and serve immediately with the spicy salt and pepper as a condiment.

Butterfly Prawns (Shrimp)

Use unpeeled, raw king or tiger prawns (jumbo shrimp)
which are succulent and packed with flavour.

Serves 4
12 unpeeled raw tiger prawns (jumbo shrimp)
2 tbsp light soy sauce
1 tbsp Chinese rice wine or dry sherry
1 tbsp cornflour (cornstarch)
2 eggs, lightly beaten
8–10 tbsp breadcrumbs
vegetable oil, for deep-frying
salt and pepper
chopped spring onions (scallions), to garnish
shredded lettuce leaves, to serve

1 Remove the heads, peel and devein the prawns (shrimp), but leave the tails intact. Split them in half from the underbelly about halfway along, leaving the tails still firmly attached. Flatten them out slightly.

2 Mix together the soy sauce, Chinese rice wine or sherry and cornflour (cornstarch)in a bowl and season to taste with salt and pepper. Add the prawns (shrimp) and turn to coat thoroughly. Marinate for about 10–15 minutes.

3 Heat the oil in a preheated wok. Pick up each prawn (shrimp) by the tail, dip it in the beaten egg, then roll it in the breadcrumbs to coat well, shaking off any excess.

4 Deep-fry the prawns (shrimp), in batches, until golden brown. Remove them with a slotted spoon and drain on kitchen paper (paper towels).

5 To serve, arrange the prawns (shrimp) on a bed of lettuce leaves and garnish with chopped spring onions (scallions), either raw or soaked in a tablespoon of the hot oil for about 30 seconds.

COOK'S VARIATION

Serve the prawns (shrimps) on a bed of Crispy Seaweed (see page 23) instead of shredded lettuce.

Sesame Prawn (Shrimp) Toasts

These small toasts are easy to prepare and are one of the most popular Chinese appetizers in the West. Make sure you serve plenty of them as they are very tasty.

Serves 4
225 g/8 oz cooked, peeled prawns (shrimp)
1 spring onion (scallion)
$^1/_4$ tsp salt
1 tsp light soy sauce
1 tbsp cornflour (cornstarch)
1 egg white, beaten
3 thin slices white bread, crusts removed
4 tbsp sesame seeds
vegetable oil, for deep-frying

COOK'S TIP

This is even better if you can obtain raw prawns (shrimp), as the cooked ones sometimes tend to become detached from the toasts.

COOK'S TIP

Fry the triangles in two batches, keeping them warm, to prevent them from sticking together and overcooking.

1 Put the prawns (shrimp) and spring onion (scallion) in a food processor and process until finely minced (ground) or chop very finely by hand. Stir in the salt, soy sauce, cornflour (cornstarch) and egg white.

2 Spread the prawn (shrimp) mixture on to one side of each slice of bread.

3 Spread the sesame seeds on top of the prawn (shrimp) mixture on each slice of bread, pressing firmly.

4 Cut each slice into four equal triangles or strips.

5 Heat the oil for deep-frying in a wok until almost smoking. Carefully place the triangles in the oil, coated side down, and cook for 2–3 minutes, until golden brown. Remove with a slotted spoon and drain on kitchen paper (paper towels). Serve hot.

Deep-Fried Spare Ribs

The spare ribs should be chopped into small bite-size
pieces before or after cooking.

Serves 4
8–10 finger spare ribs
1 tsp Chinese five-spice powder or
1 tbsp mild curry powder
1 tbsp Chinese rice wine or
dry sherry
1 egg
2 tbsp flour
vegetable oil for deep-frying
1 tsp finely shredded
spring onions (scallions)
1 tsp finely shredded fresh green or
red hot chillies, seeded
salt and pepper
Spicy Salt and Pepper
(see page 31), to serve

1 Chop the ribs into 3–4 small pieces.
Place the ribs in a bowl with the
Chinese five-spice or curry powder,
rice wine or sherry, and salt and
pepper. Turn to coat them thoroughly
and marinate for 1–2 hours.

2 Beat the egg and flour together in a
bowl to make a smooth batter. Dip the
marinated ribs in the batter, one by
one, to coat well.

3 Heat the oil in a preheated wok
until smoking. Add the ribs and deep-
fry for 4–5 minutes, then remove
with a slotted spoon and drain on
kitchen paper (paper towels).

4 Reheat the oil over a high heat, add
the ribs and deep-fry once more for
another minute. Remove with a
slotted spoon and drain again on
kitchen paper (paper towels).

5 Pour 1 tablespoon of the hot oil
over the spring onions (scallions) and
chillies and leave for 30–40 seconds.
Transfer the ribs to a serving dish and
garnish with the spring onions
(scallions) and chillies. Serve with the
spicy salt and pepper.

COOK'S TIP

You could add 1 tablespoon brown
sugar and 1 teaspoon chilli sauce to
the marinade in step 1 for a richer
and spicier flavour.

Pork with Chilli & Garlic Sauce

Any leftovers from this dish can be used for a number of other dishes, such as Hot & Sour Soup (see page 57), but it may be so popular that nothing is left.

Serves 4
450 g/1 lb boneless leg of pork, not skinned
fresh parsley, to garnish

SAUCE
1 tsp finely chopped garlic
1 tsp finely chopped spring onions (scallions)
2 tbsp light soy sauce
1 tsp red chilli oil
$1/2$ tsp sesame oil

1 Tie the pork together in one piece with kitchen string and place it in a large saucepan. Add enough cold water to cover and bring to a rolling boil over a medium heat.

2 Lower the heat, skim off the scum that rises to the surface, cover and simmer gently for 25–30 minutes.

3 Remove the pan from the heat. Leave the meat in the liquid covered, for at least 1–2 hours. Lift out the meat with 2 slotted spoons and set aside, skin side up, for 2–3 hours or until completely cold.

4 To serve, cut off and discard the skin, but leave a very thin layer of fat on top, rather like a ham joint. Cut the meat in small thin slices across the grain and arrange decoratively on a serving plate. Mix together the sauce ingredients and pour a little of the sauce evenly over the pork. Garnish with parsley and serve with the remaining sauce.

Pork Dim Sum

These small steamed parcels are classically served as an appetizer
and are very adaptable to your favourite fillings.

Serves 4
400 g/14 oz lean minced (ground) pork
2 spring onions (scallions), chopped
50 g/1³/₄ oz canned bamboo shoots, drained and chopped
1 tbsp light soy sauce
1 tbsp Chinese rice wine or dry sherry
2 tsp sesame oil
2 tsp caster (superfine) sugar
1 egg white, lightly beaten
4¹/₂ tsp cornflour (cornstarch)
24 wonton wrappers

1 Mix together the minced (ground) pork, onions, bamboo shoots, soy sauce, Chinese rice wine or sherry, sesame oil, sugar and egg white in a bowl until well incorporated.

2 Stir in the cornflour (cornstarch), mixing well.

3 Place a portion of the mixture in the centre of each wonton wrapper and lightly brush the edges of the wrappers with water.

4 Bring the wrappers together in the centre, pinching together to 'gather' at the top.

5 Line a steamer with a clean damp tea towel (dish cloth) and arrange the wontons in a single layer inside. Cover and steam for 5–7 minutes, until cooked through. Serve immediately in the steamer.

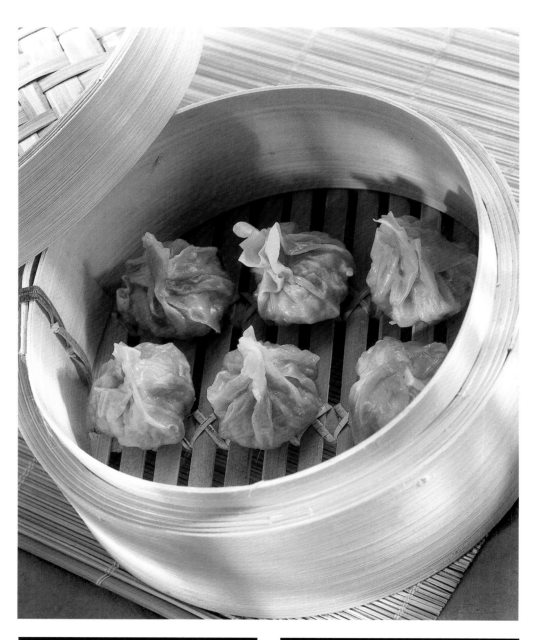

COOK'S VARIATION

You can use almost any of your favourite fillings, such as prawns (shrimp), minced (ground) chicken or crabmeat, instead of pork.

COOK'S TIP

You can use additional flavourings, such as chilli and ginger. Dim sum is traditionally served with a small bowl of soy sauce for dipping.

Barbecue Pork (Char Siu)

Also called honey-roasted pork, these are the strips of reddish meat sometimes seen
hanging in the windows of Cantonese restaurants.

Serves 4
450 g/1 lb pork fillet
150 ml/¹/₄ pint/²/₃ cup boiling water
1 tbsp clear honey, dissolved in a little hot water
shredded lettuce, to serve

MARINADE
1 tbsp sugar
1 tbsp crushed yellow bean sauce
1 tbsp light soy sauce
1 tbsp hoi-sin sauce
1 tbsp oyster sauce
¹/₂ tsp chilli sauce
1 tbsp brandy or rum
1 tsp sesame oil

1 Cut the pork into strips about
2.5 cm/1 inch thick and 18–20 cm/
7–8 inches long and place in a large
shallow dish. Thoroughly combine
the marinade ingredients in a bowl
and pour the mixture over the pork,
turning it until well coated. Cover,
and marinate for at least 3–4 hours,
turning occasionally.

2 Remove the pork strips from the
dish with a slotted spoon, reserving
the marinade. Arrange the pork strips
on a rack over a baking tin (pan). Place
the tin (pan) in a preheated oven at
220°C/425°F/Gas 7, and pour in the
boiling water. Roast for about
10–15 minutes.

3 Lower the oven temperature to
180°C/350°F/Gas 4. Baste the pork
strips with the reserved marinade and

turn them over. Roast for a further
10 minutes.

4 Remove the pork from the oven,
brush with the honey syrup, and
lightly brown under a preheated grill
(broiler) for 3–4 minutes, turning once
or twice.

5 To serve, allow the pork to cool
slightly before cutting it. Cut across
the grain into thin slices and arrange
on a bed of shredded lettuce. Make a
sauce by boiling the marinade and the
drippings in the roasting tin (pan) for
a few minutes, strain and pour over
the pork. Serve immediately.

Pot Sticker Dumplings

These dumplings obtain their name from the fact that they will stick to the
pot when steamed if they are not fried crisply enough initially.

Serves 4
DUMPLINGS
175 g/6 oz/1¹/₂ cups plain (all-purpose) flour
pinch of salt
3 tbsp vegetable oil
6–8 tbsp boiling water
oil, for deep-frying
sliced spring onion (scallion) and chives, to garnish
FILLING
150 g/5¹/₂ oz lean chicken, very finely chopped
25 g/1 oz canned bamboo shoots, drained and chopped
2 spring onions (scallions), finely chopped
¹/₂ small red (bell) pepper, seeded and finely chopped
¹/₂ tsp Chinese curry powder
1 tbsp light soy sauce
1 tsp caster (superfine) sugar
1 tsp sesame oil
salt and pepper

1 To make the dumplings, mix together the flour and salt in a bowl. Make a well in the centre, add the oil and water and mix well to form a soft dough. Knead the dough on a lightly floured surface, wrap in clear film (plastic wrap) and let stand for 30 minutes.

2 Meanwhile, mix the filling ingredients together in a bowl.

3 Divide the dough into 12 equal pieces and roll each into a 12.5-cm/ 5-inch round.

4 Spoon a portion of the filling on to one half of each round and fold the dough over the filling to form a semi-circle. Twist the edges firmly together to seal, pressing together well.

5 Heat a little oil into a heavy-based frying pan (skillet) and cook the dumplings, in batches, until browned and slightly crisp, adding more oil as necessary. Drain thoroughly, set aside and keep warm.

6 Return the dumplings to the pan (skillet) and add 125 ml/4 fl oz/¹/₂ cup water. Cover and steam for 5 minutes, or until the dumplings are cooked. Remove with a slotted spoon and serve immediately, garnished with spring onion (scallion) and chives.

Steamed Duck Buns

The dough used in this recipe may be wrapped around a multitude of fillings, such as chicken, pork or prawns (shrimp), or sweet fillings as an alternative.

Serves 4
DOUGH
300 g/10½ oz/2⅔ cups plain (all-purpose) flour
15 g/½ oz dried yeast
1 tsp caster (superfine) sugar
2 tbsp warm water
175 ml/6 fl oz/¾ cup warm milk

FILLING
300 g/10½ oz duck breasts
1 tbsp light brown sugar
1 tbsp light soy sauce
2 tbsp clear honey
1 tbsp hoi-sin sauce
1 tbsp vegetable oil
1 leek, finely chopped
1 garlic clove, crushed
1 tbsp grated fresh ginger root

1 Place the duck breast in a glass bowl. Mix together the sugar, soy sauce, honey and hoi-sin sauce. Pour the mixture over the duck and marinate for 20 minutes.

2 Remove the duck from the marinade and roast on a rack over a roasting tin (pan) in a preheated oven at 200°C/400°F/Gas 6 for 35–40 minutes. Cool, remove the meat from the bones and dice.

3 Heat the oil and stir-fry the leek, garlic and ginger for 2–3 minutes, until tender. Mix with the duck meat.

4 To make the dough, sift the flour into a mixing bowl. Mix together the yeast, sugar and water and leave in a warm place for about 15 minutes. Pour the yeast mixture into the flour, with the milk, mixing to form a firm dough. Knead the dough for 5 minutes and roll into a sausage shape 2.5 cm/ 1 inch in diameter. Cut into 16 equal pieces, cover and let stand for 20–25 minutes.

5 Flatten each dough piece into a 10-cm/4-inch round. Place 1 tbsp of filling in the centre of each round and draw up the sides, twisting at the top.

6 Place the dumplings on a damp tea towel (dish cloth) in a steamer, cover and steam for 20 minutes. Serve hot.

Chinese Omelette

This is a fairly filling omelette, as it contains chicken and prawns (shrimp).
It is cooked as a whole and sliced for serving

Serves 4
8 eggs
225 g/8 oz/2 cups shredded cooked chicken
12 large cooked prawns (shrimp), peeled and deveined
2 tbsp chopped chives
2 tsp light soy sauce
dash of chilli sauce
2 tbsp vegetable oil

COOK'S VARIATION

Substitute 150 g/5 oz cooked or canned crabmeat for the prawns (shrimp), if wished.

COOK'S TIP

Add peas or other vegetables to the omelette and serve as a main course for 2 people.

1 Lightly beat the eggs in a large mixing bowl. Add the chicken and prawns (shrimp), mixing well.

2 Stir in the chives, soy sauce and chilli sauce, mixing well.

3 Heat the oil in a large frying pan (skillet) over a medium heat and add the egg mixture, tilting the pan to coat the base. Gently stir the omelette with a fork while it is cooking.

4 When the omelette is set, slide it out of the pan and cut into squares or slices to serve.

5 Transfer to a warm serving plate and serve immediately.

Honeyed Chicken Wings

Chicken wings are ideal for a starter as they are small and perfect for eating with the fingers.

Serves 4
2 tbsp peanut oil
450 g/1 lb chicken wings
2 tbsp light soy sauce
2 tbsp hoi-sin sauce
2 tbsp clear honey
2 garlic cloves, crushed
1 tsp sesame seeds
dash of chilli sauce

1 Heat the oil in a preheated wok and cook the chicken wings, turning frequently, for 10–12 minutes, or until golden brown all over. Drain off any excess oil from the wok.

2 Add the soy sauce, hoi-sin sauce, honey, garlic, sesame seeds and chilli sauce.

3 Reduce the heat and cook for about 20–25 minutes, turning the chicken wings frequently until they are cooked through.

4 Transfer to a warm serving dish and serve immediately.

COOK'S TIP

Make the dish in advance and freeze the chicken wings. Thaw thoroughly, arrange in a single layer in an ovenproof dish and heat right through in a preheated oven at 180°C/350°F/Gas 4.

Salads & Pickles

Western-style salads rarely appear in China, but combinations of lightly cooked and raw dressed vegetables, served either warm or cold, are popular. The best and freshest vegetables are always used and ingredients are matched so that crunchy and melt-in-the-mouth textures and sweet and spicy flavours simultaneously delight the palate. Try Sweet & Sour Tofu (Bean Curd) Salad or Hot & Sour Duck Salad, for example. Dressings often feature citrus juice, particularly lime, as well as soy and fish sauces. Nuts and seeds provide a garnish, as well as 'crunch factor', and honey adds a touch of sweetness and an attractive glaze.

Pickling fresh vegetables in the summer for eating in the winter is a long-standing tradition in China. They are used in soups and stir-fries, as a condiment and served as appetizers. Pickled vegetables are frequently spiced with chillies or a sweet-and-sour combination of vinegar and honey.

Sweet & Sour Tofu (Bean Curd) Salad

Tofu (bean curd) mixed with crisp stir-fried vegetables, then tossed in a piquant sweet-and-sour dressing makes an ideal light meal or starter.

Serves 4–6
2 tbsp vegetable oil
1 garlic clove, crushed
450 g/1 lb tofu (bean curd), cubed
1 onion, sliced
1 carrot, cut into julienne strips
1 celery stick, sliced
2 small red (bell) peppers, seeded and sliced
225 g/8 oz mangetout (snow peas), trimmed and halved
115 g/4 oz broccoli, trimmed and divided into florets
115 g/4 oz thin French (green) beans, halved
2 tbsp oyster sauce
1 tbsp tamarind concentrate
1 tbsp fish sauce
1 tbsp tomato purée (paste)
1 tbsp light soy sauce
1 tbsp chilli sauce
2 tbsp sugar
1 tbsp white vinegar
pinch of ground star anise
1 tsp cornflour (cornstarch)
300 ml/$\frac{1}{2}$ pint/1$\frac{1}{4}$ cups water

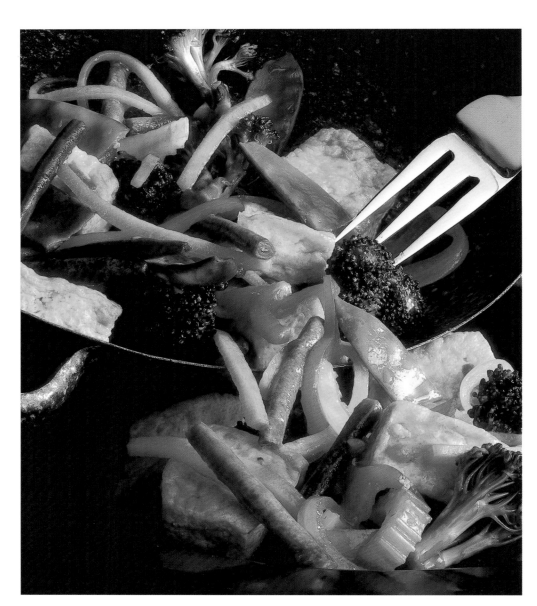

1 Heat the vegetable oil in a preheated wok or large, heavy-based frying pan (skillet). Add the crushed garlic and stir-fry for a few seconds.

2 Add the tofu (bean curd), in batches, and stir-fry over a low heat, until golden on all sides. Remove with a slotted spoon and keep warm.

3 Add the onion, carrot, celery, red (bell) pepper, mangetout (snow peas), broccoli and green beans to the pan and stir-fry for about 2–3 minutes, or until tender-crisp.

4 Add the oyster sauce, tamarind concentrate, fish sauce, tomato purée (paste), soy sauce, chilli sauce, sugar, vinegar and star anise, mixing well to coat the vegetables. Stir-fry for a further 2 minutes.

5 Mix the cornflour (cornstarch) with the water to make a smooth paste and add to the wok or frying pan (skillet), together with the fried tofu (bean curd). Stir-fry gently until the sauce boils and thickens slightly.

6 Serve the salad immediately, on warm plates.

Sweet & Sour Cucumber

Chunks of cucumber are marinated in vinegar and sweetened
with honey to make a sweet-and-sour appetizer.

Serves 4
1 cucumber
1 tsp salt
2 tsp honey
2 tbsp rice vinegar
3 tbsp chopped fresh coriander (cilantro)
2 tsp sesame oil
$^1/_4$ tsp crushed red peppercorns
strips of red and yellow (bell) pepper, to garnish

1 Peel thin strips off the cucumber along the length. This gives a pretty striped effect. Cut the cucumber in quarters lengthways and then into 2.5-cm/1-inch long pieces. Place them in a colander.

2 Sprinkle the salt over the cucumber and set aside for 30 minutes to allow the salt to draw out excess water. Wash the cucumber thoroughly under cold running water to remove the salt, drain and pat dry with kitchen paper (paper towels).

3 Place the cucumber in a bowl. Combine the honey with the vinegar and pour the mixture over the cucumber. Mix together and marinate for 15 minutes.

4 Stir in the coriander (cilantro) and sesame oil, and place in a serving bowl.

5 Sprinkle the crushed red peppercorns on top of the salad. Serve garnished with strips of red and yellow (bell) pepper.

Chinese Hot Salad

Stir-fried vegetables with a little touch of chilli. To serve cold, add French dressing as the vegetables cool, toss well and serve.

Serves 4
1 tbsp dark soy sauce
1^{1}/$_{2}$–2 tsp sweet chilli sauce
2 tbsp dry sherry
1 tbsp brown sugar
1 tbsp wine vinegar
2 tbsp sunflower oil
1 garlic clove, crushed
4 spring onions (scallions), sliced thinly diagonally
225 g/8 oz courgettes (zucchini), cut into julienne strips about 4 cm/1^{1}/$_{2}$ inches long
225 g/8 oz carrots, cut into julienne strips about 4 cm/1^{1}/$_{2}$ inches long
1 red or green (bell) pepper, cored, seeded and sliced thinly
400 g/14 oz can beansprouts, well drained
125 g/4^{1}/$_{2}$ oz French (green) or fine beans, cut into 5-cm/2-inch lengths
1 tbsp sesame oil
salt and pepper
1–2 tsp sesame seeds, to garnish

1 Blend the soy sauce, chilli sauce, sherry, sugar, vinegar, and salt and pepper together.

2 Heat the 2 tablespoons of sunflower oil in a preheated wok, swirling it around until it is really hot.

3 Add the garlic and spring onions (scallions) to the wok and stir-fry for 1–2 minutes.

4 Add the courgettes (zucchini), carrots and (bell) pepper and stir-fry for 1–2 minutes, then add the soy sauce mixture and bring to the boil.

5 Add the beansprouts and French (green) beans and stir-fry for about 1–2 minutes, making sure all the vegetables are coated with the sauce.

6 Drizzle the sesame oil over the vegetables. Stir–fry for 30 seconds and sprinkle with sesame seeds.

7 Transfer to a serving dish and serve immediately or cool and serve with French dressing.

Oriental Salad

This colourful crisp salad has a fresh orange dressing
and is topped with crunchy vermicelli.

Serves 4–6

25 g/1 oz/¼ cup dried vermicelli

½ head Chinese leaves (cabbage)

115 g/4 oz/½ cup beansprouts

6 radishes

115 g/4 oz mangetout
(snow peas)

1 large carrot

115 g/4 oz sprouting beans

DRESSING

juice of 1 orange

1 tbsp sesame seeds, toasted

1 tsp honey

1 tsp sesame oil

1 tbsp hazelnut oil

1 Break the vermicelli into small
strands. Heat a wok or frying pan
(skillet) and dry-fry the vermicelli
until lightly golden. Remove from the
pan and set aside.

2 Shred the Chinese leaves (cabbage)
and wash with the beansprouts. Drain
thoroughly and place in a large bowl.
Slice the radishes. Trim the
mangetout (snow peas) and cut each
into 3. Cut the carrot into thin
matchsticks. Add the sprouting beans
and prepared vegetables to the bowl.

3 Place all the dressing ingredients in
a screw-top jar and shake until well-
blended. Pour the dressing over the
salad and toss.

4 Transfer the salad to a serving bowl
and sprinkle over the reserved
vermicelli before serving.

Pickled Vegetables

Pickled vegetables can be marinated for as little
as 30 minutes or for several days.

Serves 4
PICKLED CUCUMBER
1 cucumber, about 30 cm/12 inches long
1 tsp salt
2 tsp caster (superfine) sugar
1 tsp rice vinegar
1 tsp red chilli oil
a few drops of sesame oil
MIXED PICKLED VEGETABLES
350 g/12 oz Chinese leaves (cabbage), cut into bite-size pieces
50 g/1³/₄ oz French (green) beans, topped and tailed
115 g/4 oz carrots, diced
3 fresh red chillies, seeded and finely chopped
2 tsp Szechuan peppercorns
2 tbsp coarse salt
2 tbsp rice wine

1 To make Pickled Cucumber, halve the cucumber, unpeeled, lengthways. Scrape off and discard the seeds and cut the flesh across into thick chunks.

2 Sprinkle the cucumber with the salt and mix thoroughly. Set aside for at least 20–30 minutes, longer if possible, then pour the accumulated juice away.

3 Mix the cucumber with the sugar, vinegar and chilli oil.

4 Transfer the pickled cucumber to a serving dish and lightly sprinkle with the sesame oil just before serving.

5 To make Mixed Pickled Vegetables, place the Chinese leaves (cabbage), beans and carrots in a glass bowl, together with the chillies, Szechuan peppercorns, salt and rice wine. Stir the mixture well, cover and leave to marinate in the refrigerator for about 4 days, stirring from time to time. Serve the mixed pickled vegetables cold, as a salad.

Hot & Sour Duck Salad

This is a lovely tangy salad, drizzled with a lime juice and fish sauce dressing. It makes a splendid starter or light main course dish.

Serves 4

2 heads crisp salad lettuce,
washed and separated into leaves

2 shallots, thinly sliced

4 spring onions
(scallions), chopped

1 celery stick, cut
into julienne strips

5-cm/2-inch piece cucumber,
cut into julienne strips

115 g/4 oz/$\frac{1}{2}$ cup beansprouts

200 g/7 oz can water chestnuts,
drained and sliced

4 duck breast fillets, roasted
and sliced

orange slices, to serve

DRESSING

3 tbsp fish sauce

1$\frac{1}{2}$ tbsp lime juice

2 garlic cloves, crushed

1 fresh red chilli, seeded and
very finely chopped

1 fresh green chilli, seeded and
very finely chopped

1 tsp palm sugar
or demerara (raw crystal) sugar

1 Mix the lettuce leaves with the shallots, spring onions (scallions), celery, cucumber, beansprouts and water chestnuts. Place the mixture on a large serving platter.

2 Arrange the duck breast slices on top of the salad in an attractive overlapping pattern.

3 To make the dressing, put the fish sauce, lime juice, garlic, chillies and sugar into a small pan. Heat gently, stirring constantly. Taste and adjust the piquancy if liked by adding more lime juice, or add more fish sauce to reduce the sharpness.

4 Drizzle the warm salad dressing over the duck salad and serve.

COOK'S TIP

Fish sauce, also known as *nam pla*, is made from salted anchovies and has a very strong flavour. It is commonly used in oriental cooking.

Cucumber & Beansprout Salad

This is a very light dish and is ideal on its own
for a summer meal or as a starter.

Serves 4
350 g/12 oz/1¹/₂ cups beansprouts
1 small cucumber
1 green (bell) pepper, seeded and cut into matchsticks
1 carrot, cut into matchsticks
2 tomatoes, finely chopped
1 celery stick, cut into matchsticks
1 garlic clove, crushed
dash of chilli sauce
2 tbsp light soy sauce
1 tsp wine vinegar
2 tsp sesame oil
16 chives

COOK'S TIP

Mung beansprouts are the most
commonly available, but you could
also try soya, aduki (adzuki), alfalfa,
lentil or chick pea (garbanzo
bean) sprouts.

COOK'S TIP

The vegetables may be prepared
in advance, but do not assemble
the dish until just before serving,
otherwise the beansprouts
will discolour.

1 Blanch the beansprouts in boiling
water for 1 minute. Drain and rinse
under cold water. Drain well again.

2 Halve the cucumber lengthways.
Scoop out the seeds with a teaspoon
and discard. Cut the flesh into
matchsticks and mix with the
beansprouts, (bell) pepper, carrot,
tomatoes and celery.

3 Mix together the garlic, chilli sauce,
soy sauce, vinegar and sesame oil.
Pour the dressing over the vegetables,
tossing well to coat and spoon on to
serving plates. Garnish with chives
and serve.

Broccoli, (Bell) Pepper & Almond Salad

This is a colourful, crunchy salad with a delicious dressing. It is better
left overnight if possible for the flavours to mingle.

Serves 4
450 g/1 lb small broccoli florets
50 g/1¾ oz baby corn cobs, halved, lengthways
1 red (bell) pepper, seeded and cut into thin strips
50 g/2 oz blanched almonds
DRESSING
1 tbsp sesame seeds
1 tbsp peanut oil
2 garlic cloves, crushed
2 tbsp light soy sauce
1 tbsp clear honey
2 tsp lemon juice
pepper
lemon zest, to garnish

1 Blanch the broccoli and baby corn cobs in boiling water for 5 minutes. Drain well, rinse under cold running water and drain thoroughly again.

2 Transfer the broccoli and baby corn cobs to a large mixing bowl and add the (bell) pepper and almonds.

3 To make the dressing, heat a wok or small heavy-based frying pan (skillet) and add the sesame seeds. Dry-fry, stirring constantly, for about 1 minute, or until the sesame seeds are lightly browned and are giving off a delicious aroma.

4 Mix the peanut oil, garlic, soy sauce, honey and lemon juice together and season with pepper to taste. Add the sesame seeds and mix together well.

5 Pour the dressing over the salad, cover and set aside in the refrigerator for a minimum of 4 hours and preferably overnight.

6 Garnish the salad with lemon zest and serve.

COOK'S TIP

Take care when browning the sesame seeds, as they will quickly burn. Dry-fry over a low heat and stir constantly.

Soups

In China, soup is not usually served as a separate course, but is one of several dishes forming the main part of the meal. Chinese soups are usually clear broths flavoured with finely sliced vegetables, spices and herbs. They sometimes contain meat, poultry, fish or seafood and many include noodles, wontons and dumplings. Some of the recipes in this chapter are substantial enough to provide a light lunch – try (Small) Shrimp Dumpling Soup.

Their basis is a good quality stock, together with the freshest vegetables. It is always better to use home-made stock (see page 16), as stock and bouillon cubes tend to be rather salty and lack depth of flavour.

Most Chinese soups are a balance of two flavours – crab and ginger, for example. The solid ingredients, meat, vegetables or seafood, are cooked until crisply tender so that they retain their texture and colour, making the soup visually appealing.

Mixed Vegetable Soup

Select three or four vegetables for this soup: the Chinese like to blend different colours, flavours and textures to create harmony as well as contrast.

Serves 4

about 25–60 g/1–2 oz each of 3 or 4 of the following:
mushrooms, carrots, asparagus, mangetout (snow peas),
bamboo shoots, baby corn cobs, watercress, cucumber, tomatoes,
spinach, lettuce,
Chinese leaves (cabbage),
tofu (bean curd)

600 ml/1 pint/2¹/₂ cups Chinese Stock (see page 16)

1 tbsp light soy sauce

a few drops of sesame oil (optional)

salt and pepper

finely chopped spring onions (scallions), to garnish

1 Cut your selection of vegetables into roughly uniform shapes and sizes (slices, shreds or cubes).

2 Bring the stock to a rolling boil in a wok and add the vegetables of your choice – some require a longer cooking time than others: add carrots and baby corn cobs first, cook for 2 minutes, then add asparagus, mushrooms, mangetout (snow peas), Chinese leaves (cabbage) and tofu (bean curd) and cook for 1 minute.

3 Add the spinach, lettuce, watercress, cucumber and tomato. Stir and bring back to the boil.

4 Add the soy sauce and sesame oil, and adjust the seasoning. Serve immediately, garnished with spring onions (scallions).

Hot & Sour Soup

This is the favourite soup in Chinese restaurants throughout the world.

Serves 4

4–6 dried Chinese mushrooms, soaked in warm water for 30 minutes

115 g/4 oz cooked pork or chicken

1 cake tofu (bean curd)

50 g/1¾ oz canned sliced bamboo shoots, drained

600 ml/1 pint/2½ cups Chinese Stock (see page 16) or water

1 tbsp Chinese rice wine or dry sherry

1 tbsp light soy sauce

2 tbsp rice vinegar

1 tbsp Cornflour (Cornstarch) Paste (see page 16)

salt and pepper

2–3 spring onions (scallions), thinly sliced, to garnish

1 Drain the mushrooms, squeeze dry and discard the hard stalks. Thinly slice the mushroom caps.

2 Using a Chinese cleaver or very sharp knife, thinly slice the meat, tofu (bean curd) and bamboo shoots into narrow shreds.

3 Bring the stock or water to a rolling boil in a wok or large pan and add the mushrooms, pork or chicken, tofu (bean curd) and bamboo shoots. Bring back to the boil, lower the heat and simmer for about 1 minute.

4 Add the Chinese rice wine or sherry, soy sauce and vinegar, and season to taste with salt and pepper.

5 Bring back to the boil and stir in the cornflour (cornstarch) paste. Transfer to warm soup bowls, sprinkle with the spring onions (scallions) and serve.

Vegetarian Hot & Sour Soup

This is a popular Chinese soup, which is unusual in that it is thickened.
The 'hot' flavour is achieved by the addition of plenty of black pepper.

Serves 4
4 Chinese dried mushrooms (or open-cup mushrooms)
115 g/4 oz firm tofu (bean curd)
50 g/1¾ oz/1 cup canned bamboo shoots, drained
600 ml/1 pint/2½ cups vegetable stock or water
50 g/1¾ oz/⅓ cup peas
1 tbsp dark soy sauce
2 tbsp white wine vinegar
2 tbsp cornflour (cornstarch)
salt and pepper
sesame oil, to serve

1 Place the dried mushrooms in a bowl and cover with warm water. Set aside to soak for 20–25 minutes.

2 Drain the mushrooms and squeeze out the excess water, reserving the soaking water. Remove the stalks and tough centres and cut the mushroom caps into thin shreds. Shred the tofu (bean curd) and bamboo shoots.

3 Bring the stock or water to the boil in a large saucepan. Add the mushrooms, tofu (bean curd), bamboo shoots and peas. Bring back to the boil, lower the heat and simmer for 2 minutes.

4 Mix together the soy sauce, vinegar and cornflour (cornstarch) with 2 tablespoons of the reserved mushroom soaking liquid to make a smooth paste. Stir the into the soup, together with the remaining mushroom soaking liquid. Bring to the boil and season with salt and plenty of pepper. Simmer for 2 minutes.

5 Ladle the soup into individual warm bowls with a few drops of sesame oil in each and serve.

Chinese Cabbage Soup

This is a piquant soup, which is slightly sweet-and-sour in flavour. Cabbage is cooked in a vegetable broth with sugar, vinegar and chilli and served as a hearty meal or appetizer.

Serves 4

450 g/1 lb Chinese cabbage

600 ml/1 pint/2¹/₂ cups vegetable stock

1 tbsp rice wine vinegar

1 tbsp light soy sauce

1 tbsp caster (superfine) sugar

1 tbsp Chinese rice wine or dry sherry

1 fresh red chilli, thinly sliced

1 tbsp cornflour (cornstarch)

2 tbsp water

1 Trim the cabbage and shred the leaves. Heat the stock in a large saucepan, add the cabbage and cook for 10–15 minutes.

2 Mix the vinegar, soy sauce, sugar and Chinese rice wine or sherry together and add to the broth, together with the chilli. Bring to the boil and cook for 2–3 minutes.

3 Blend the cornflour (cornstarch) with the water to form a smooth paste. Gradually stir the cornflour (cornstarch) mixture into the soup, stirring constantly until the broth thickens. Cook for a further 4–5 minutes. Ladle the soup into warm bowls and serve immediately.

COOK'S TIP

Cook a little rice and spoon into the base of the soup dishes. Ladle the soup over the rice and serve immediately.

Wonton Soup

Filled wontons are served in a clear soup. The recipe for the wonton skins makes 24 but the soup requires only 12 – freeze the rest for another time.

Serves 4
WONTON SKINS
1 egg
6 tbsp water
225 g/8 oz/2 cups plain (all-purpose) flour
FILLING
115 g/4 oz/$^1/_2$ cup frozen chopped spinach, thawed
15 g/$^1/_2$ oz/1 tbsp pine nuts, toasted and chopped
25g/1 oz/$^1/_4$ cup minced (ground) Quorn (mycoprotein)
salt
SOUP
600 ml/1 pint/2$^1/_2$ cups vegetable stock
1 tbsp dry sherry
1 tbsp light soy sauce
2 spring onions (scallions), chopped

1 Beat the egg lightly in a bowl and mix with the water. Stir in the flour to form a stiff dough. Knead lightly, then cover with a damp cloth and set aside to rest for 30 minutes.

2 Roll the dough out into a large sheet about 5 mm/¼ inch thick. Cut out 24 × 7-cm/3-inch squares. Dust each one with flour. Only 12 squares are required so freeze the rest.

3 To make the filling, squeeze out the excess water from the spinach. Mix the spinach with the pine nuts and Quorn (mycoprotein). Season with salt.

4 Divide the mixture into 12 and place one portion in the centre of each square. Seal by pressing the opposite corners of each square together.

5 To make the soup, bring the vegetable stock, sherry and soy sauce

to the boil in a large saucepan. Add the wontons and boil rapidly for 2–3 minutes.

6 Add the spring onions (scallions) to the soup, ladle into warm bowls and serve immediately

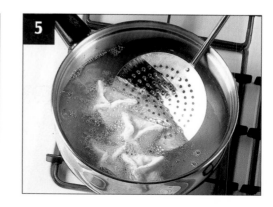

Spinach & Tofu (Bean Curd) Soup

This is a very colourful and delicious soup. If spinach is not in season,
watercress or lettuce can be used instead.

Serves 4
1 cake tofu (bean curd)
115 g/4 oz spinach leaves without stems
700 ml/1¼ pints/3 cups Chinese Stock (see page 16) or water
1 tbsp light soy sauce
salt and pepper

1 Cut the tofu (bean curd) into small
pieces about 5 mm/¼ inch thick. Wash
the spinach leaves and cut them into
small pieces or shreds, discarding any
discoloured leaves and tough stalks.
(If possible, use fresh young spinach
leaves, which have not yet developed
tough ribs. Otherwise, it is important
to cut out all the ribs and stems for
this soup.)

2 In a wok or large pan, bring the
stock to a rolling boil. Add the tofu
(bean curd) and soy sauce, bring back
to the boil and simmer for about
2 minutes over a medium heat.

3 Add the spinach and simmer for
1 more minute.

4 Skim the surface of the soup to
make it clear, adjust the seasoning
and serve immediately.

COOK'S TIP

For a stronger flavour, you could
use smoked or marinated tofu
(bean curd).

Beef & Vegetable Noodle Soup

Thin strips of beef are marinated in soy sauce and garlic to form the basis of this delicious soup. Served with noodles, it is both filling and delicious.

Serves 4
225 g/8 oz lean beef, cut into thin strips
1 garlic clove, crushed
2 spring onions (scallions), chopped
3 tbsp soy sauce
1 tsp sesame oil
225 g/8 oz egg noodles
850 ml/1¹/₂ pints/3³/₄ cups beef stock
13 baby corn cobs, sliced
¹/₂ leek, shredded
125 g/4¹/₂ oz broccoli florets
pinch of chilli powder

COOK'S VARIATION

If wished, add 1 tablespoon grated fresh ginger root to the marinade in step 1 for a spicier flavour.

COOK'S TIP

Vary the vegetables used, or use those to hand. If desired, use a few drops of chilli sauce in place of chilli powder, but remember it is very hot.

1 Put the beef in a shallow glass bowl with the garlic and spring onions (scallions). Add the soy sauce and sesame oil, cover and marinate for 30 minutes.

2 Cook the noodles in boiling water for 3–4 minutes, drain and reserve.

3 Bring the beef stock to the boil in a large saucepan and add the beef, together with the marinade, the baby corn cobs, leek and broccoli. Cover and simmer for 7–10 minutes, until the beef and vegetables are cooked through and tender.

4 Stir in the noodles and chilli powder and cook for a further 2–3 minutes. Serve immediately.

Noodles in Soup

Noodles in soup (tang mein) are more popular than fried noodles (chow mein) in China.
You can use different ingredients for the dressing, if preferred.

Serves 4
225 g/8 oz cooked chicken fillet, pork fillet (tenderloin), or other cooked meat
3–4 Chinese dried mushrooms, soaked in warm water for 30 minutes
115 g/4 oz canned sliced bamboo shoots, rinsed and drained
115 g/4 oz spinach leaves, lettuce hearts, or Chinese leaves (cabbage), shredded
2 spring onions (scallions), shredded finely
225 g/8 oz egg noodles
about 600 ml/1 pint/2½ cups Chinese Stock (see page 16)
2 tbsp light soy sauce
2 tbsp vegetable oil
1 tsp salt
½ tsp sugar
2 tsp Chinese rice wine or dry sherry
a few drops of sesame oil
1 tsp red chilli oil (optional)

1 Cut the meat into thin shreds. Squeeze dry the soaked mushrooms and discard the hard stalks.

2 Thinly shred the mushrooms, bamboo shoots, spinach leaves and spring onions (scallions).

3 Cook the noodles in boiling water according to the instructions on the packet, then drain and rinse under cold water. Place in a bowl. Bring the stock to a boil, add about 1 tablespoon soy sauce and pour it over the noodles. Keep warm.

4 Heat the oil in a preheated wok, add the meat, vegetables and about half the spring onions (scallions). Stir-fry for about 2–3 minutes. Add the salt, sugar, Chinese rice wine or sherry, sesame oil and chilli oil, if using.

5 Pour the mixture in the wok over the noodles, garnish with the remaining spring onions (scallions) and serve immediately.

Mushroom & Cucumber Noodle Soup

A light, refreshing clear soup of mushrooms, cucumber and small pieces of rice noodles, flavoured with soy sauce and a touch of garlic.

Serves 4
115 g/4 oz flat or open-cup mushrooms
½ cucumber
2 spring onions (scallions)
1 garlic clove
2 tbsp vegetable oil
25 g/1 oz/¼ cup Chinese rice noodles
¾ tsp salt
1 tbsp soy sauce

1 Wash the mushrooms and slice thinly. Do not remove the peel as this adds more flavour. Halve the cucumber lengthways. Scoop out and discard the seeds, using a teaspoon, and slice the cucumber thinly.

2 Chop the spring onions (scallions) finely and cut the garlic clove into thin strips.

3 Heat the oil in a preheated wok or large saucepan. Add the spring onions (scallions) and garlic, and stir-fry for 30 seconds. Add the mushrooms and stir-fry for 2–3 minutes.

4 Stir in 600 ml/1 pint/2½ cups water. Break the noodles into short lengths and add them to the soup. Bring to the boil.

5 Add the cucumber slices, salt and soy sauce, and simmer for 2–3 minutes.

6 Serve the soup in warm bowls, distributing the noodles and vegetables evenly among them.

Fish Soup with Wontons

This soup is topped with small wontons filled with prawns (shrimp),
making it both very tasty and satisfying.

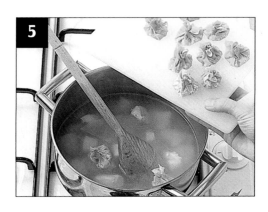

Serves 4
125 g/4¹/₂ oz large, cooked, peeled prawns (shrimp)
1 tsp chopped chives
1 small garlic clove, finely chopped
1 tbsp vegetable oil
12 wonton wrappers
1 small egg, beaten
850 ml/1¹/₂ pints/3³/₄ cups fish stock
175 g/6 oz white fish fillet, diced
dash of chilli sauce
sliced fresh red chilli and chives, to garnish

1 Roughly chop a quarter of the prawns (shrimp) and mix together with the chives and garlic.

2 Heat the oil in a preheated wok or heavy-based frying pan (skillet) and stir-fry the mixture for 1–2 minutes. Set aside to cool completely.

3 Spread out the wonton wrappers on a work surface (counter) and spoon a little of the filling into the centre of each. Brush the edges with beaten egg and fold in half, pressing out the air and sealing the edges well. Pinch into a round shape. Let stand while you are preparing the soup.

4 Pour the fish stock into a large saucepan and bring to the boil. Add the white fish fillet and the remaining prawns (shrimp). Cook over a medium heat for 5 minutes.

5 Add the chilli sauce and the wontons and cook for a further 5 minutes. Ladle the soup into warm individual serving bowls, garnish with red chilli slices and chives and serve immediately.

COOK'S VARIATION

Replace the prawns (shrimp) with cooked crabmeat for an alternative flavour.

Seafood & Tofu (Bean Curd) Soup

Use prawn (shrimp), squid or scallops, or a combination
of all three for this delicious soup.

Serves 4
225 g/8 oz seafood, such as peeled prawns (shrimp), squid, scallops, thawed if frozen
1/2 egg white, beaten lightly
1 tbsp Cornflour (Cornstarch) Paste (see page 16)
1 cake tofu (bean curd)
700 ml/1¼ pints/3 cups Chinese Stock (see page 16)
1 tbsp light soy sauce
salt and pepper
fresh coriander (cilantro) leaves, to garnish (optional)

1 Small prawns (shrimp) can be left whole; larger ones should be cut into smaller pieces. Cut the squid and scallops into small pieces.

2 If raw, mix the prawns (shrimp) and scallops with the egg white and cornflour (cornstarch) paste to prevent them from becoming tough when they are cooked.

3 Cut the tofu (bean curd) into about 24 small cubes.

4 Bring the stock to a rolling boil. Add the tofu (bean curd) and soy sauce, bring back to the boil and simmer for 1 minute.

5 Stir in the seafood, raw pieces first, cooked ones last. Bring back to boil and simmer for just 1 minute. Adjust the seasoning and serve garnished with coriander (cilantro) leaves, if using.

(Small) Shrimp Dumpling Soup

These dumplings filled with (small) shrimp and pork may be made
slightly larger and served as dim sum on their own.

Serves 4

FOR THE DOUGH

150 g/5¹/₂ oz/1²/₃ cups plain
(all-purpose) flour

50 ml/2 fl oz/¹/₄ cup
boiling water

5 tsp cold water

1¹/₂ tsp vegetable oil

FOR THE FILLING

125 g/4¹/₂ oz minced (ground) pork

125 g/4¹/₂ oz cooked
peeled (small) shrimp, chopped

50 g/1³/₄ oz canned water chestnuts,
drained and chopped

1 celery stick, chopped

1 tsp cornflour (cornstarch)

1 tbsp sesame oil

1 tbsp light soy sauce

FOR THE SOUP

850 ml/1¹/₂ pints/3³/₄ cups
fish stock

50 g/1³/₄ oz transparent
(cellophane) noodles

1 tbsp Chinese rice wine or
dry sherry

chopped chives,
to garnish

1 First make the dumplings. Mix together the flour, boiling water, cold water and oil in a bowl to make a pliable dough. Knead on a lightly floured surface for 5 minutes and cut into 16 equal-size pieces.

2 Roll the dough into rounds approximately 7.5 cm/3 inches in diameter.

3 Mix the filling ingredients together and spoon a little of the mixture into the centre of each round. Bring the dough together along the centre of the filling to form small, long dumplings. Press the edges together to seal and twist the dough along the seam.

4 Pour the fish stock into a large saucepan and bring to the boil. Add the noodles, dumplings and Chinese rice wine or dry sherry, bring back to the boil and simmer over a medium heat for 4–5 minutes, until the noodles and dumplings are cooked.

5 Ladle the soup into warm individual bowls, garnish with chopped chives and serve immediately.

Fish & Vegetable Soup

A chunky fish soup with strips of vegetables, flavoured with ginger and lemon, makes a meal in itself.

Serves 4
225 g/8 oz white fish fillets, such as cod, halibut, haddock, sole
1/2 tsp ground ginger
1/2 tsp salt
1 small leek, trimmed and sliced
1 tbsp sunflower oil
1 large carrot, cut into julienne strips
8 canned water chestnuts, drained and thinly sliced
1.2 litres/2 pints/5 cups fish or vegetable stock
1 tbsp lemon juice
1 tbsp light soy sauce
1 large courgette (zucchini), cut into julienne strips
2–4 crab sticks (optional), thawed if frozen
pepper

1 Remove any skin from the fish and cut the flesh into cubes, about 2.5 cm/1 inch. Combine the ground ginger and salt and rub into the fish. Marinate for at least 30 minutes.

2 Meanwhile, divide the green and white parts of the leek. Cut each part into 2.5-cm/1-inch lengths and then into julienne strips down the length of each piece, keeping the two parts separate. Slice the crab sticks into 1-cm/1/2-inch pieces.

3 Heat the oil in a wok. Add the white part of the leek and stir-fry for 1–2 minutes, then add the carrots and water chestnuts and stir-fry for 1–2 minutes.

4 Add the stock and bring to the boil, then add the lemon juice and soy sauce, lower the heat and simmer for 2 minutes.

5 Add the fish and continue to cook for about 5 minutes, until the fish begins to break up a little, then add the green part of the leek and the courgettes (zucchini) and simmer for about 1 minute. Add the sliced crab sticks, if using, and season to taste with pepper. Simmer for a further minute or so until piping hot. Ladle into warm individual soup bowls and serve immediately.

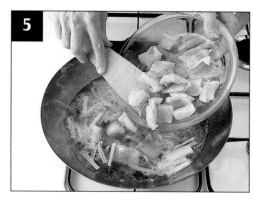

Crab & Ginger Soup

Two classic ingredients in Chinese cooking are blended together
in this recipe for a special soup.

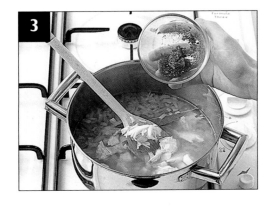

Serves 4

1 carrot, chopped
1 leek, chopped
1 bay leaf
850 ml/1½ pints/3¾ cups stock
2 medium-size cooked crabs
2.5-cm/1-inch piece fresh ginger root, grated
½ tsp ground star anise
5 ml/1 tsp light soy sauce
salt and pepper

COOK'S TIP

Loosen the crab by banging the
back underside with your fist, then
force the body away from the shell
with your thumbs.

COOK'S TIP

If freshly cooked crabs are
unavailable, use drained canned
crabmeat or thawed frozen
crabmeat instead.

1 Put the carrot, leek, bay leaf and
fish stock in a large saucepan and
bring to the boil. Reduce the heat,
cover and cook for 10 minutes.

2 Meanwhile, remove all the meat
from the cooked crabs. Break off the
claws, break the joints and remove all
the meat. You may require a fork or
skewer for this. Add the crabmeat to
the fish stock.

3 Add the ginger, soy sauce and star
anise to the fish stock and bring to
the boil. Simmer for 10 minutes and
adjust the seasoning to taste.

4 Spoon into warm individual
serving bowls and garnish with crab
claws. Serve immediately.

Three-Flavour Soup

Ideally, use raw prawns (shrimp) in this soup. If that is not possible,
add ready-cooked ones at the very last stage.

Serves 4

115 g/4 oz boneless skinless
chicken breast

115 g/4 oz raw peeled
prawns (shrimp)

salt

$1/2$ egg white, beaten lightly

2 tsp Cornflour (Cornstarch)
Paste (see page 16)

115 g/4 oz honey-roast ham

700 ml/1$1/4$ pints/3 cups Chinese
Stock (see page 16) or water

finely chopped spring onions
(scallions), to garnish

1 Thinly slice the chicken into small
shreds. If the prawns (shrimp) are
large, cut each in half lengthways,
otherwise leave whole.

2 Place the chicken and prawns
(shrimp) in a bowl and mix with a
pinch of salt, the egg white and
cornflour (cornstarch) paste until
thoroughly coated.

3 Cut the ham into small thin slices
approximately the same size as the
chicken pieces.

4 Bring the stock or water to a rolling
boil, add the chicken, the raw prawns
(shrimps) and the ham. Bring the
soup back to the boil and simmer for
1 minute.

5 Adjust the seasoning and ladle the
soup into warm individual bowls.
Garnish with the spring onions
(scallions) and serve immediately.

Curried Chicken & Sweetcorn (Corn) Soup

Tender cooked chicken strips and baby corn cobs are the main flavours in this delicious clear soup, with just a hint of ginger.

Serves 4
175 g/6 oz can sweetcorn (corn), drained
850 ml/1¹⁄₂ pints/3³⁄₄ cups chicken stock
350 g/12 oz cooked, lean chicken, cut into strips
16 baby corn cobs
1 tsp Chinese curry powder
1-cm/¹⁄₂-inch piece fresh ginger root, grated
3 tbsp light soy sauce
2 tbsp chopped chives

1 Put the canned sweetcorn (corn) in a food processor with 150 ml/¹⁄₄ pint/²⁄₃ cup of the chicken stock and process until smooth. Rub through a strainer, pressing with the back of a spoon to remove any husks.

2 Pour the remaining stock into a large saucepan and add the chicken strips. Stir in the sweetcorn (corn) purée.

3 Add the baby corn cobs and bring the soup to the boil. Boil for 10 minutes, then add the curry powder, ginger and soy sauce. Cook for a further 10–15 minutes and stir in the chives. Serve immediately in warm bowls.

COOK'S TIP

Prepare the soup up to 24 hours in advance without adding the chicken, then cool, cover and store in the refrigerator. Add the chicken just before serving and heat through.

Prawn (Shrimp) Soup

A mixture of textures and flavours make this an interesting and colourful soup. The egg may be made into a flat omelette and added as thin strips.

Serves 4
2 tbsp sunflower oil
2 spring onions (scallions), thinly sliced diagonally
1 carrot, coarsely grated
115 g/4 oz large closed-cup mushrooms, sliced thinly
1 litre/1³/₄ pints/4 cups fish or vegetable stock
¹/₂ tsp Chinese five-spice powder
1 tbsp light soy sauce
115 g/4 oz large peeled and deveined cooked prawns (shrimp), or peeled and deveined cooked tiger prawns (jumbo shrimp), thawed if frozen
¹/₂ bunch of watercress, trimmed and roughly chopped
1 egg, beaten well
salt and pepper
4 large prawns (shrimp) in shells, to garnish (optional)

1 Heat the oil in a preheated wok. Add the spring onions (scallions) and stir-fry for a minute, then add the carrots and mushrooms and continue to stir-fry for about 2 minutes.

2 Add the stock and bring to the boil, then season to taste with salt and pepper, five-spice powder and soy sauce. Lower the heat and simmer for 5 minutes.

3 If the prawns (shrimp) are really large, cut them in half before adding them to the wok, then continue to simmer for 3–4 minutes.

4 Add the roughly chopped watercress to the wok and mix well, then slowly pour in the beaten egg in a circular movement so that it cooks in threads in the soup.

5 Adjust the seasoning to taste and ladle the soup into warm individual soup bowls. Top each serving with a whole prawn (shrimp) and serve immediately.

Sweetcorn (Corn) & Crabmeat Soup

You should use American-style creamed sweetcorn (corn) for this soup since it originated among the Chinese community in the United States. Chicken can be used instead of the crabmeat.

Serves 4

115 g/4 oz crabmeat, or cooked chicken breast

¹/₄ tsp finely chopped fresh ginger root

2 egg whites

2 tbsp milk

1 tbsp Cornflour (Cornstarch) Paste (see page 16)

600 ml/1 pint/2¹/₂ cups Chinese Stock (see page 16)

225 g/8 oz can American-style creamed sweetcorn (corn)

salt and pepper

finely chopped spring onions (scallions), to garnish

1 Flake the crabmeat (or coarsely chop the chicken breast) and mix with the ginger.

2 Beat the egg whites until frothy, add the milk and cornflour (cornstarch) paste and beat again until smooth. Blend in the crabmeat or chicken.

3 Put the stock in a wok or large frying pan (skillet) and bring the stock to the boil. Add the creamed sweetcorn (corn), bring back to the boil and lower the heat.

4 Stir in the crabmeat or chicken pieces and egg-white mixture, adjust the seasoning and stir gently until the mixture is thoroughly blended. Ladle into warm individual soup bowls, garnish with chopped spring onions (scallions) and serve immediately.

Peking Duck Soup

This is a hearty and robustly flavoured soup, containing pieces of duck and vegetables cooked in a rich stock.

Serves 4
850 ml/1^1/$_2$ pints/3^3/$_4$ cups chicken or duck stock
1 tbsp Chinese rice wine or dry sherry
1 tbsp light soy sauce
225 g/8 oz Chinese leaves (cabbage), shredded
125 g/4^1/$_2$ oz lean duck breast meat, finely diced
2 garlic cloves, crushed
pinch of ground star anise
1 tbsp sesame seeds
1 tsp sesame oil
1 tbsp chopped fresh parsley

1 Bring the stock to the boil in a large saucepan. Add the sherry or rice wine, soy sauce, Chinese leaves (cabbage) and duck. Reduce the heat and simmer for 15 minutes.

2 Stir in the garlic and star anise and cook for a further 10–15 minutes, until the duck is tender.

3 Meanwhile, dry-fry the sesame seeds in a hot, wok or heavy-based frying pan (skillet), stirring constantly. Remove from the pan and stir into the soup, together with the sesame oil and parsley. Ladle into warm individual soup bowls and serve immediately.

COOK'S TIP

If Chinese leaves (cabbage) are unavailable, use green cabbage.

Chicken & Sweetcorn (Corn) Soup

A hint of chilli and sherry flavour this chicken and sweetcorn (corn) soup, which contains red (bell) pepper and tomato for colour and flavour.

Serves 4
1 boneless skinless chicken breast, about 175 g/6 oz
2 tbsp sunflower oil
2–3 spring onions (scallions), thinly sliced diagonally
1 small or ½ large red (bell) pepper, cored, seeded and thinly sliced
1 garlic clove, crushed
115 g/4 oz baby corn cobs, thinly sliced
1 litre/1¾ pints/4 cups chicken stock
200 g/7 oz can sweetcorn kernels, well drained
2 tbsp sherry
2–3 tsp sweet chilli sauce
2–3 tsp cornflour (cornstarch)
2 tomatoes, peeled, quartered, seeded and sliced
salt and pepper
chopped fresh coriander (cilantro) or parsley, to garnish

1 Cut the chicken breast into 4 strips lengthways, then cut each strip into narrow slices across the grain.

2 Heat the oil in a preheated wok. Add the chicken and stir-fry for 3–4 minutes, spreading it out well in the wok, until it is well sealed and golden all over and almost completely cooked.

3 Add the spring onions (scallions), (bell) pepper and garlic and continue to stir-fry for 2–3 minutes, then add the baby corn cobs and stock and bring to the boil.

4 Add the corn kernels, rice wine or sherry, sweet chilli sauce and salt to taste and simmer for 5 minutes, stirring from time to time.

5 Blend the cornflour (cornstarch) with a little cold water, add to the soup and bring to the boil. Add the strips of tomato, adjust the seasoning and simmer for a few minutes. Ladle the soup into warm individual soup bowls, sprinkle finely chopped coriander (cilantro) or parsley on top and serve immediately.

Clear Chicken & Egg Soup

This tasty chicken soup has the addition of poached eggs, making it both delicious and filling. Use fresh, home-made chicken stock for a better flavour.

Serves 4
1 tsp salt
1 tbsp rice wine vinegar
4 eggs
850 ml/1^1/$_2$ pints/3^3/$_4$ cups chicken stock
1 leek, sliced
125 g/4^1/$_2$ oz broccoli florets
125 g/4^1/$_2$ oz/1 cup shredded cooked chicken
2 open-cap mushrooms, sliced
1 tbsp Chinese rice wine or dry sherry
dash of chilli sauce
chilli powder, to garnish

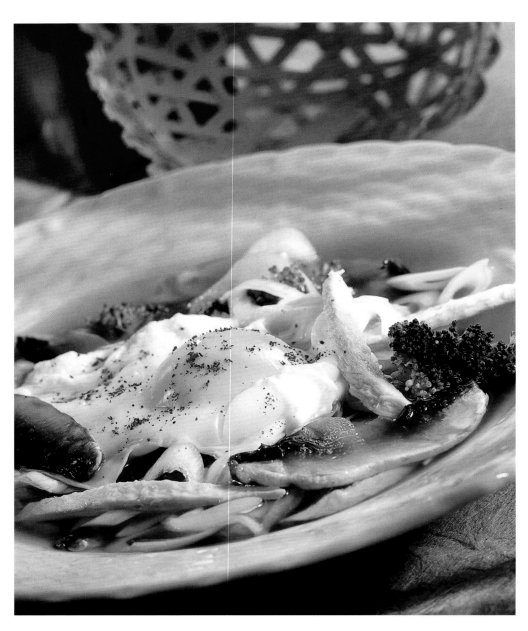

1 Bring a large saucepan of water to the boil and add the salt and vinegar. Reduce the heat so that it is just simmering and carefully break the eggs into the water, one at a time. Poach for 1 minute and remove with a slotted spoon.

2 Bring the chicken stock to the boil in a separate pan and add the leek, broccoli, chicken, mushrooms and sherry and season with chilli sauce to taste. Cook for 10–15 minutes.

3 Add the poached eggs to the soup and cook for a further 2 minutes. Ladle the soup into warm individual soup bowls, dividing the eggs among them. Dust with a little chilli powder and serve immediately.

COOK'S VARIATION

For a vegetarian version, use vegetable stock and 115 g/4 oz shredded firm tofu (bean curd) instead of the chicken.

COOK'S TIP

Use 4 dried Chinese mushrooms, rehydrated according to the packet instructions, in place of the open-cap mushrooms.

Chicken Soup with Almonds

This soup can also be made using turkey or pheasant breasts.
Pheasant gives a stronger, gamey flavour.

Serves 4
1 large or 2 small boneless skinless chicken breasts
1 tbsp sunflower oil
4 spring onions (scallions), thinly sliced diagonally
1 carrot, cut into julienne strips
700 ml/1¼ pints/3 cups chicken stock
finely grated rind of ½ lemon
40 g/1½ oz/⅓ cup ground almonds
1 tbsp light soy sauce
1 tbsp lemon juice
25 g/1 oz/¼ cup flaked (slivered) almonds, toasted
salt and pepper

1 Using a very sharp knife, cut each chicken breast into 4 strips lengthways, then slice the strips very thinly across the grain to produce fine shreds of chicken.

2 Heat the oil in a preheated wok. Add the chicken and stir-fry for 3–4 minutes, until sealed and almost completely cooked through. Then add the carrot and continue to stir-fry for 2–3 minutes. Add the spring onions (scallions) and stir-fry for a further 2 minutes.

3 Add the stock to the wok and bring to the boil. Add the lemon rind, ground almonds, soy sauce and lemon juice and season to taste with salt and pepper. Bring back to the boil, lower the heat and simmer, uncovered, for 5 minutes, stirring occasionally.

4 Add most of the toasted flaked (slivered) almonds and continue to cook for a further 1–2 minutes. Check and adjust the seasoning.

5 Ladle the soup into warm individual soup bowls, sprinkle with the remaining almonds to garnish and serve immediately.

Lamb & Rice Soup

This is a very filling soup, as it contains rice and tender pieces of lamb.
Serve before a light main course.

Serves 4
50 g/1³/₄ oz/¹/₄ cup rice
850 ml/1¹/₂ pints/3³/₄ cups lamb stock
150 g/5¹/₂ oz lean lamb, cut into strips
1 leek, sliced
1 garlic clove, thinly sliced
2 tsp light soy sauce
1 tsp rice wine vinegar
1 medium open-cap mushroom, sliced

1 Cook the rice in boiling salted water for 10–15 minutes. Drain and rinse under cold running water.

2 Meanwhile, bring the lamb stock to the boil in a large saucepan. Add the lamb strips, leek, garlic, soy sauce and vinegar. Reduce the heat, cover and simmer for 10 minutes, until the lamb is cooked through.

3 Add the mushroom slices and the rice and cook for a further 2–3 minutes, until the mushroom is cooked.

4 Ladle into warm individual bowls and serve immediately.

COOK'S TIP

Use a few dried Chinese mushrooms, rehydrated according to the packet instructions and chopped, instead of the open-cap mushroom. Add with the lamb.

Pork & Szechuan Vegetable Soup

Sold in cans, Szechuan preserved vegetable is pickled mustard root,
which is quite hot and salty, so rinse in water before use.

Serves 4
225 g/8 oz pork fillet (tenderloin)
2 tsp Cornflour (Cornstarch) Paste (see page 16)
115 g/4 oz Szechuan preserved vegetable
700 ml/1¼ pints/3 cups Chinese Stock (see page 16) or water
salt and pepper
a few drops of sesame oil (optional)
2–3 spring onions (scallions), sliced, to garnish

1 Cut the pork across the grain into thin shreds and place in a bowl. Add the cornflour (cornstarch) paste and mix thoroughly.

2 Wash and rinse the Szechuan preserved vegetable, then cut into thin shreds approximately the same size as the pork.

3 Bring the stock or water to a rolling boil, add the pork and stir to separate the shreds. Bring back to the boil.

4 Add the Szechuan preserved vegetable and bring back to the boil once more. Adjust the seasoning and sprinkle with sesame oil, if using. Ladle into warm individual soup bowls, garnish with spring onions (scallions) and serve immediately.

Fish & Seafood

China's extensive coastline and the many rivers and inland lakes ensure an abundance of fresh fish and seafood. They are prepared in a variety of ways, often marinated with herbs and spices, and cooked in combination with fresh vegetables. Steaming is a favourite technique for cooking whole fish, while seafood is frequently stir-fried. Whole fish and fillets are also braised or poached.

Shellfish may be fried at a high temperature in a flavoured oil, which penetrates the shells to create a delicious sauce.

Black bean sauce, fresh chillies, ginger, pineapple and other fruits, soy sauce, lemon grass, cashew nuts and rice wine are typical ingredients used to flavour many fish dishes.

The recipes in this chapter reflect the different regional approaches to preparing fish. Try Fish in Szechuan Hot Sauce for a spicy way of serving freshwater fish, which abound in western China, or Fried Squid Flowers, a Cantonese seafood speciality.

Trout with Pineapple

Pineapple is widely used in Chinese cooking. The tartness of fresh pineapple complements fish particularly well.

Serves 4

4 trout fillets, skinned

2 tbsp vegetable oil

2 garlic cloves, cut into slivers

4 slices fresh pineapple,
peeled and diced

1 celery stick, sliced

1 tbsp light soy sauce

50 ml/2 fl oz/¼ cup fresh
or unsweetened pineapple juice

150 ml/¼ pint/⅔ cup
fish stock

1 tsp cornflour (cornstarch)

2 tsp water

shredded celery leaves and fresh
red chilli strips, to garnish

1 Using a sharp knife, cut the trout fillets into strips.

2 Heat 1 tablespoon of the oil in a preheated wok until almost smoking and cook the fish for 2 minutes, stirring well. Remove from the wok and set aside.

3 Add the remaining oil, reduce the heat and stir-fry the garlic, pineapple and celery for 1–2 minutes.

4 Add the soy sauce, pineapple juice and stock to the wok. Bring to the boil and cook for 2–3 minutes to reduce the sauce.

5 Blend the cornflour (cornstarch) with the water to form a paste and stir it into the wok. Bring the sauce to the boil and cook, stirring constantly, until the sauce thickens and clears.

6 Return the fish to the wok, and cook, stirring gently, until heated through.

7 Transfer to a warm serving dish, garnish with shredded celery leaves and red chilli strips and serve.

COOK'S TIP

Use canned pineapple instead of fresh, choosing slices in unsweetened, natural juice in preference to a syrup.

Fish with Black Bean Sauce

Any firm steaks such as salmon or turbot
can be cooked by the same method.

Serves 4–6

1 sea bass or trout, weighing about
675g/1¹/₂ lb, cleaned

1 tsp salt

1 tbsp sesame oil

2–3 spring onions (scallions),
cut in half lengthways

1 tbsp light soy sauce

1 tbsp Chinese rice wine
or dry sherry

1 tbsp finely shredded
ginger root

1 tbsp oil

2 tbsp crushed black bean sauce

2 spring onions (scallions),
shredded finely

TO GARNISH

fresh coriander (cilantro) leaves
(optional)

lemon slices

4 Heat the oil in a preheated wok or saucepan until hot, then stir in the black bean sauce. Remove the fish from the steamer and transfer to a serving dish. Pour the hot black bean sauce over the whole length of the fish and place the shredded spring onions (scallions) on top. Serve garnished with coriander (cilantro) leaves, if using, and lemon slices.

1 Using a sharp knife, score both sides of the fish with diagonal cuts at 2.5-cm/1-inch intervals. Rub both the inside and outside of the fish with the salt and sesame oil.

2 Place the spring onions (scallions) on a heatproof platter and put the fish on top. Blend the soy sauce and wine with the ginger shreds and pour the mixture evenly all over the fish.

3 Place the fish on the platter in a bamboo steamer or inside a wok on a rack. Cover tightly and steam vigorously for 12–15 minutes, adding more water if necessary, until the fish is tender and cooked through.

Crispy Fish with Chillies

This is a hot dish, not for the faint hearted. It may be made without the chilli flavourings if preferred.

Serves 4
450 g/1 lb white fish fillets

FOR THE BATTER

50 g/1³/₄ oz/¹/₂ cup plain (all-purpose) flour
1 egg, separated
1 tbsp peanut oil
4 tbsp milk
vegetable oil, for deep-frying

FOR THE SAUCE

1 fresh red chilli, chopped
2 garlic cloves, crushed
pinch of chilli powder
3 tbsp tomato purée (paste)
1 tbsp rice wine vinegar
2 tbsp dark soy sauce
2 tbsp Chinese rice wine
2 tbsp water
pinch of caster (superfine) sugar

1 Cut the fish into 2.5-cm/1-inch cubes and set aside. Sift the flour into a mixing bowl and make a well in the centre. Add the egg yolk and oil to the bowl and gradually stir in the milk, incorporating the flour to form a smooth batter. Let stand for 20 minutes.

2 Beat the egg white until it forms peaks and fold it into the batter. Heat the oil in a preheated wok. Dip the fish into the batter and fry it, in batches, for 8–10 minutes, until cooked through and golden. Remove the fish from the wok with a slotted spoon and keep warm while you cook the remaining batches.

3 Pour off all but 1 tbsp of oil from the wok and return it to the heat. Add the chilli, garlic, chilli powder, tomato purée (paste), vinegar, soy sauce, wine, water and sugar and cook, stirring, for 3–4 minutes.

4 Return the fish to the wok and stir gently to coat it thoroughly in the sauce. Cook for 2–3 minutes, until completely heated through. Transfer the fish and sauce to a warm serving dish and serve immediately.

Braised Fish Fillets

Any white fish is ideal for this dish. Lemon sole is particularly
delicious cooked in this way.

Serves 4
3–4 small Chinese dried mushrooms
300–350 g/10$^1/_2$–12 oz fish fillets
1 tsp salt
$^1/_2$ egg white, lightly beaten
1 tsp Cornflour (Cornstarch) Paste (see page 16)
600 ml/1 pint/2$^1/_2$ cups vegetable oil
1 tsp finely chopped fresh ginger root
2 spring onions (scallions), finely chopped
1 garlic clove, finely chopped
$^1/_2$ small green (bell) pepper, seeded and cut into small cubes
$^1/_2$ small carrot, thinly sliced
50 g/1$^3/_4$ oz canned sliced bamboo shoots, rinsed and drained
$^1/_2$ tsp sugar
1 tbsp light soy sauce
1 tsp Chinese rice wine or dry sherry
1 tbsp chilli bean sauce
2–3 tbsp Chinese Stock (see page 16) or water
a few drops of sesame oil

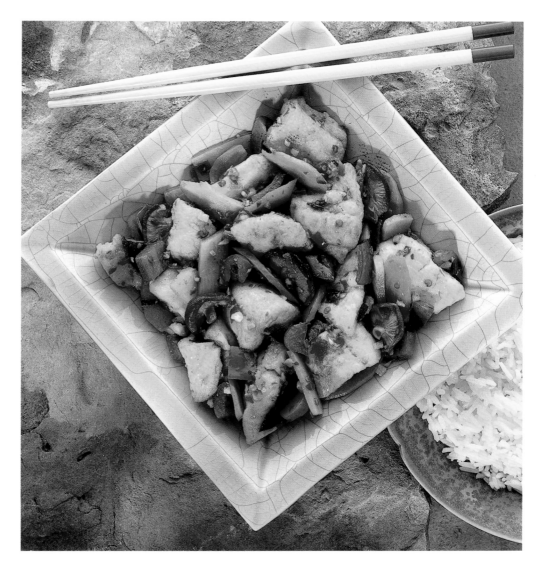

1 Soak the dried mushrooms in warm water for 30 minutes, then drain on kitchen paper (paper towels), reserving the soaking water for stock. Squeeze the mushrooms to extract all the moisture, cut off and discard any hard stems and slice the caps thinly.

2 Cut the fish into bite-size pieces, then place in a shallow dish and mix with a pinch of salt, the egg white and cornflour (cornstarch) paste, turning the fish to coat well.

3 Heat the oil and deep-fry the fish pieces for about 1 minute. Remove with a slotted spoon and drain on kitchen paper (paper towels).

4 Pour off the oil, leaving about 1 tablespoon in the wok. Add the ginger, spring onions (scallions) and garlic to flavour the oil for a few seconds, then add the vegetables and stir-fry for about 1 minute.

5 Add the sugar, soy sauce, wine or sherry, chilli bean sauce, stock or water, and remaining salt, and bring to the boil. Add the fish pieces, stir to coat well with the sauce, and braise for another minute. Sprinkle with sesame oil and serve immediately.

Mullet with Ginger

Ginger is used widely in Chinese cooking for its strong, pungent flavour. Always use fresh ginger where possible, but ground ginger may be used as an alternative when fresh is not available.

Serves 4
1 whole mullet, cleaned and scaled
2 spring onions (scallions), finely chopped
1 tsp grated fresh ginger root
125 ml/4 fl oz/¹/₂ cup garlic wine vinegar
125 ml/4 fl oz/¹/₂ cup light soy sauce
3 tsp caster (superfine) sugar
dash of chilli sauce
125 ml/4 fl oz/¹/₂ cup fish stock
1 green (bell) pepper, seeded and thinly sliced
1 large tomato, peeled, seeded and cut into thin strips
salt and pepper
sliced tomato, to garnish

1 Wash the fish inside and out and pat dry with kitchen paper (paper towels).

2 Make three diagonal slits in the flesh on each side of the fish. Season the fish with salt and pepper inside and out.

3 Place the fish on a heatproof plate and scatter the spring onions (scallions) and ginger over the top. Cover and steam for 10 minutes, or until the fish is cooked through.

4 Meanwhile, place the vinegar, soy sauce, sugar, chilli sauce, fish stock, (bell) pepper and tomato in a saucepan and bring to the boil. Cook over a high heat to reduce and thicken the sauce slightly.

5 Transfer the fish to a serving dish, pour the sauce over it, garnish with tomato slices and serve immediately.

COOK'S TIP

Use fillets of fish for this recipe if wished and reduce the cooking time for the fish to 5–7 minutes.

Fish in Szechuan Hot Sauce

This is a classic Szechuan recipe. When served in a restaurant,
the fish head and tail are removed before cooking.

Serves 4

1 carp, bream, sea bass, trout,
grouper or grey mullet,
about 750 g/1 lb 10 oz, gutted

1 tbsp light soy sauce

1 tbsp Chinese rice wine
or dry sherry

vegetable oil, for deep-frying

flat-leaf parsley or coriander
(cilantro) sprigs, to garnish

SAUCE

2 garlic cloves, finely chopped

2–3 spring onions (scallions),
finely chopped

1 tsp finely chopped ginger root

2 tbsp chilli bean sauce

1 tbsp tomato purée (paste)

2 tsp sugar

1 tbsp rice vinegar

125 ml/4 fl oz/$^{1}/_{2}$ cup Chinese
Stock (see page 16)
or water

1 tbsp Cornflour (Cornstarch)
Paste (see page 16)

$^{1}/_{2}$ tsp sesame oil

1 Wash the fish and dry well on
kitchen paper (paper towels). Score
both sides of the fish to the bone with
a sharp knife, making diagonal cuts at
intervals of about 2.5 cm/1 inch. Rub
the fish with the soy sauce and wine
on both sides, then marinate in the
refrigerator for 10–15 minutes.

2 Heat the oil in a preheated wok
until smoking. Deep-fry the fish in
the hot oil for about 3–4 minutes on
both sides, or until golden brown.

3 Pour off the oil, leaving about
1 tablespoon in the wok. Push the fish
to one side of the wok and add the
garlic, the white parts of the spring
onions (scallions), ginger, chilli bean
sauce, tomato purée (paste), sugar,
vinegar and stock. Bring to the boil and
braise the fish in the sauce for

4–5 minutes, turning it over once, until
it is tender and cooked through.

4 Add the green parts of the spring
onions (scallions) and stir in the
cornflour (cornstarch) paste. Sprinkle
with sesame oil and serve, garnished
with parsley or coriander (cilantro).

Steamed Snapper with Fruit & Ginger Stuffing

Red mullet may be used in place of the whole snapper, although they are a little more difficult to stuff because their size. Use one mullet per person.

Serves 4

1.4 kg/3 lb whole snapper,
cleaned and scaled

175 g/6 oz spinach

orange slices and shredded
spring onion (scallion),
to garnish

FOR THE STUFFING

50 g/1³/₄ oz/2 cups cooked
long-grain rice

1 tsp grated fresh
ginger root

2 spring onions (scallions),
finely chopped

2 tsp light soy sauce

1 tsp sesame oil

¹/₂ tsp ground star anise

1 orange,
segmented and chopped

1 Wash the fish inside and out and pat dry with kitchen paper (paper towels). Blanch the spinach for 40 seconds, then drain well. Arrange the spinach on a heatproof plate and place the fish on top.

2 Thoroughly mix all the stuffing ingredients together.

3 Spoon the stuffing into the body cavity of the fish, pressing it in well with a spoon.

4 Cover the plate and cook in a steamer for 10 minutes, or until the fish is cooked through. Garnish with orange slices and shredded spring onion (scallion) and serve.

Scallops In Ginger Sauce

Scallops are both attractive and delicious and make this a special dish. Cooked with ginger and orange, this dish is perfect served with plain rice.

Serves 4
2 tbsp vegetable oil
450 g/1 lb scallops, cleaned and halved
2.5-cm/1-inch piece fresh ginger root, finely chopped
3 garlic cloves, crushed
2 leeks, shredded
75 g/3 oz/³/₄ cup shelled peas
125 g/4¹/₂ oz canned bamboo shoots, drained
2 tbsp light soy sauce
2 tbsp unsweetened orange juice
1 tsp caster (superfine) sugar
orange zest, to garnish

1 Heat the oil in a preheated wok. Add the scallops and stir-fry for 1–2 minutes. Remove the scallops from the wok with a slotted spoon and set aside.

2 Add the ginger and garlic to the wok and stir-fry for 30 seconds.

3 Stir in the leeks and peas and cook, stirring, for a further 2 minutes.

4 Add the bamboo shoots and return the scallops to the wok.

5 Stir in the soy sauce, orange juice and sugar and cook for 1–2 minutes.

6 Transfer to a warm serving dish, garnish with the orange zest and serve immediately.

COOK'S TIP

The edible parts of the scallop are the round white muscle and the coral or roe. Use the skirt for making stock.

COOK'S TIP

Frozen scallops may be thawed and used in this recipe, adding them at the end of cooking to prevent them from breaking up.

Spiced Scallops

Scallops are available both fresh and frozen.
Make sure they are completely thawed before cooking.

Serves 4
12 large scallops with coral attached, thawed if frozen, or 350 g/12 oz small scallops without coral, thawed
4 tbsp sunflower oil
4–6 spring onions (scallions), thinly sliced diagonally
1 garlic clove, crushed
2.5-cm/1-inch piece fresh ginger root, finely chopped
225 g/8 oz mangetout (snow peas)
115 g/4 oz button or closed-cup mushrooms, sliced
2 tbsp Chinese rice wine or dry sherry
2 tbsp light soy sauce
1 tbsp clear honey
1/4 tsp ground allspice
1 tbsp sesame seeds, toasted
salt and pepper

1 Wash and dry the scallops, discarding any black pieces. Detach the corals, if using. Slice each scallop into 3–4 pieces and halve the corals if they are large.

2 Heat 2 tablespoons of oil in a preheated wok. Add the spring onions (scallions), garlic and ginger, and stir-fry for a minute or so. Add the mangetouts (snow peas) and continue to stir-fry for 2–3 minutes. Remove from the wok with a slotted spoon and transfer to a bowl.

3 Add the remaining oil to the wok. When it is really hot, add the scallops and corals, and stir-fry for 2–3 minutes. Add the mushrooms and continue to cook for a further 1–2 minutes.

4 Add the wine or sherry, soy sauce, honey and allspice, with salt and pepper to taste. Mix thoroughly, then return the vegetable mixture to the wok.

5 Season well and toss together over a high heat for a minute or so, until piping hot. Serve immediately, sprinkled with sesame seeds.

Stir-Fried Prawns (Shrimp) & Vegetables

This colourful and delicious dish is cooked with vegetables.
Vary them according to seasonal availability.

Serves 4
50 g/1³/₄ oz mangetout (snow peas)
¹/₂ small carrot, thinly sliced lengthways
50 g/1³/₄ oz baby corn cobs
50 g/1³/₄ oz straw mushrooms
175–225 g/6–8 oz raw tiger prawns (jumbo shrimp), peeled and deveined
salt
¹/₂ egg white, beaten lightly
1 tsp Cornflour (Cornstarch) Paste (see page 16)
about 300 ml/¹/₂ pint/1¹/₄ cups vegetable oil
1 spring onion (scallion), cut into short sections
4 slices fresh ginger root, finely chopped
¹/₂ tsp caster (superfine) sugar
1 tbsp light soy sauce
1 tsp Chinese rice wine or dry sherry
a few drops of sesame oil

1 Top and tail the mangetout (snow peas). Cut the carrot into slices the same size as the mangetouts (snow peas). Halve the baby corn cobs and straw mushrooms.

2 Mix the prawns (shrimp) with a pinch of salt, the egg white and cornflour (cornstarch) paste.

3 Heat the oil in a preheated wok. Add the prawns (shrimp), stirring to separate them. Stir-fry and remove from the wok with a slotted spoon as soon as their colour changes.

4 Pour off the oil, leaving about 1 tablespoon in the wok. Add the mangetouts (snow peas), carrot, baby corn, mushrooms, spring onion (scallion) and ginger root. Stir-fry for about 1 minute.

5 Return the prawns (shrimp) to the wok and add the sugar, soy sauce and Chinese rice wine or dry sherry. Blend well. Sprinkle with the sesame oil, transfer to a warm serving dish and serve immediately.

Stir-Fried Prawns (Shrimp)

This quick and easy dish has a subtle flavour and would make an excellent light lunch
served with plain boiled rice.

Serves 4
175 g/6 oz raw prawns (shrimp), peeled and deveined
1 tsp salt
¼ tsp egg white
2 tsp Cornflour (Cornstarch) Paste (see page 16)
300 ml/½ pint/1¼ cups vegetable oil
1 spring onion (scallion), cut into short sections
2.5-cm/1-inch piece fresh ginger root, thinly sliced
1 small green (bell) pepper, seeded and cubed
½ tsp caster (superfine) sugar
1 tbsp light soy sauce
1 tsp Chinese rice wine or dry sherry
a few drops of sesame oil

1 Mix the prawns (shrimp) with a
pinch of salt, the egg white and
cornflour (cornstarch) paste until they
are all well coated.

2 Heat the oil in a preheated wok and
stir-fry the prawns (shrimp) for
30–40 seconds only. Remove and
drain on kitchen paper (paper towels).

3 Pour off the oil, leaving about
1 tablespoon in the wok. Add the
spring onion (scallion) and ginger to
flavour the oil for a few seconds, then
add the green (bell) pepper and stir-
fry for about 1 minute.

4 Add the remaining salt and the
sugar followed by the prawns

(shrimp). Continue stirring for
another minute or so, then add the
soy sauce and Chinese rice wine or
sherry and blend well. Sprinkle with
sesame oil, transfer to a warm serving
dish and serve immediately.

COOK'S VARIATION

The green (bell) peppers can be
replaced by either mangetout
(snow peas) or broccoli.

Seafood Combination

Use any combination of fish and shellfish in this delicious dish
of coated fish served in a wine sauce.

Serves 4
2 tbsp dry white wine
1 egg white, lightly beaten
¹/₂ tsp Chinese five-spice powder
1 tsp cornflour (cornstarch)
300 g/10¹/₂ oz raw prawns (shrimp), peeled and deveined
125 g/4¹/₂ oz prepared squid, cut into rings
125 g/4¹/₂ oz white fish fillets, cut into strips
vegetable oil, for deep-frying
1 green (bell) pepper, seeded and cut into thin strips
1 carrot, cut into thin strips
4 baby corn cobs, halved lengthways

1 Mix together the wine, egg white, Chinese five-spice powder and cornflour (cornstarch) in a large bowl.

2 Add the prawns (shrimp), squid and fish fillets to the mixture and stir to evenly coat. Remove the mixed fish with a slotted spoon, reserving any remaining cornflour (cornstarch) mixture.

3 Heat the oil in a preheated wok and deep-fry the prawns (shrimp), squid and fish for 2–3 minutes. Remove the seafood from the wok with a slotted spoon and set aside.

4 Pour off all but 1 tablespoon of the oil from the wok and return to the heat. Add the (bell) pepper, carrot and corn cobs to the wok and stir-fry for 4–5 minutes.

5 Return the seafood to the wok with any reserved cornflour (cornstarch) mixture and toss well to heat through thoroughly.

6 Transfer to a warm serving dish and serve immediately.

COOK'S TIP

Using a sharp knife, open up the squid rings and score a lattice pattern on the flesh to make them look more attractive.

Szechuan Prawns (Shrimp)

This spicy dish would make an excellent light main course.
Serve with rice or noodles and a leafy green salad.

Serves 4
225–300 g/8–10¹/₂ oz raw tiger prawns (jumbo shrimp)
pinch of salt
¹/₂ egg white, lightly beaten
1 tsp Cornflour (Cornstarch) Paste (see page 16)
600 ml/1 pint/2¹/₂ cups vegetable oil
fresh coriander (cilantro) leaves, to garnish

SAUCE

1 tsp finely chopped fresh ginger root
2 spring onions (scallions), finely chopped
1 garlic clove, finely chopped
3–4 small dried red chillies, seeded and chopped
1 tbsp light soy sauce
1 tsp Chinese rice wine or dry sherry
1 tbsp tomato purée (paste)
1 tbsp oyster sauce
2–3 tbsp Chinese Stock (see page 16) or water
a few drops of sesame oil

1 Peel and devein the prawns (shrimp), then mix with the salt, egg white and cornflour (cornstarch) paste until coated all over.

2 Heat the oil in a preheated wok until it is smoking, then deep-fry the prawns (shrimp) for about 1 minute. Remove with a slotted spoon and drain on kitchen paper (paper towels).

3 Pour off the oil, leaving about 1 tablespoon in the wok. Add all the ingredients for the sauce, bring to the boil and stir until smooth and thoroughly blended.

4 Add the prawns (shrimp) to the sauce, stirring to blend. Garnish with coriander (cilantro) leaves and serve.

COOK'S TIP

If raw prawns are not available, omit steps 1 and 2 and add the cooked prawns before the sauce in step 3.

Sizzled Chilli Prawns (Shrimp)

Large prawns (shrimp) are marinated in a chilli mixture then
stir-fried with cashews. Serve with fluffy rice and braised vegetables.

Serves 4
5 tbsp soy sauce
5 tbsp Chinese rice wine or dry sherry
3 dried red chillies, seeded and chopped
2 garlic cloves, crushed
2 tsp grated fresh ginger root
5 tbsp water
500 g/1 lb 2 oz peeled cooked tiger prawns (jumbo shrimp), deveined
1 large bunch spring onions (scallions), chopped
75 g/2¾ oz/¾ cup salted cashew nuts
3 tbsp vegetable oil
2 tsp cornflour (cornstarch)
boiled rice and braised vegetables, to serve

1 Mix the soy sauce with the Chinese
rice wine or sherry, chillies, garlic,
ginger and water in a large bowl.

2 Add the prawns (shrimp), spring
onions (scallions) and cashew nuts
and mix thoroughly so that they are
well coated. Cover tightly and
marinate in the refrigerator for at
least 2 hours, stirring occasionally.

3 Heat the oil in a preheated wok or
large, heavy-based frying pan (skillet).
Remove the prawns (shrimp), spring
onions (scallions) and cashews from
the marinade with a slotted spoon
and add to the wok or pan, reserving
the marinade. Stir-fry over a high heat
for 1–2 minutes.

4 Mix the marinade and cornflour
(cornstarch). Add to the pan and cook
for 30 seconds, until the marinade
forms a slightly thickened shiny glaze
over the prawn (shrimp) mixture.

5 Transfer the chilli prawns (shrimp)
to a warm serving dish and serve
immediately, with plenty of boiled
rice and a selection of braised
vegetables.

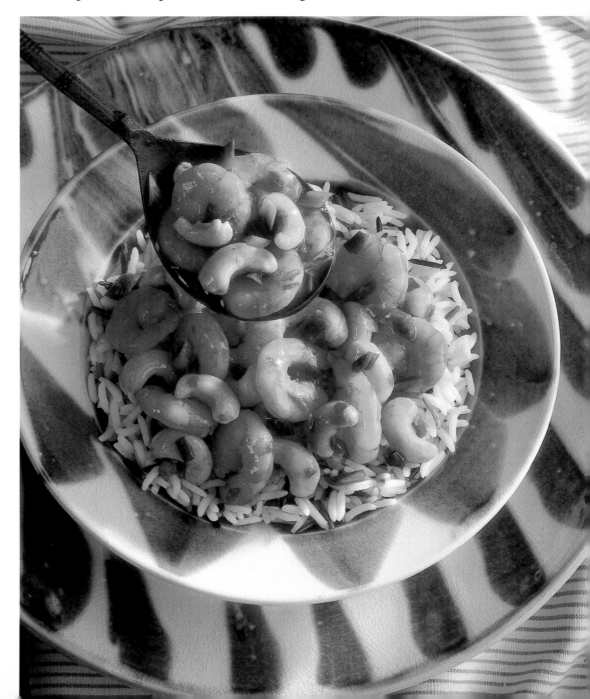

Prawn (Shrimp) Stir-Fry with Lemon Grass

A very quick and tasty stir-fry using prawns (shrimp),
cucumber and oyster mushrooms, flavoured with lemon grass.

Serves 4
¹/₂ cucumber
2 tsp cornflour (cornstarch)
2 tbsp water
1 tbsp dark soy sauce
¹/₂ tsp fish sauce
2 tbsp sunflower oil
6 spring onions (scallions), halved lengthways and cut into 4-cm/1¹/₂-inch lengths
1 stalk lemon grass, thinly sliced
1 garlic clove, chopped
1 tsp chopped fresh red chilli
115 g/4 oz oyster mushrooms, torn into pieces
1 tsp chopped fresh ginger root
350 g/12 oz cooked peeled prawns (shrimp), deveined
2 tbsp Chinese rice wine or dry sherry
boiled rice, to serve

1 Cut the cucumber into thin strips measuring about 5 mm x 4 cm/ ¹/₄ x 1³/₄ inches.

2 In a small bowl, mix together the cornflour (cornstarch), water, soy sauce and fish sauce until smooth and set aside.

3 Heat the oil in a preheated wok or large frying pan (skillet). Add the spring onions (scallions), cucumber, lemon grass, garlic, chilli, mushrooms and ginger and stir-fry for 2 minutes.

4 Add the prawns (shrimp) and stir-fry for a further minute.

5 Stir the cornflour (cornstarch) and soy sauce mixture and Chinese rice wine or dry sherry into the ingredients in the wok or pan and heat through, stirring constantly, until the sauce has thickened and is piping hot.

6 Transfer to a warm serving dish and serve immediately with boiled rice.

(Small) Shrimp Fu Yong

The classic ingredients of this popular dish are eggs, carrots and (small) shrimp.
Add extra ingredients such as peas or crabmeat if wished.

Serves 4
2 tbsp vegetable oil
1 carrot, grated
5 eggs, beaten
225 g/8 oz raw shrimp, peeled and deveined
1 tbsp light soy sauce
pinch of Chinese five-spice powder
2 spring onions (scallions), chopped
2 tsp sesame seeds
1 tsp sesame oil

1 Heat the oil in a preheated wok. Add the carrot and stir-fry for 1–2 minutes. Push the carrot to one side of the wok and add the eggs. Cook, stirring gently, for 1–2 minutes.

2 Stir in the shrimp, soy sauce and five-spice powder and stir-fry for 2–3 minutes, until the shrimp change colour and the fu yong is almost dry.

3 Turn out on to a warm serving plate, sprinkle with spring onions (scallions), sesame seeds and sesame oil and serve immediately.

COOK'S TIP

If only cooked prawns (shrimp) are available, add just before the end of cooking, but make sure they are fully incorporated into the fu yong.

Sweet & Sour Prawns (Shrimp) with Chilli

This colourful dish is a mouth-watering combination of sweet-and-sour and spicy flavours. Serve with plain rice or noodles.

Serves 4

175–225 g/6–8 oz peeled raw tiger prawns (jumbo shrimp), deveined

pinch of salt

1 tsp egg white

1 tsp Cornflour (Cornstarch) Paste (see page 16)

300 ml/1/2 pint/1 1/4 cups vegetable oil

SAUCE

1 tbsp vegetable oil

1/2 small green (bell) pepper, seeded and thinly sliced

1/2 small carrot, thinly sliced

115 g/4 oz canned water chestnuts, drained and sliced

1/2–1 tsp salt

1 tbsp light soy sauce

2 tbsp caster (superfine) sugar

3 tbsp rice or sherry vinegar

1 tsp Chinese rice wine or dry sherry

1 tbsp tomato sauce

1/2–1 tsp chilli sauce

3–4 tbsp Chinese Stock (see page 16) or water

2 tsp Cornflour (Cornstarch) Paste (see page 16)

a few drops of sesame oil

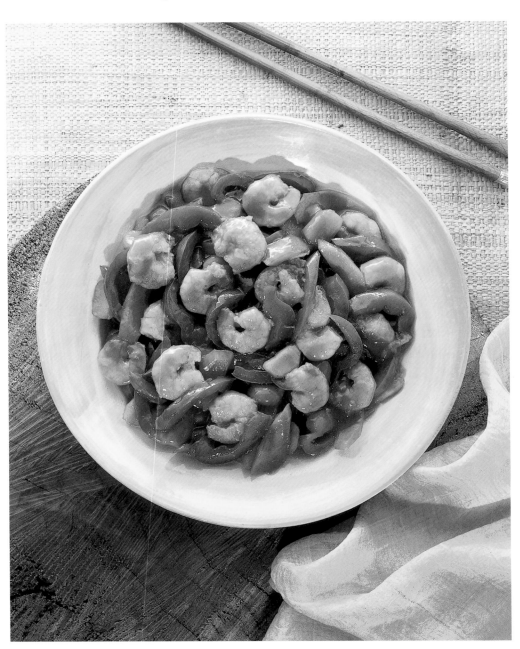

1 In a large bowl, mix together the prawns (shrimp), salt, egg white and cornflour (cornstarch) paste.

2 Heat the oil in a preheated wok. Add the prawns (shrimp) and stir-fry for 30–40 seconds only. Remove them from the wok and drain on kitchen paper (paper towels).

3 Pour off the oil and wipe the wok clean. To make the sauce, heat the oil in the wok. Add the vegetables and stir-fry for about 1 minute, then add the seasonings, together with the stock or water and bring to the boil.

4 Add the prawns (shrimp) and stir until blended well. Thicken the sauce with the cornflour (cornstarch) paste and stir until smooth. Sprinkle with sesame oil, transfer to a warm serving dish and serve immediately.

Cantonese Prawns (Shrimp)

This prawn (shrimp) dish is very simple and is ideal
for supper or lunch when time is short.

Serves 4

5 tbsp vegetable oil

4 garlic cloves, crushed

675 g/1½ lb raw prawns (shrimp),
peeled and deveined

5-cm/2-inch piece fresh
ginger root, chopped

175 g/6 oz lean pork, diced

1 leek, sliced

3 eggs, beaten

shredded leek and red (bell) pepper
matchsticks, to garnish

SAUCE

2 tbsp Chinese rice wine or dry sherry

2 tbsp light soy sauce

2 tsp caster (superfine) sugar

150 ml/¼ pint/⅔ cup fish stock

4½ tsp cornflour (cornstarch)

3 tbsp water

1 Heat 2 tablespoons of the oil in a
preheated wok and stir-fry the garlic
for 30 seconds. Stir in the prawns
(shrimp) and stir-fry for 5 minutes,
until they change colour. Remove the
prawns (shrimp) from the wok with a
slotted spoon and keep warm.

2 Add the remaining oil to the wok
and stir-fry the ginger, pork and leek
for 4–5 minutes, until the pork is
lightly browned and sealed.

3 To make the sauce, add the rice
wine, sherry, soy sauce, sugar and fish
stock to the wok. Blend the cornflour
with the water to form a smooth paste
and stir it into the wok. Cook, stirring,
until the sauce thickens and clears.

4 Return the prawns (shrimp) to the
wok and add the beaten eggs. Cook for
5–6 minutes, gently stirring
occasionally, until the egg sets.
Transfer to a serving dish, garnish
with shredded leek and (bell) pepper
matchsticks and serve immediately.

COOK'S TIP

Do not stir too vigorously after
adding the eggs in step 4, or they
will beak up into small hard pieces.
They should be lightly scrambled.

Sweet & Sour Prawns (Shrimp)

A favourite with everyone, this superb dish tastes as wonderful as it looks and takes only minutes to prepare.

Serves 4
300–350 g/10¹/₂–12 oz unpeeled raw king or tiger prawns (jumbo shrimp)
vegetable oil for deep-frying
fresh coriander (cilantro) leaves, to garnish

SAUCE

1 tbsp vegetable oil
2 tsp finely chopped spring onions (scallions)
1 tsp finely chopped fresh ginger root
1 tbsp light soy sauce
2 tbsp sugar
3 tbsp rice vinegar
1 tsp Chinese rice wine or dry sherry
125 ml/4 fl oz/¹/₂ cup Chinese Stock (see page 16) or water
1 tbsp Cornflour (Cornstarch) Paste (see page 16)
a few drops of sesame oil
coriander (cilantro) leaves, to garnish

1 Remove the heads and legs from the prawns (shrimp), but leave the body shells intact

2 Heat the oil in a preheated wok. Deep-fry the prawns (shrimp) in hot oil for about 45–50 seconds, or until they become bright orange. Remove with a slotted spoon and drain on kitchen paper (paper towels).

3 To make the sauce, heat the oil in a preheated wok and add the spring onions (scallions), ginger, soy sauce,

sugar, rice vinegar, Chinese rice wine or sherry and stock or water. Bring to the boil.

4 Add the prawns (shrimp) to the sauce, blend well, then thicken the

sauce with the cornflour (cornstarch) paste. Stir until smooth and then add the sesame oil.

5 Serve hot, garnished with coriander (cilantro) leaves.

Fried Prawns (Shrimp) with Cashews

Cashew nuts are delicious as part of a stir-fry with almost any other ingredients.
Use the unsalted variety in cooking.

Serves 4

2 garlic cloves, crushed

1 tbsp cornflour (cornstarch)

pinch of caster (superfine) sugar

450 g/1 lb raw tiger prawns
(jumbo shrimp),
peeled and deveined

4 tbsp vegetable oil

1 leek, sliced

125 g/4$^{1}/_{2}$ oz broccoli florets

1 orange (bell) pepper,
seeded and diced

75 g/2$^{3}/_{4}$ oz/$^{3}/_{4}$ cup
unsalted cashew nuts

SAUCE

175 ml/6 fl oz/$^{3}/_{4}$ cup
fish stock

1 tbsp cornflour (cornstarch)

dash of chilli sauce

2 tsp sesame oil

1 tbsp Chinese rice wine or
dry sherry

1 Mix together the garlic, cornflour (cornstarch) and sugar in a bowl. Stir the prawns (shrimp) into the mixture until thoroughly coated.

2 Heat the oil in a preheated wok and add the prawn (shrimp) mixture. Stir-fry over a high heat for 20–30 seconds, until the prawns (shrimp) change colour. Remove the prawns (shrimp) from the wok with a slotted spoon and set aside.

3 Add the leek, broccoli and (bell) pepper to the wok and stir-fry for 2 minutes.

4 To make the sauce, mix the stock, cornflour (cornstarch), chilli sauce, oil and rice wine or dry sherry together and add to the wok, together with the cashew nuts. Return the prawns (shrimp) to the wok and cook for 1 minute. Transfer to a warm serving dish and serve immediately.

COOK'S VARIATION

This recipe also works well with chicken, pork or beef strips instead of the prawns (shrimp). Use 225 g/8 oz meat instead of 450 g/1 lb prawns (shrimp).

Baked Crab with Ginger

The crab is interchangeable with lobster. In Chinese restaurants, only live crabs
and lobsters are used, but ready-cooked ones can be used at home.

Serves 4
1 large or 2 medium crabs, weighing about 675 g/1½ lb in total
2 tbsp Chinese rice wine or dry sherry
1 egg, lightly beaten
1 tbsp cornflour (cornstarch)
3–4 tbsp vegetable oil
1 tbsp finely chopped fresh ginger root
3–4 spring onions (scallions), cut into sections
2 tbsp light soy sauce
1 tsp sugar
about 75 ml/5 tbsp/⅓ cup Chinese Stock (see page 16) or water
½ tsp sesame oil
coriander (cilantro) leaves, to garnish

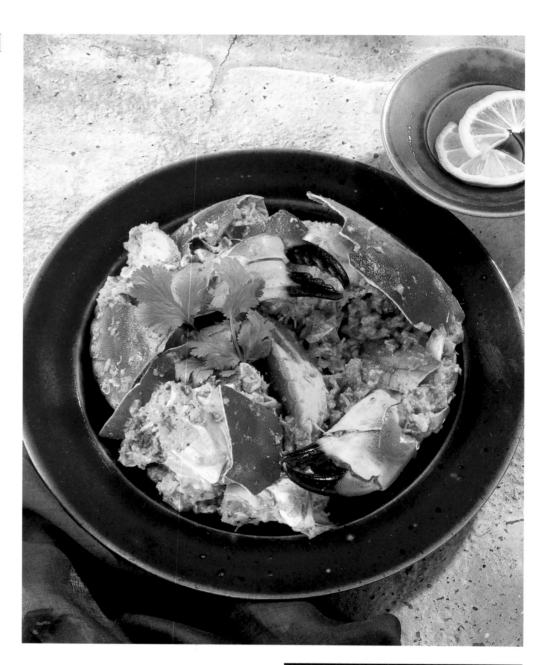

1 Cut the crab in half from the under-belly. Break off the claws and crack them with the back of the cleaver or a large kitchen knife.

2 Discard the legs and crack the shell, breaking it into several pieces. Discard the feathery gills and the stomach sac. Place in a bowl with the wine, egg and cornflour (cornstarch) and marinate for 10–15 minutes.

3 Heat the oil in a large preheated wok and stir-fry the crab with the ginger and spring onions (scallions) for 2–3 minutes.

4 Add the soy sauce, sugar and stock or water, blend well and bring to the boil. Cover and cook for 3–4 minutes, then remove the lid from the wok. Sprinkle with sesame oil and transfer to a warm serving dish. Garnish with fresh coriander (cilantro) leaves and serve immediately.

COOK'S TIP

Provide finger bowls for your guests as the only way to tackle this dish is with the hands.

Squid in Oyster Sauce & Vegetables

Squid is a delicious fish, which contrary to popular belief, is not rubbery. If prepared and cooked correctly, it is a quick-cooking, attractive and tasty ingredient.

Serves 4
450 g/1 lb prepared squid
150 ml/¼ pint/²⁄₃ cup vegetable oil
1-cm/½-inch piece fresh ginger root, grated
50 g/1¾ oz mangetout (snow peas)
5 tbsp hot fish stock
red (bell) pepper triangles, to garnish

SAUCE
1 tbsp oyster sauce
1 tbsp light soy sauce
pinch of caster (superfine) sugar
1 garlic clove, crushed

1 First prepare the squid by cutting down the centre of the bodies lengthways. Flatten the squid out, inside uppermost, and score a lattice design with a sharp knife, deep into the flesh.

2 Prepare the sauce by combining the oyster sauce, soy sauce, sugar and crushed garlic.

3 Heat the oil in a preheated wok until almost smoking. Lower the heat slightly and cook the squid until they curl. Remove with a slotted spoon and drain on kitchen paper (paper towels).

4 Pour off all but 2 tablespoons of the oil and return the wok to the heat. Add the ginger and mangetout (snow peas) and stir-fry for 1 minute. Return the squid to the wok and pour in the sauce and stock. Simmer for 3 minutes, until thickened and heated through.

5 Transfer to a warm serving dish, garnish with (bell) pepper triangles and serve immediately.

COOK'S TIP

Take care not to overcook the squid, otherwise it will become rubbery and unappetizing.

Fried Squid Flowers

The addition of green (bell) pepper and black bean sauce to the squid
makes a colourful and delicious dish from the Cantonese school.

Serves 4
350–400 g/12–14 oz prepared and cleaned squid
1 green (bell) pepper, seeded
3–4 tbsp vegetable oil
1 garlic clove, finely chopped
$\frac{1}{4}$ tsp finely chopped fresh ginger root
2 tsp finely chopped spring onions (scallions)
$\frac{1}{2}$ tsp salt
2 tbsp crushed black bean sauce
1 tsp Chinese rice wine or dry sherry
a few drops of sesame oil

1 Open up the squid and score the inside of the flesh deeply in a criss-cross pattern with a cleaver or sharp knife.

2 Cut the squid into pieces about the size of an oblong postage stamp. Blanch in a bowl of boiling water for a few seconds. Drain and dry well on kitchen paper (paper towels).

3 Cut the (bell) pepper into small triangular pieces. Heat the oil in a preheated wok and stir-fry the (bell) pepper for about 1 minute. Add the garlic, ginger, spring onions (scallions), salt and squid. Continue stirring for another minute.

4 Finally add the black bean sauce and wine, and blend well. Transfer to a warm serving dish, sprinkle with sesame oil and serve immediately.

Fish & Ginger Stir-fry

This delicious and spicy recipe is a really quick fish dish, ideal for midweek
family meals or light lunches at weekends.

Serves 4
4 tbsp cornflour (cornstarch)
$1/2$ tsp ground ginger
675 g/$1^1/_2$ lb firm white fish fillets, skinned and cubed
3 tbsp peanut oil
2.5-cm/1-inch fresh ginger root, grated
1 leek, thinly sliced
1 tbsp white wine vinegar
2 tbsp Chinese rice wine or dry sherry
3 tbsp dark soy sauce
1 tsp caster (superfine) sugar
2 tbsp lemon juice

1 Mix the cornflour (cornstarch) and
ginger in a bowl. Add the cubes of fish
in batches, turning to coat evenly.

2 Heat the oil in a preheated wok.
Add the ginger and leek and stir-fry
for 1 minute.

3 Add the coated fish and cook for a
further 5 minutes, until browned,
stirring to prevent the fish from
sticking.

4 Add the remaining ingredients and
cook over a low heat for 3–4 minutes,
until the fish is cooked through.
Transfer to a serving dish and serve.

COOK'S TIP

Use any firm white fish which
will hold its shape, such as cod,
haddock or monkfish.

Poultry Dishes

Chinese cooks fully appreciate the versatility of poultry. Chicken is probably second only to pork in its popularity and duck is usually served on special occasions. Chicken lends itself perfectly to fast-cooking methods, such as stir-frying. The meat can easily be shredded, sliced or diced and its delicate flavour blends with other ingredients, from ginger and chillies to lemon and honey.

Recipes in this chapter include many Western favourites: Chicken with Cashew Nuts & Vegetables and Lemon Chicken.

Duck, with its strong flavour and richer, fattier meat, is usually prepared with piquant or fruity sauces as a counterbalance. It is sometimes cooked with its skin on, which becomes deliciously crisp. Although Aromatic & Crispy Duck is a universally favourite dish, do not overlook the other superb duck recipes in this chapter, including Duck with Mangoes.

Chinese Chicken Salad

This is a refreshing dish suitable for a summer meal or light lunch.
Its delicate combination of flavours provides an interesting alternative
to western-style salads.

Serves 4
225 g/8 oz skinless, boneless chicken breast
2 tsp light soy sauce
1 tsp sesame oil
1 tsp sesame seeds
2 tbsp vegetable oil
125 g/4¹/₂ oz beansprouts
1 red (bell) pepper, seeded and thinly sliced
1 carrot, cut into matchsticks
3 baby corn cobs, sliced
snipped chives and carrot matchsticks, to garnish
SAUCE
2 tsp rice wine vinegar
1 tbsp light soy sauce
dash of chilli oil

1 Place the chicken in a shallow glass dish. Mix together the soy sauce and sesame oil in a small bowl and pour the mixture over the chicken. Sprinkle with sesame seeds and let stand for 20 minutes.

2 Remove the chicken from the marinade and cut the meat into thin slices. Heat the vegetable oil in a preheated wok and stir-fry the chicken for 4–5 minutes, until cooked through. Remove with a slotted spoon and cool.

3 Add the beansprouts, (bell) pepper, carrot and baby corn cobs to the wok and stir-fry for 2–3 minutes. Remove from the wok with a slotted spoon and cool.

4 Mix the sauce ingredients together. Arrange the chicken and vegetables together on a serving plate. Spoon the sauce over the salad, garnish with chives and carrot matchsticks and serve immediately.

COOK'S VARIATION

Add 150 g/5 oz mangetout(snow peas) instead of the (bell) pepper, if wished.

Chicken with Beansprouts

This is the basic Chicken Chop Suey to be found in almost every
Chinese restaurant all over the world.

Serves 4

115 g/4 oz boneless skinless
chicken breasts

1 tsp salt

$^1/_4$ egg white, beaten lightly

2 tsp Cornflour (Cornstarch)
Paste (see page 16)

about 300 ml/$^1/_2$ pint/1$^1/_4$ cups
vegetable oil

1 small onion, thinly sliced

1 small green (bell) pepper,
seeded and cut into
thin matchsticks

1 small carrot, cut into
thin matchsticks

115 g/4 oz/2 cups fresh
beansprouts

$^1/_2$ tsp sugar

1 tbsp light soy sauce

1 tsp Chinese rice wine or
dry sherry

2–3 tbsp Chinese Stock (see page 16)

a few drops of sesame oil

chilli sauce, to serve

1 Thinly shred the chicken and mix
with a pinch of the salt, the egg white
and cornflour (cornstarch) paste in
that order.

2 Heat the oil in a preheated wok.
Add the chicken and stir-fry for about
1 minute, until no longer pink,
stirring to separate the shreds.
Remove with a slotted spoon and
drain on kitchen paper (paper towels).

3 Carefully pour off the excess oil
from the wok, leaving about
2 tablespoons. Add the onion, green
(bell) pepper and carrot and stir-fry
for about 2 minutes, until tender, but
still crisp. Then add the beansprouts
and stir-fry for a few seconds, until
just tender.

4 Add the chicken with the remaining
salt, sugar, soy sauce and Chinese rice
wine or sherry. Blend well and add the
stock or water. Sprinkle with the
sesame oil and serve at once.

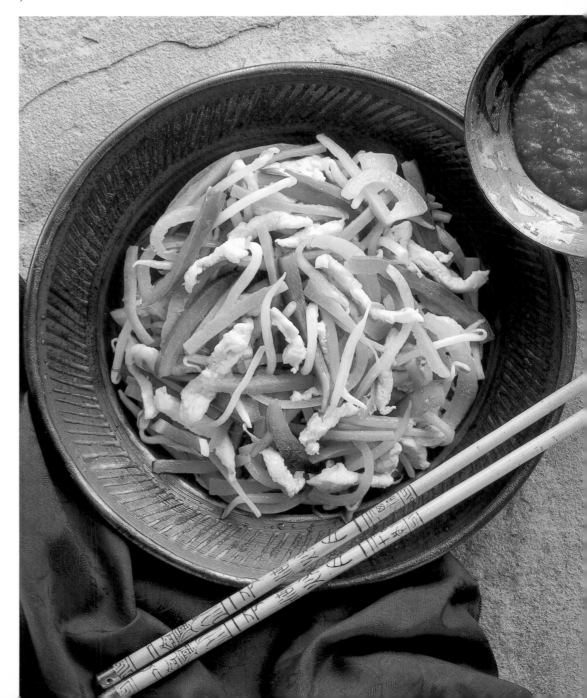

Kung Po Chicken with Cashew Nuts

Beware – this is quite a fiery dish, so if you prefer a milder flavour,
reduce the number of dried chillies.

Serves 4
225–300 g/8–10$^{1}/_{2}$ oz boneless skinless chicken breasts
$^{1}/_{4}$ tsp salt
$^{1}/_{3}$ egg white
1 tsp Cornflour (Cornstarch) Paste (see page 16)
1 green (bell) pepper, seeded
4 tbsp vegetable oil
1 spring onion (scallion), cut into short sections
a few small slices of fresh ginger root
4–5 small dried red chillies, soaked, seeded and shredded
2 tbsp crushed yellow bean sauce
1 tsp Chinese rice wine or dry sherry
115 g/4 oz roasted cashew nuts
a few drops of sesame oil
boiled rice, to serve

pepper. Stir-fry for 1 minute, then add
the chicken, together with the yellow
bean sauce and rice wine or sherry.
Blend well and stir-fry for another
minute. Finally, stir in the cashew
nuts and sesame oil. Serve hot.

COOK'S VARIATION

Peanuts, walnuts or almonds can be
used instead of the cashew nuts
if wished.

1 Cut the chicken into small cubes
about the size of sugar lumps. Place in
a small bowl and mix with a pinch of
salt, the egg white and the cornflour
(cornstarch) paste, in that order.

2 Cut the green (bell) pepper into
cubes or triangles about the same size
as the chicken pieces.

3 Heat the oil in a preheated wok,
add the chicken cubes and stir-fry for
about 1 minute, or until the colour
changes. Remove with a slotted spoon
and keep warm.

4 Add the spring onion (scallion),
ginger, chillies and green (bell)

Chicken with Cashew Nuts & Vegetables

This is a popular dish in Chinese restaurants in the West, although nothing beats making it yourself.

Serves 4
300 g/10^1/$_2$ oz boneless, skinless chicken breast, sliced into thin strips
1 tbsp cornflour (cornstarch)
1 tsp sesame oil
1 tbsp hoi-sin sauce
1 tsp light soy sauce
3 garlic cloves, crushed
2 tbsp vegetable oil
75 g/2^3/$_4$ oz unsalted cashew nuts
25 g/1 oz mangetout (snow peas)
1 celery stick, sliced
1 onion, cut into eight
50 g/1^3/$_4$ oz/^{1}/$_4$ cup beansprouts
1 red (bell) pepper, seed and diced

SAUCE
2 tsp cornflour (cornstarch)
2 tbsp hoi-sin sauce
200 ml/7 fl oz/1 cup Chinese Stock (see page 16) or chicken stock

1 Coat the chicken pieces in the cornflour (cornstarch), shaking off any excess. Place the chicken in a shallow glass dish. Mix together the sesame oil, hoi-sin sauce, soy sauce and 1 garlic clove . Pour this mixture over the chicken, turning to coat thoroughly. Marinate for 20 minutes.

2 Heat half the oil in a preheated wok. Add the cashew nuts and stir-fry for 1 minute, until browned. Add the mangetout (snow peas), celery,

remaining garlic, onion, beansprouts and (bell) pepper and cook for 2–3 minutes. Remove the vegetables from the wok and set aside.

3 Heat the remaining oil in the wok. Remove the chicken from the

marinade and stir-fry for 3–4 minutes. Return the vegetables to the wok.

4 Mix the sauce ingredients together and pour into the wok. Bring to the boil and cook, stirring, until thickened and clear. Serve immediately.

Lemon Chicken

Lemon sauce is a Cantonese speciality, easily available from oriental stores, or you can make your own.

Serves 4

350 g/12 oz boneless skinless
chicken breasts

1 tbsp Chinese rice wine or
dry sherry

1 egg, beaten

4 tbsp plain (all-purpose) flour, blended
with 2 tbsp water

vegetable oil, for deep-frying

salt and pepper

slices of fresh lemon, to garnish

LEMON SAUCE

1 tbsp vegetable oil

250 ml/9 fl oz/1 cup
Chinese Stock (see page 16)

1 tbsp caster (superfine) sugar

1 tbsp lemon juice

1 tbsp cornflour (cornstarch)

1 tsp salt

1 tsp lemon rind

1 To make the lemon sauce, heat the oil in a wok until hot, reduce the heat and add all the other sauce ingredients. Blend well, then bring to the boil and stir until smooth.

2 Cut the chicken into thin slices and place in a shallow dish with the rice wine or sherry, and salt and pepper. Marinate for 25–30 minutes.

3 Make a batter with the egg and the flour paste. Place the chicken slices in the batter and turn to coat well.

4 Heat the oil in a wok or deep-fryer. Add the chicken slices and fry until golden brown, remove with a slotted

spoon and drain thoroughly on absorbent kitchen paper (paper towels). Cool slightly, then cut the chicken slices into bite-size pieces.

5 Heat about 1 tablespoon of oil in a wok. Stir in the lemon sauce until well blended and pour evenly over the chicken. Garnish with lemon slices.

Chicken with Yellow Bean Sauce

Ready-made yellow bean sauce is available from supermarkets and Chinese foodstores.
It is made from yellow soya beans and is quite salty in flavour.

Serves 4
450 g/1 lb skinless, boneless chicken breasts
1 egg white, beaten
1 tbsp cornflour (cornstarch)
1 tbsp wine vinegar
1 tbsp light soy sauce
1 tsp caster (superfine) sugar
3 tbsp vegetable oil
1 garlic clove, crushed
1-cm/½-inch piece fresh ginger root, grated
1 green (bell) pepper, seeded and diced
2 large mushrooms, sliced
3 tbsp yellow bean sauce
red or green (bell) pepper strips, to garnish

Stir in the vinegar and soy sauce mixture and return the chicken to the wok. Cook, stirring, for 1–2 minutes. Transfer to a warm serving dish, garnish with (bell) pepper strips and serve immediately.

VARIATION

Although darker in colour, black bean sauce would work equally well in this recipe.

1 Cut the chicken into 2.5-cm/1-inch cubes. Mix the egg white and cornflour (cornstarch) and dip the chicken pieces into the mixture to coat. Set aside for 20 minutes.

2 Mix the vinegar, soy sauce and sugar in a bowl. Remove the chicken from the egg white mixture with a slotted spoon. Heat the oil in a preheated wok and stir-fry the chicken for 3–4 minutes, until golden brown. Remove the chicken from the wok and set aside.

3 Add the garlic, ginger, (bell) pepper and mushrooms to the wok and stir-fry for 1–2 minutes.

4 Add the yellow bean sauce and cook, stirring constantly, for 1 minute.

Peanut Sesame Chicken

A quick-to-make chicken and vegetable dish, sesame seeds and peanuts give it crunch and the fruit juice glaze gives a lovely shiny coating to the sauce.

Serves 4
2 tbsp vegetable oil
2 tbsp sesame oil
450 g/1 lb boneless skinless chicken breasts, sliced into strips
225 g/8 oz broccoli, divided into small florets
225 g/8 oz baby or dwarf corn cobs, halved if large
1 small red (bell) pepper, seeded and sliced
2 tbsp soy sauce
250 ml/9 fl oz/1 cup orange juice
2 tsp cornflour (cornstarch)
2 tbsp toasted sesame seeds
50 g/1¾ oz/½ cup roasted, shelled, unsalted peanuts
rice or noodles, to serve

1 Heat the oils in a preheated wok or large, heavy-based frying pan (skillet), add the chicken strips and stir-fry for about 4–5 minutes, until browned.

2 Add the broccoli, corn cobs and red (bell) pepper and stir-fry for a further 1–2 minutes.

3 Meanwhile, mix together the soy sauce, orange juice and cornflour (cornstarch). Stir into the chicken and vegetable mixture and cook, stirring constantly, until the sauce has thickened slightly and a glaze has developed.

4 Stir in the sesame seeds and peanuts, mixing well. Heat for a further 3–4 minutes. Serve at once, with rice or noodles.

Braised Chicken

This is a delicious way to cook a whole chicken. It has a
wonderful glaze, which is served as a sauce.

Serves 4
1.5 kg/3 lb 5 oz chicken
3 tbsp vegetable oil
1 tbsp peanut oil
2 tbsp dark brown sugar
5 tbsp dark soy sauce
150 ml/¼ pint/⅔ cup water
2 garlic cloves, crushed
1 small onion, chopped
1 fresh red chilli, chopped
celery leaves and snipped chives, to garnish

1 Clean the chicken inside and out
with damp kitchen paper (paper
towels).

2 Put the oil in a large wok, add the
sugar and heat gently until the sugar
caramelizes. Stir in the soy sauce until
thoroughly mixed.

3 Add the chicken and turn it in the
mixture to coat all over.

4 Add the water, garlic, onion and
chilli. Cover and simmer, turning the
chicken from time to time, for
approximately 1 hour, until it is
tender and cooked through.

5 Remove the chicken from the wok
and set aside to rest. Increase the heat
and reduce the sauce in the wok until
it has thickened. Cut the chicken into
individual portions and arrange on a
warm serving plate.

6 Garnish with celery leaves and
chives and serve with the sauce.

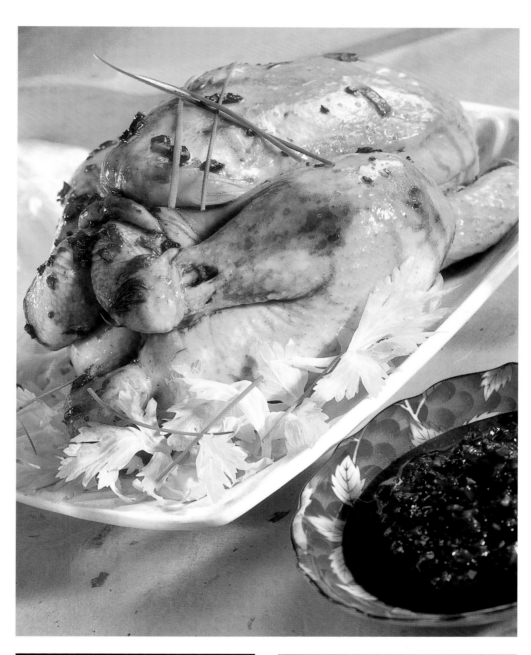

COOK'S TIP

You could prepare this recipe with
chicken portions, reducing the
cooking time to 25–30 minutes.

COOK'S TIP

When caramelizing the sugar, do
not have the heat too high,
otherwise it may burn.

Chicken with (Bell) Pepper

Golden brown, deep-fried strips of chicken are perfectly complemented
by the tender-crisp green (bell) pepper and the hint of chilli.

Serves 4
300 g/10¹/₂ oz boneless skinless chicken breasts
1 tsp salt
¹/₂ egg white
2 tsp Cornflour (Cornstarch) Paste (see page 16)
1 green (bell) pepper, seeded
300 ml/¹/₂ pint/1¹/₄ cups vegetable oil
1 spring onion (scallion), finely shredded
a few strips of ginger root, finely shredded
1–2 fresh red chillies, seeded and finely shredded
¹/₂ tsp sugar
1 tbsp Chinese rice wine or dry sherry
a few drops of sesame oil

1 Cut the chicken breasts into strips, then mix in a bowl with a pinch of the salt, the egg white and cornflour (cornstarch) paste, in that order.

2 Cut the (bell) pepper into thin shreds the same size and length as the chicken strips.

3 Heat the oil in a preheated wok, and deep-fry the chicken strips, in batches, for about 1 minute, or until no longer pink. Remove the chicken strips with a slotted spoon, set aside and keep warm.

4 Pour off the excess oil from the wok, leaving about 1 tablespoon. Add the spring onion (scallion), ginger, chillies and (bell) pepper. Stir-fry for about 1 minute, then return the chicken to the wok. Add the remaining salt, the sugar and wine or sherry. Stir-fry for another minute, sprinkle with sesame oil, transfer to a warm dish and serve immediately.

COOK'S VARIATION

To make chicken with celery, substitute 4–6 thinly sliced celery sticks for the (bell) pepper, following the same method.

Spicy Peanut Chicken

This quick dish has many variations, but is a classic combination of ingredients, with peanuts, chicken and chillies blending to give a wonderfully flavoured dish.

Serves 4

300 g/10½ oz skinless, boneless chicken breasts

2 tbsp peanut oil

125 g/4½ oz/1 cup shelled peanuts

1 fresh red chilli, sliced

1 green (bell) pepper, seeded and cut into strips

fried rice, to serve

SAUCE

150 ml/¼ pint/⅔ cup chicken stock

1 tbsp Chinese rice wine or dry sherry

1 tbsp light soy sauce

1½ tsp light brown sugar

2 garlic cloves, crushed

1 tsp grated fresh ginger root

1 tsp wine vinegar

1 tsp sesame oil

3 Heat the sauce without boiling and stir in the chicken, chilli and (bell) pepper. Sprinkle the sesame oil into the wok, stir and cook for 1 minute. Transfer to serving plates and serve hot with fried rice.

COOK'S TIP

If necessary, blend the peanuts with a little of the stock to form a softer paste.

1 Cut the chicken into 2.5-cm/1-inch cubes and set aside. Heat the peanut oil in a preheated wok and stir-fry the peanuts for 1 minute. Remove with a slotted spoon and set aside. Add the chicken and cook for 1–2 minutes. Stir in the chilli and green (bell) pepper and cook for 1 minute. Remove the ingredients from the wok with a slotted spoon and set aside.

2 Blend half the peanuts in a food processor or crush with a rolling pin until almost smooth. Return the peanuts to the wok and add the chicken stock, Chinese rice wine or sherry, soy sauce, sugar, garlic, ginger and vinegar.

Chicken Fu Yong

Most people associate fu yong with an omelette, however, a fu yong dish should use egg whites only to create a very delicate texture.

Serves 4
175 g/6 oz boneless skinless chicken breasts
1 tsp Chinese rice wine or dry sherry
1 tbsp cornflour (cornstarch)
3 eggs, beaten
1/2 tsp finely chopped spring onions (scallions)
3 tbsp vegetable oil
115 g/4 oz/1 cup peas
1 tsp light soy sauce
salt and pepper
few drops of sesame oil

1 Cut the chicken across the grain into very small, paper-thin slices, using a cleaver. Place the slices in a shallow dish, add 1/2 teaspoon salt, pepper, the rice wine or sherry and cornflour (cornstarch), and turn in the mixture until they are well coated.

2 Beat the eggs in a small bowl with a pinch of salt and add the spring onions (scallions).

3 Heat the oil in a preheated wok, add chicken slices and stir-fry for about 1 minute, making sure that the slices are kept separated. Pour the beaten eggs over the chicken, and lightly scramble until set. Do not stir too vigorously, or the mixture will break up in the oil. Stir the oil from the bottom of the wok so that the fu yong rises to the surface.

4 Add the peas, soy sauce and salt to taste and blend well. Sprinkle with sesame oil and serve immediately.

Bang-Bang Chicken

The cooked chicken meat is tenderized by beating with a rolling pin,
hence the name for this very popular Szechuan dish.

Serves 4

1 litre/1¾ pints/4 cups water

2 chicken quarters
(breast half and leg)

1 cucumber, cut into
matchstick shreds

SAUCE

2 tbsp light soy sauce

1 tsp sugar

1 tbsp finely chopped spring
onions (scallions)

1 tsp red chilli oil

¼ tsp pepper

1 tsp white sesame seeds

2 tbsp peanut butter, creamed
with a little sesame oil

1 Bring the water to a rolling boil in a wok or a large pan. Add the chicken pieces, reduce the heat, cover and cook for 30–35 minutes.

2 Remove the chicken from the pan and immerse it in a bowl of cold water for at least 1 hour to cool it.

3 Remove the chicken pieces and drain well. Pat dry with kitchen paper (paper towels), then take the meat off the bone.

4 On a flat surface, pound the chicken with a rolling pin, then tear the meat into shreds with 2 forks. Mix with the shredded cucumber and arrange in a shallow serving dish.

5 To serve, mix the sauce ingredients and pour on to the chicken.

Chilli Chicken

This is quite a hot dish, using fresh chillies. If you prefer
a milder dish, halve the number of chillies used.

Serves 4
350 g/12 oz skinless, boneless chicken
¹/₂ tsp salt
1 egg white, lightly beaten
2 tbsp cornflour (cornstarch)
4 tbsp vegetable oil
2 garlic cloves, crushed
1-cm/¹/₂-inch piece fresh ginger root, grated
1 red (bell) pepper, seeded and diced
1 green (bell) pepper, seeded and diced
2 fresh red chillies, chopped
2 tbsp light soy sauce
1 tbsp Chinese rice wine or dry sherry
1 tbsp wine vinegar

1 Cut the chicken into cubes and place in a mixing bowl. Add the salt, egg white, cornflour (cornstarch) and 1 tbsp of the oil. Turn the chicken in the mixture to coat.

2 Heat the remaining oil in a preheated wok. Add the garlic and ginger and stir-fry for 30 seconds.

3 Add the chicken pieces to the wok and stir-fry for 2–3 minutes, until golden brown.

4 Stir in the (bell) peppers, chillies, soy sauce, rice wine or sherry and wine vinegar and cook for a further 2–3 minutes, until the chicken is cooked through. Transfer to a warm serving dish and serve immediately.

COOK'S VARIATION

This recipe also works well with lean tender steak, cut into thin strips.

COOK'S TIP

When preparing the chillies, wear rubber gloves to prevent the juices burning and irritating your hands.

Szechuan Chilli Chicken

In China, the chicken pieces are chopped through the bone for this dish,
but if you do not possess a cleaver, use boneless chicken meat.

Serves 4
450 g/1 lb chicken thighs
¼ tsp pepper
1 tbsp caster (superfine) sugar
2 tsp light soy sauce
1 tsp dark soy sauce
1 tbsp Chinese rice wine or dry sherry
2 tsp cornflour (cornstarch)
2–3 tbsp vegetable oil
1–2 garlic cloves, crushed
2 spring onions (scallions), cut into short sections, with the green and white parts separated
4–6 small dried red chillies, soaked and seeded
2 tbsp yellow bean sauce
about 150 ml/¼ pint/⅔ cup Chinese Stock (see page 16) or water

1 Cut or chop the chicken thighs into bite-size pieces and place in a shallow dish. Mix together the pepper, sugar, soy sauce, Chinese rice wine or sherry and cornflour (cornstarch). Pour the mixture over the chicken, turning to coat, and marinate for 25–30 minutes.

2 Heat the oil in a preheated wok, add the chicken pieces and stir-fry for about 1–2 minutes, until lightly brown. Remove the chicken pieces with a slotted spoon, set aside and keep warm.

3 Add the garlic, the white parts of the spring onions (scallions), the chillies and yellow bean sauce to the wok. Stir-fry for about 30 seconds, blending well.

4 Return the chicken pieces to the wok and stir-fry for approximately 1–2 minutes. Add the stock or water, bring to the boil, lower the heat and cover. Braise over a medium heat for

5–6 minutes, stirring once or twice. Transfer to a warm serving dish, garnish with the green parts of the spring onions (scallions) and serve immediately.

Chicken Chop Suey

Both well known and popular, chop suey dishes are easy to make and delicious. They are based on beansprouts and soy sauce with a meat or vegetable flavouring.

Serves 4
4 tbsp light soy sauce
2 tsp light brown sugar
500 g/1 lb 2 oz skinless, boneless chicken, cut into strips
3 tbsp vegetable oil
2 onions, quartered
2 garlic cloves, crushed
350 g/12 oz/1½ cups beansprouts
3 tsp sesame oil
1 tbsp cornflour (cornstarch)
3 tbsp water
425 ml/¾ pint/2 cups Chinese Stock (see page 16) or chicken stock
shredded leek, to garnish

(cornstarch) paste and bring to the boil, stirring until the sauce is thickened and clear.

6 Transfer to a warm serving dish, garnish with shredded leek and serve.

VARIATION

This recipe may be made with beef, pork or mixed vegetables, changing the flavour of the stock accordingly.

1 Mix the soy sauce and sugar together. Place the chicken in a shallow glass dish and spoon the soy mixture over it, turning to coat. Let stand for 20 minutes.

2 Heat the vegetable oil in a preheated wok. Add the chicken and stir-fry for 2–3 minutes, until golden brown all over.

3 Add the onion quarters and the garlic and stir-fry for a further 2 minutes.

4 Add the beansprouts and cook for a further 4–5 minutes. Stir in the sesame oil.

5 Blend the cornflour (cornstarch) with the water to form a smooth paste. Pour the stock into the wok, together with the cornflour

Chicken with Mushrooms

Chinese dried mushrooms should be used for this dish – otherwise use
fresh shiitake mushrooms rather than fresh white mushrooms.

Serves 4

300–350 g/10$^{1}/_{2}$–12 oz boneless skinless
chicken breasts

$^{1}/_{2}$ tsp sugar

1 tbsp light soy sauce

1 tsp Chinese rice wine or
dry sherry

2 tsp cornflour (cornstarch)

4–6 Chinese dried mushrooms,
soaked in warm water
for 30 minutes

1 tbsp finely shredded
fresh ginger root

salt and pepper

a few drops of sesame oil

fresh coriander (cilantro) or
flat leaf parsley leaves,
to garnish

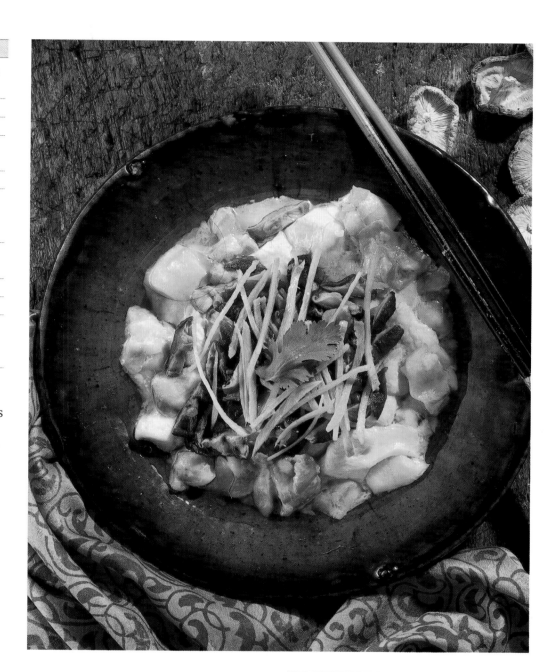

1 Cut the chicken into bite-size pieces and place in a bowl. Mix together the sugar, soy sauce, Chinese rice wine or sherry and cornflour (cornstarch). Pour the mixture over the chicken, turning to coat thoroughly. Marinate for 25–30 minutes.

2 Drain the mushrooms and pat dry with absorbent kitchen paper (paper towels). Slice the mushrooms into thin shreds, discarding any hard pieces of stem.

3 Place the chicken pieces, well spread out, on a heatproof dish that will fit inside a bamboo steamer. Arrange the mushroom and ginger shreds on top of the chicken and sprinkle with salt, pepper and sesame oil to taste.

4 Place the dish on the rack inside a hot steamer or on a rack in a wok filled with hot water and steam over high heat for 20 minutes. Serve immediately, garnished with coriander (cilantro) or parsley leaves.

COOK'S TIP

If using fresh shiitake mushrooms, be careful not to overcook them, as they will then become tough.

Crispy Chicken

In this recipe the chicken is brushed in a syrup and deep-fried until golden.
It is a little time consuming, but well worth the effort.

Serves 4
1.5 kg/3 lb 5 oz oven-ready chicken
2 tbsp clear honey
2 tsp Chinese five-spice powder
2 tbsp wine vinegar
850 ml/1½ pints/3¾ cups vegetable oil, for frying
chilli sauce, to serve

1 Wash the chicken inside and out and pat dry with kitchen paper (paper towels). Bring a large saucepan of water to the boil and remove from the heat. Place the chicken in the water, cover and set aside for 20 minutes. Remove the chicken from the water and pat thoroughly dry with kitchen paper (paper towels). Chill in the refrigerator overnight.

2 Mix the honey, Chinese five-spice powder and vinegar together. Brush some of the mixture over the chicken and return the chicken to the refrigerator for 20 minutes. Repeat this process until all the glaze has been used. Return the chicken to the refrigerator for at least 2 hours after the final coating.

3 Using a cleaver or a very sharp knife, open the chicken out by splitting it down the centre through the breast and then cut each half into four pieces.

4 Heat the oil for deep-frying in a wok until almost smoking. Reduce the heat and fry each piece of chicken for

5–7 minutes, until golden and cooked through. Remove from the oil and drain on absorbent kitchen paper (paper towels). Serve hot with a little chilli sauce.

COOK'S TIP

If it is easier, buy chicken portions and use instead of a whole chicken.

Chicken with Celery & Cashew Nuts

Yellow bean sauce, widely available in bottles, gives this quick and easy dish
a really authentic taste. Pecan nuts can be used in place of cashews.

Serves 4
500 g/1 lb 2 oz boneless skinless chicken breasts
2 tbsp sunflower or vegetable oil
115 g/4 oz/1 cup unsalted cashew nuts
4–6 spring onions (scallions), thinly sliced diagonally
5–6 celery sticks, thinly sliced diagonally
175 g/6 oz jar yellow bean sauce
salt and pepper
celery leaves, to garnish (optional)
boiled rice, to serve

1 Cut the chicken into thin slices
across the grain using a Chinese
cleaver or very sharp knife.

2 Heat the oil in a preheated wok.
Add the cashew nuts and stir-fry until
they begin to brown, then add the
chicken and stir-fry until well sealed
and almost cooked through.

3 Add the spring onions (scallions)
and celery and continue to stir-fry for
2–3 minutes.

4 Add the yellow bean sauce, season
lightly with salt and pepper and toss
until the chicken and vegetables are
thoroughly coated with the sauce and
piping hot.

5 Transfer to a warm serving dish,
garnish with the celery leaves, if
using, and serve immediately with
boiled rice.

Stir-Fried Duck with Broccoli & (Bell) Peppers

This is an attractive dish using different coloured (bell) peppers
and broccoli to make it both tasty and appealing to the eye.

Serves 4	
1 egg white	
2 tbsp cornflour (cornstarch)	
450 g/1 lb skinless, boneless duck meat	
vegetable oil, for deep-frying	
1 red (bell) pepper, seeded and diced	
1 yellow (bell) pepper, seeded and diced	
125 g/4½ oz small broccoli florets	
1 garlic clove, crushed	
2 tbsp light soy sauce	
2 tsp Chinese rice wine or dry sherry	
1 tsp light brown sugar	
125 ml/4 fl oz/½ cup Chinese Stock (see page 16) or chicken stock	
2 tsp sesame seeds	

1 Beat the egg white and cornflour (cornstarch) together in a mixing bowl. Cut the duck into 2.5-cm/1-inch cubes and stir into the egg white mixture. Let stand for 30 minutes.

2 Heat the oil for deep-frying in a wok until almost smoking. Remove the duck from the egg white mixture and fry in the oil for 4–5 minutes, until crisp. Remove the duck from the oil with a slotted spoon and drain on kitchen paper (paper towels).

3 Add the (bell) peppers and broccoli to the wok and fry for 2–3 minutes. Remove with a slotted spoon and drain on kitchen paper (paper towels).

4 Pour all but 2 tablespoons of oil from the wok and return it to the heat. Add the garlic and stir-fry for 30 seconds. Stir in the soy sauce, rice wine or sherry, sugar and stock and bring to the boil. Stir in the duck and vegetables and cook for 1–2 minutes. Spoon the duck and vegetables on to a warm serving plate and sprinkle with sesame seeds. Serve immediately.

Aromatic & Crispy Duck

The pancakes traditionally served with this dish take ages to make.
Buy ready-made ones from Chinese foodstores, or use crisp lettuce instead.

Serves 4
2 large duck quarters
1 tsp salt
3–4 pieces star anise
1 tsp Szechuan red peppercorns
1 tsp cloves
2 cinnamon sticks, broken into pieces
2–3 spring onions (scallions), cut into short sections
4–5 small slices fresh ginger root
3–4 tbsp Chinese rice wine or dry sherry
vegetable oil, for deep-frying
TO SERVE
12 ready-made pancakes or 12 crisp lettuce leaves
hoi-sin or plum sauce
$^{1}/_{4}$ cucumber, thinly shredded
3–4 spring onions (scallions), thinly shredded

1 Rub the duck pieces with the salt and arrange the star anise, peppercorns, cloves and cinnamon on top. Sprinkle with the spring onions (scallions), ginger and wine or sherry. Marinate for at least 3–4 hours.

2 Arrange the duck pieces (with the marinade spices) on a plate that will fit inside a bamboo steamer. Pour some hot water into a wok, place the bamboo steamer in the wok, sitting on a trivet. Put in the duck and cover with the bamboo lid. Steam the duck pieces (with the marinade) over high heat for at least 2–3 hours, until tender and cooked through. Top up the hot water from time to time as required.

3 Remove the duck and set aside to cool for at least 4–5 hours – this is very important, for unless the duck is cold and dry, it will not be crispy.

4 Pour off the water and wipe the wok dry. Pour in the oil and heat until smoking. Deep-fry the duck pieces, skin-side down, for 4–5 minutes, or until crisp and brown. Remove and drain on kitchen paper (paper towels).

5 Scrape the meat off the bones on to a dish. Put the pancakes or lettuce, hoisin or plum sauce, cucumber and spring onions (scallions) on serving dishes. To serve, place 1 teaspoon of hoi-sin or plum sauce on the centre of a pancake (or lettuce leaf), add a few pieces of cucumber and spring onion (scallion), with a portion of the duck meat. Wrap up to form a small parcel and eat with your fingers.

Duck in Spicy Sauce

Chinese five-spice powder gives a lovely flavour to this sliced duck,
and the chilli adds a little subtle heat.

Serves 4
1 tbsp vegetable oil
1 tsp grated fresh ginger root
1 garlic clove, crushed
1 fresh red chilli, chopped
350 g/12 oz skinless, boneless duck meat, cut into strips
125 g/4^1/$_2$ oz cauliflower florets
50 g/1^3/$_4$ oz mangetout (snow peas)
50 g/1^3/$_4$ oz baby corn cobs, halved lengthways
300 ml/^{1}/$_2$ pint/1^1/$_4$ cups chicken stock
1 tsp Chinese five-spice powder
2 tsp Chinese rice wine or dry sherry
1 tsp cornflour (cornstarch)
2 tsp water
1 tsp sesame oil

1 Heat the vegetable oil in a preheated wok. Add the ginger, garlic, chilli and duck and stir-fry for 2–3 minutes. Remove with a slotted spoon and set aside.

2 Add the vegetables to the wok and stir-fry for 2–3 minutes. Pour off any excess oil from the wok.

3 Return the duck to the wok and pour in the stock. Sprinkle the Chinese five-spice powder over the top, stir in the Chinese rice wine or sherry and cook over a low heat for 15 minutes, until the duck is tender.

4 Blend the cornflour (cornstarch) with the water to form a smooth paste and stir it into the wok, together with the sesame oil. Bring to the boil, stirring until the sauce has thickened and cleared. Transfer the duck in spicy sauce to a warm serving dish and serve immediately.

COOK'S TIP

Omit the chilli for a milder dish, or seed the chilli before adding it to remove some of the heat.

Honey & Soy Glazed Duck

This honey and soy glaze gives a wonderful sheen and flavour to the duck skin.
It is so simple, yet utterly delicious.

Serves 4
1 tsp dark soy sauce
2 tbsp clear honey
1 tsp garlic vinegar
2 garlic cloves, crushed
1 tsp ground star anise
2 tsp cornflour (cornstarch)
2 tsp water
2 large boneless duck breasts, about 225g/8 oz each

TO GARNISH

celery leaves
cucumber matchsticks
snipped chives

1 Mix together the soy sauce, honey, vinegar, garlic and star anise.

2 Blend the cornflour (cornstarch) with the water to form a smooth paste and stir it into the honey and soy sauce mixture.

3 Place the duck breasts in a shallow ovenproof dish and brush the soy marinade over them, turning to coat them completely. Cover and marinate in the refrigerator for at least 2 hours or overnight if possible.

4 Cook the duck in a preheated oven at 220°C/425°F/Gas Mark 7 for about 20–25 minutes, basting frequently with the glaze.

5 Remove the duck from the oven and cook under a preheated grill (broiler) for 3–4 minutes to caramelize the top of the duck.

6 Transfer the duck to a chopping board and cut into thin slices.

7 Arrange the duck slices on a warm serving plate, garnish with celery leaves, cucumber matchsticks and snipped chives and serve.

COOK'S TIP

The duck breasts are cooked through if the juices run clear when a knife is inserted into the thickest part of the flesh.

Duck with Pineapple

For best results, use ready-cooked duck meat, widely available from many Chinese restaurants and supermarkets.

Serves 4

115–175 g/4–6 oz cooked
duck meat

3 tbsp vegetable oil

1 small onion, thinly sliced

2–3 slices fresh ginger root,
thinly shredded

1 spring onion (scallion),
thinly shredded

1 small carrot, cut into thin strips

115 g/4 oz canned pineapple,
cut into small slices

$1/2$ tsp salt

1 tbsp red rice vinegar

2 tbsp syrup from the pineapple

1 tbsp Cornflour (Cornstarch)
Paste (see page 16)

black bean sauce, to serve
(optional)

1 Cut the cooked duck meat into thin strips using a Chinese cleaver or very sharp knife.

2 Heat the oil in a preheated wok. Add the onion and stir-fry for 1–2 minutes. Add the ginger, spring onion (scallion) and carrot and stir-fry for 1 minute.

3 Add the duck shreds and pineapple to the wok, together with the salt, rice vinegar and the pineapple syrup. Stir until the mixture is well blended.

4 Add the cornflour (cornstarch) paste and stir for 1–2 minutes, until the sauce has thickened. Transfer to a warm serving dish and serve with black bean sauce, if wished.

Duck With Mangoes

Use fresh mangoes in this recipe for a terrific flavour and colour.
If unavailable, use canned mangoes and rinse them before using.

Serves 4
2 medium-size ripe mangoes
300 ml/^{1}/$_2$ pint/1^1/$_4$ cups chicken stock
2 large skinless duck breasts, about 225 g/8 oz each
2 garlic cloves, crushed
1 tsp grated fresh ginger root
3 tbsp vegetable oil
1 tsp wine vinegar
1 tsp light soy sauce
1 leek, sliced
freshly chopped parsley, to garnish

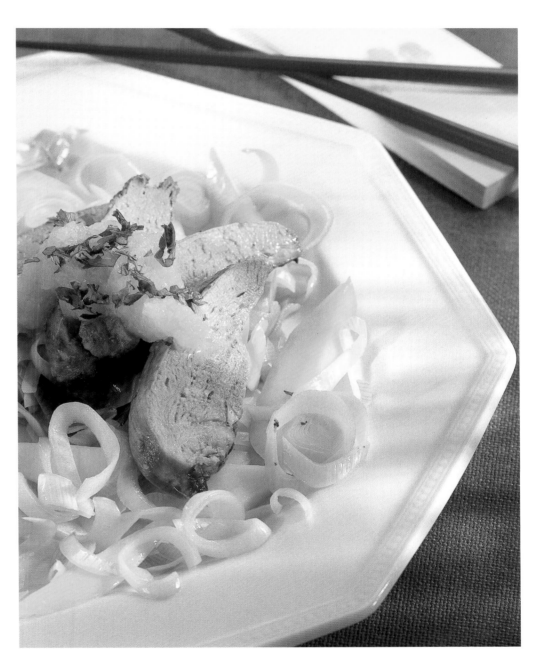

1 Peel the mangoes and cut the flesh from each side of the stone (pit). Cut the flesh into strips.

2 Put half the mango pieces and the stock in a food processor and process until smooth. Alternatively, press half the fruit through a fine strainer and mix with the stock.

3 Rub the duck with the garlic and ginger. Heat the oil in a preheated wok and cook the duck breasts, turning, until sealed. Reserve the oil in the wok and remove the duck. Place on a rack over a roasting tin (pan) and cook in a preheated oven at 220°C/425°F/Gas 7 for 20 minutes, until cooked through.

4 Meanwhile, place the mango and stock mixture in a saucepan and add the vinegar and soy sauce. Bring to the boil and cook over a high heat until reduced by half.

5 Heat the oil reserved in the wok. Add the leek and remaining mango and stir-fry for 1 minute. Remove from the wok with a slotted spoon, arrange on the base of a serving dish and keep warm.

6 Slice the cooked duck breasts and arrange the slices on top of the leek and mango mixture.

7 Pour the sauce on top and serve immediately.

Meat Dishes

The most popular meat throughout China is pork, as it is both economical and versatile. All cuts are tender and suitable for all cooking techniques, including stir-frying, braising and steaming. A spit-roasted pig is an essential feature of a festive occasion, such as a wedding. For everyday meals, the richness of the meat is balanced by spicy or fruity marinades and sauces and crisp

vegetables.

Lamb is popular in northern China, but is rarely eaten elsewhere. Most lamb recipes are light and simple.

Beef is eaten in all regions of China, but as it is much less versatile and economic than pork, it is not so popular. Only certain cuts, such as fillet and sirloin, lend themselves to fast-cooking techniques. Other cuts of beef are usually braised.

Two meat dishes, one of which is usually pork, are served at family meals. For a formal dinner, at least two meat dishes would form part of the appetizers, as well.

Lamb Meatballs in Soy Sauce

These small meatballs are made with minced (ground) lamb and spiced with
chilli, garlic, parsley and Chinese curry powder for a delicious flavour.

Serves 4
450 g/1 lb minced (ground) lamb
3 garlic cloves, crushed
2 spring onions (scallions), finely chopped
1/2 tsp chilli powder
1 tsp Chinese curry powder
1 tbsp chopped fresh parsley
25 g/1 oz/1/2 cup fresh white breadcrumbs
1 egg, beaten
3 tbsp vegetable oil
125 g/41/2 oz Chinese cabbage, shredded
1 leek, sliced
1 tbsp cornflour (cornstarch)
2 tbsp water
300 ml/1/2 pint/11/4 cups lamb stock
1 tbsp dark soy sauce
shredded leek, to garnish

1 Mix the lamb, garlic, spring onions (scallions), chilli powder, Chinese curry powder, chopped parsley and breadcrumbs together in a bowl. Work the egg into the mixture, bringing it together until firm. Roll into 16 small balls of even size between the palms of your hands.

2 Heat the oil in a preheated wok. Add the cabbage and leek and stir-fry for 1 minute. Remove from the wok with a slotted spoon and set aside.

3 Add the meatballs to the wok and fry, turning gently but frequently, for 3–4 minutes, until browned all over and almost cooked through.

4 Mix the cornflour (cornstarch) and water to a smooth paste. Pour the stock and soy sauce into the wok and cook for 2–3 minutes. Stir in the cornflour (cornstarch) paste. Bring to the boil, stirring until thick and clear.

5 Return the cabbage and leek to the wok and cook for 1 minute, until heated through. Transfer the cabbage and leek to a warm serving dish, top with the meatballs and garnish with the shredded leek. Serve immediately.

Hot Lamb

This really is quite a spicy dish, using 2 chillies in the rich sauce. Halve the number
of chillies to reduce the heat or seed the chillies before using if desired.

Serves 4
450 g/1 lb lean boneless lamb, cut into 2.5-cm/1-inch cubes
2 tbsp hoi-sin sauce
1 tbsp dark soy sauce
1 garlic clove, crushed
2 tsp grated fresh ginger root
2 tbsp vegetable oil
2 onions, sliced
1 fennel bulb, sliced
4 tbsp water

SAUCE

1 large fresh red chilli, cut into thin strips
1 fresh green chilli, cut into thin strips
2 tbsp rice wine vinegar
2 tsp light brown sugar
2 tbsp peanut oil
1 tsp sesame oil

1 Place the lamb in a shallow glass
dish. Mix together the hoi-sin sauce,
soy sauce, garlic and ginger in a bowl.
Pour the mixture over the lamb,
turning it to coat well. Marinate for
20 minutes.

2 Heat the vegetable oil in a
preheated wok until nearly smoking.
Lower the heat slightly, add the lamb
and stir-fry for 1–2 minutes. Add the
onions and fennel and cook for a
further 2 minutes, until they begin to
brown. Stir in the water, cover and
cook for 2–3 minutes.

3 Meanwhile, make the sauce. Put
the chillies, vinegar, sugar, peanut oil
and sesame oil in a saucepan and cook
over a low heat for 3–4 minutes,
stirring occasionally.

4 Transfer the lamb and onions to a
warm serving dish, top with the sauce
and serve immediately.

VARIATION

Use beef, pork or duck instead of
the lamb and vary the vegetables,
using leeks or celery instead of the
onion and fennel.

Lamb & Ginger Stir-fry

Fillet of lamb (or beef or pork) is cooked with garlic, ginger and shiitake mushrooms.
Serve with noodles, or plain boiled rice if preferred.

Serves 4
450 g/1 lb lamb fillet (tenderloin), or beef or pork
2 tbsp sunflower oil
1 tbsp chopped fresh ginger root
2 garlic cloves, chopped
6 spring onions (scallions), white and green parts diagonally sliced
225 g/8 oz shiitake mushrooms, sliced
175 g/6 oz mangetout (snow peas)
1 tsp cornflour (cornstarch)
2 tbsp Chinese rice wine or dry sherry
1 tbsp light soy sauce
1 tsp sesame oil
1 tbsp sesame seeds, toasted
Chinese egg noodles, to serve

1 Cut the lamb into 5-mm/¼-inch thick slices using a very sharp knife.

2 Heat the oil in a preheated wok or large, heavy-based frying pan (skillet). Add the lamb and stir-fry for about 2 minutes.

3 Add the ginger, garlic, spring onions (scallions), mushrooms and mangetout (snow peas) and stir-fry for a further 2 minutes.

4 Mix the cornflour (cornstarch) with the rice wine or sherry, add to the wok with the soy sauce and sesame oil and cook, stirring, for 1 minute, until thickened. Sprinkle with the sesame seeds and serve with Chinese egg noodles.

Stir-fried Lamb with Sesame Seeds

This is a very simple, but delicious dish, in which lean pieces of lamb are cooked in sugar and soy sauce and sprinkled with sesame seeds, then served on a bed of leeks and carrot.

Serves 4
2 tbsp peanut oil
450 g/1 lb boneless lean lamb, cut into strips
2 leeks, sliced
1 carrot, cut into matchsticks
2 garlic cloves, crushed
75 ml/3 fl oz/$\frac{1}{3}$ cup lamb or vegetable stock
2 tsp light brown sugar
1 tbsp dark soy sauce
$4\frac{1}{2}$ tsp sesame seeds

1 Heat the peanut oil in a large preheated wok.

2 Add the lamb and stir-fry for 2–3 minutes. Remove the lamb from the wok with a slotted spoon, set aside and keep warm.

3 Add the leek, carrot and garlic and stir-fry in the remaining oil for 1–2 minutes. Remove the vegetables from the wok and carefully drain off any remaining oil.

4 Place the stock, sugar and soy sauce in the wok and add the lamb. Cook, stirring constantly, for 2–3 minutes, or until the lamb is thoroughly coated with the sauce.

5 Sprinkle the sesame seeds over the top, turning the lamb to coat.

6 Spoon the leek and carrot mixture on to a warm serving plate and top with the sesame-coated lamb. Serve immediately.

COOK'S TIP

To bring out the full flavour and fragrance of the sesame seeds, dry–fry or toast them briefly before sprinkling them over the lamb.

COOK'S TIP

Be careful not to burn the sugar in the wok when heating and coating the meat, otherwise the flavour of the dish will be spoiled.

Five-Spiced Lamb

Chinese five-spice powder is a blend of cinnamon, fennel, star anise, ginger and cloves. It gives an authentic Chinese flavour to many dishes.

Serves 4
675 g/1½ lb lean boneless lamb (leg or fillet)
2 tsp Chinese five-spice powder
3 tbsp sunflower oil
1 red (bell) pepper, seeded and thinly sliced
1 green (bell) pepper, seeded and thinly sliced
1 yellow or orange (bell) pepper, seeded and thinly sliced
4–6 spring onions (scallions), thinly sliced diagonally
175 g/6 oz French (green) or fine beans, cut into 4-cm/1½-inch lengths
2 tbsp soy sauce
4 tbsp Chinese rice wine or dry sherry
salt and pepper
Chinese noodles, to serve

TO GARNISH

strips of red and yellow (bell) pepper
fresh coriander (cilantro) leaves

1 Cut the lamb into narrow strips, about 4 cm/1½ inches long, across the grain. Place in a bowl, add the five-spice powder and ¼ teaspoon salt, mix well, cover and marinate in a cool place for at least an hour or up to 24 hours.

2 Heat half the oil in a preheated wok until it is almost smoking. Lower the heat slightly, add the lamb and stir-fry briskly for 3–4 minutes, until almost cooked. Remove from the wok with a slotted spoon and keep warm.

3 Add the remaining oil to the wok and when hot, add the (bell) peppers and spring onions (scallions). Stir-fry for 2–3 minutes, then add the beans and stir-fry for 1–2 minutes.

4 Add the soy sauce and rice wine or sherry to the wok. Return the lamb to

the wok, together with any juices. Cook, stirring, for 1–2 minutes until the lamb is hot and thoroughly coated in the sauce. Season to taste.

5 Serve with noodles, garnished with strips of red and green (bell) pepper and fresh coriander (cilantro).

Lamb in Mushroom Sauce

Use a lean cut of lamb, such as fillet, for this recipe
for both flavour and tenderness.

Serves 4
350 g/12 oz lean boneless lamb
2 tbsp vegetable oil
3 garlic cloves, crushed
1 leek, sliced
1 tsp cornflour (cornstarch)
4 tbsp light soy sauce
3 tbsp Chinese rice wine or dry sherry
3 tbsp water
$\frac{1}{2}$ tsp chilli sauce
175 g/6 oz large mushrooms, sliced
$\frac{1}{2}$ tsp sesame oil
fresh red chilli strips, to garnish

1 Cut the lamb into strips. Heat the oil in a preheated wok. Add the lamb, garlic and leek and stir-fry for 2–3 minutes.

2 Mix together the cornflour (cornstarch), soy sauce, Chinese rice wine or sherry, water and chilli sauce and set aside. Add the mushrooms to the wok and stir-fry for 1 minute. Stir in the sauce and cook for about 2–3 minutes, until the lamb is cooked through. Sprinkle the sesame oil over the top, garnish with red chilli strips and serve hot.

COOK'S TIP

Use rehydrated dried Chinese mushrooms obtainable from specialist shops or Chinese supermarkets for a really authentic flavour.

Lamb in Garlic Sauce

This dish contains Szechuan pepper which is quite hot
and may be replaced with black pepper if preferred.

Serves 4
450 g/1 lb lamb fillet or loin
2 tbsp dark soy sauce
2 tsp sesame oil
2 tbsp Chinese rice wine or dry sherry
$\frac{1}{2}$ tsp Szechuan pepper
4 tbsp vegetable oil
4 garlic cloves, crushed
50 g/1$\frac{3}{4}$ oz canned water chestnuts, drained and quartered
1 green (bell) pepper, seeded and sliced
1 tbsp wine vinegar
1 tbsp sesame oil

1 Cut the lamb into 2.5-cm/1-inch
pieces and place in a shallow dish.

2 Mix together 1 tablespoon of the
soy sauce, the sesame oil, Chinese
rice wine or sherry and Szechuan
pepper in a bowl.

3 Pour the mixture over the lamb,
turning to coat, and marinate for
30 minutes.

4 Heat the vegetable oil in a large
preheated wok.

5 Remove the lamb from the
marinade and add to the wok,
together with the garlic. Stir-fry for
2–3 minutes.

6 Add the water chestnuts and (bell)
pepper and stir-fry for 1 minute. Add
the remaining soy sauce and the
wine vinegar.

7 Add the sesame oil and cook for
1–2 minutes. Transfer to a warm
serving dish and serve immediately.

Oyster Sauce Beef

This is a standard meat and vegetables recipe, which can be adapted for most kinds of meat and whatever vegetables are in season.

Serves 4
350 g/12 oz steak
1 tsp caster (superfine) sugar
1 tbsp light soy sauce
1 tsp Chinese rice wine or dry sherry
1 tsp Cornflour (Cornstarch) Paste (see page 16)
1/2 small carrot
50 g/1³/₄ oz mangetout (snow peas)
50 g/1³/₄ oz canned bamboo shoots, drained
50 g/1³/₄ oz canned straw mushrooms
about 300 ml/1/2 pint/1¹/₄ cups vegetable oil
1 spring onion (scallion), cut into short sections
2–3 small slices fresh ginger root
1/2 tsp salt
2 tbsp oyster sauce
2–3 tbsp Chinese Stock (see page 16) or water

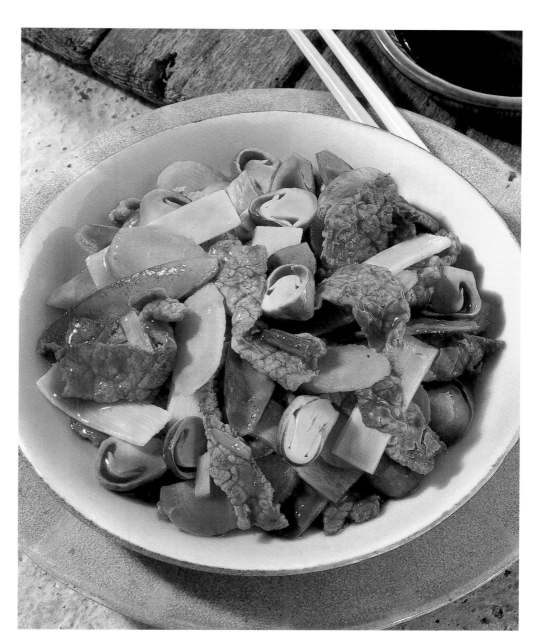

1 Cut the steak into small, thin slices. Place in a shallow dish with the sugar, soy sauce, wine and cornflour (cornstarch) paste and marinate for 25–30 minutes.

2 Slice the carrot, mangetout (snow peas), bamboo shoots and straw mushrooms so that as far as possible the vegetable pieces are of uniform size and thickness.

3 Heat the oil in a preheated wok and add the beef slices. Stir-fry for about 1 minute, then remove with a slotted spoon and keep warm.

4 Carefully pour off the excess oil, leaving about 1 tablespoon in the wok. Add the carrot, mangetout (snow peas), bamboo shoots, straw mushrooms, spring onion (scallion) and ginger and stir-fry for about 2 minutes.

5 Return the steak to the wok and add the salt, oyster sauce and stock or water. Blend well and cook, stirring constantly, until heated through.

6 Transfer to a warmed serving dish and serve immediately.

Beef & Pak Choi

A colourful selection of vegetables is stir-fried with tender strips of steak to make this tasty, nutritious and quick dish.

Serves 4
1 large head of pak choi, about 250–275 g/9–9¹/₂ oz, torn into large pieces
2 tbsp vegetable oil
2 garlic cloves, crushed
450 g/1 lb rump or fillet steak, cut into thin strips
150 g/5¹/₂ oz mangetout (snow peas), trimmed
150 g/5¹/₂ oz baby corn cobs
6 spring onions (scallions), chopped
2 red (bell) peppers, seeded and thinly sliced
2 tbsp oyster sauce
1 tbsp fish sauce
1 tbsp caster (superfine) sugar
boiled rice or noodles, to serve

1 Steam the pak choi leaves over boiling water until they are just tender. Remove from the steamer and keep warm.

2 Heat the oil in a preheated wok or a large, heavy-based frying pan (skillet). Add the garlic and strips of steak and stir-fry for 1–2 minutes, until just browned all over.

3 Add the mangetout (snow peas), baby corn cobs, spring onions (scallions), (bell) pepper, oyster sauce, fish sauce and sugar, mixing thoroughly. Stir-fry for a further 2–3 minutes until the vegetables are just tender, but still remain crisp and firm to the bite.

4 Arrange the pak choi leaves on the base of a warm serving dish and spoon the beef and vegetable mixture into the centre. Serve the stir-fry immediately, with plain boiled rice or noodles.

VARIATION

Chinese flat cabbage or Chinese flowering cabbage could be used instead of pak choi.

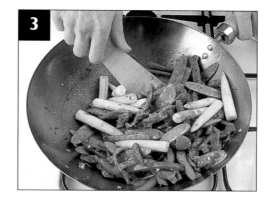

Spicy Beef & Broccoli Stir-Fry

This is a great combination of ingredients in terms of colour and flavour,
and is so simple and quick to prepare.

Serves 4
225 g/8 oz lean steak, trimmed
2 garlic cloves, crushed
dash of chilli oil
1-cm/$^1/_2$-inch piece fresh ginger root, grated
$^1/_2$ tsp Chinese five-spice powder
2 tbsp dark soy sauce
2 tbsp vegetable oil
150 g/5$^1/_2$ oz broccoli florets
1 tbsp light soy sauce
150 ml/$^1/_4$ pint/$^2/_3$ cup beef stock
2 tsp cornflour (cornstarch)
4 tsp water
carrot strips, to garnish

1 Cut the steak into thin strips and
place in a shallow glass dish. Mix
together the garlic, chilli sauce, ginger,
five-spice powder and dark soy sauce
in a bowl. Pour the mixture over the
steak, tossing to coat the strips evenly.

2 Heat 1 tablespoon of the oil in a
preheated wok. Add the broccoli and
stir-fry for 4–5 minutes. Remove from
the wok with a slotted spoon and
set aside.

3 Heat the remaining oil in the wok.
Add the steak, together with the
marinade, and stir-fry for 2–3
minutes, until the beef is sealed.
Return the broccoli to the wok and stir
in the light soy sauce and stock.

4 Blend the cornflour (cornstarch)
with the water to form a smooth paste
and stir it into the wok. Bring to
the boil, stirring constantly until
thickened and clear. Cook for 1 further
minute. Transfer to a warm serving
dish, garnish with the carrot strips
arranged in a lattice pattern on top
and serve immediately.

COOK'S TIP

Marinate the beef for several hours
for a fuller flavour. Cover and
marinate in the refrigerator if
preparing in advance.

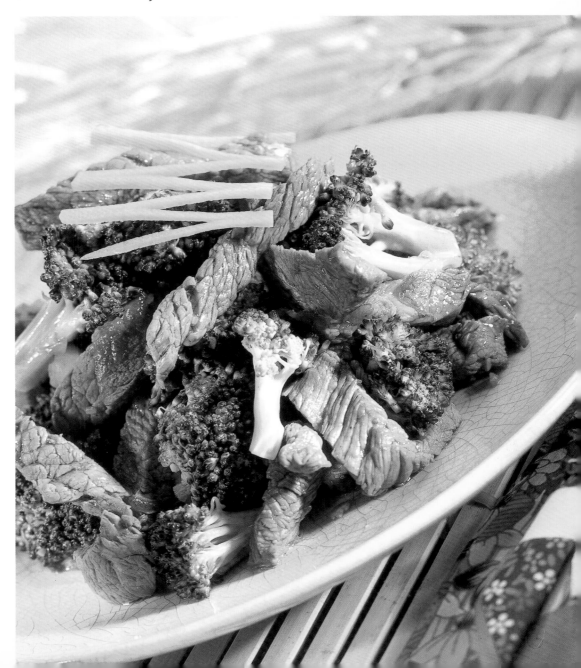

Beef & Chilli Black Bean Sauce

It is not necessary to use the expensive cuts of steak for this recipe:
the meat will be tender as it is cut into small, thin slices and marinated.

Serves 4
225–275 g/8–9¹/₂ oz steak (such as rump)
1 small onion
1 small green (bell) pepper, seeded
about 300 ml/¹/₂ pint/1¹/₄ cups vegetable oil
1 spring onion (scallion), cut into short sections
a few small slices of fresh ginger root
1–2 small green or red chillies, seeded and sliced
2 tbsp crushed black bean sauce

MARINADE

¹/₂ tsp bicarbonate of soda (baking soda) or baking powder
¹/₂ tsp sugar
1 tbsp light soy sauce
2 tsp Chinese rice wine or dry sherry
2 tsp Cornflour (Cornstarch) Paste (see page 16)
2 tsp sesame oil

1 Cut the steak into small thin strips. Mix together all the marinade ingredients in a shallow dish, add the steak strips, turn to coat and marinate for at least 2–3 hours.

2 Cut the onion and green (bell) pepper into small equal-size squares.

3 Heat the oil in a preheated wok. Add the steak strips and stir-fry for about 1 minute, or until the colour changes. Remove with a slotted spoon and drain on kitchen paper (paper towels).

4 Pour off the excess oil, leaving about 1 tablespoon in the wok. Add the spring onion (scallion), ginger, chillies, onion and green (bell) pepper and stir-fry for about 1 minute. Add the black bean sauce and stir until smooth. Return the steak strips to the wok, blend well and stir-fry for another minute. Transfer to a warm serving dish and serve immediately.

Beef & Green Beans

The green of the beans complements the dark colour
of the beef, served in a rich sauce.

Serves 4

450 g/1 lb rump or fillet steak, cut
into 2.5-cm/1-inch pieces

MARINADE

2 tsp cornflour (cornstarch)

2 tbsp dark soy sauce

2 tsp peanut oil

SAUCE

2 tbsp vegetable oil

3 garlic cloves, crushed

1 small onion, cut into eight

225 g/8 oz thin green
beans, halved

25 g/1 oz/¼ cup
unsalted cashew nuts

25 g/1 oz canned bamboo
shoots, drained

2 tsp dark soy sauce

2 tsp Chinese rice wine or
dry sherry

125 ml/4 fl oz/½ cup beef stock

2 tsp cornflour (cornstarch)

4 tsp water

salt and pepper

1 Mix the marinade ingredients together in a shallow glass dish. Add the steak, turn to coat, cover and marinate for at least 30 minutes.

2 Heat the oil for the sauce in a preheated wok. Add the garlic, onion, beans, cashews and bamboo shoots and stir-fry for 2–3 minutes.

3 Drain the beef from the marinade, add to the wok and stir-fry for 3–4 minutes.

4 Mix the soy sauce, Chinese rice wine or sherry and stock together and stir the mixture into the wok. Blend the cornflour (cornstarch) with the water to form a smooth paste and stir it into the wok. Bring the sauce to the boil, stirring until thickened and clear. Reduce the heat and simmer for 2–3 minutes. Season to taste with salt and pepper. Transfer the beef and green beans to a warm serving dish and serve immediately.

(Bell) Peppered Beef Cashew

A simple but stunning dish of tender strips of beef mixed with crunchy cashew nuts, coated in a hot sauce. Serve with rice noodles.

Serves 4
1 tbsp peanut or sunflower oil
1 tbsp sesame oil
1 onion, sliced
1 garlic clove, crushed
1 tbsp grated fresh ginger root
450 g/1 lb fillet or rump steak, cut into thin strips
2 tsp palm sugar or demerara (raw crystal) sugar
2 tbsp light soy sauce
1 small yellow (bell) pepper, seeded and sliced
1 red (bell) pepper, seeded and sliced
4 spring onions (scallions), finely chopped
2 celery stalks, chopped
4 large open-cap mushrooms, thinly sliced
4 tbsp roasted cashew nuts
3 tbsp stock or white wine
rice noodles, to serve

1 Heat the peanut or sunflower oil and the sesame oil in a preheated wok or large, heavy-based frying pan (skillet). Add the onion, garlic and ginger, and stir-fry for about 2 minutes, until the onion is softened and lightly coloured.

2 Add the steak strips and stir-fry for a further 2–3 minutes, until the meat has browned all over.

3 Add the sugar and soy sauce, mixing thoroughly. Stir in the (bell) peppers, spring onions (scallions), celery, mushrooms and cashews.

4 Add the stock or wine and stir-fry for 2–3 minutes, until the steak is cooked through and the vegetables are tender-crisp. Transfer to a warm serving dish and serve immediately with rice noodles.

COOK'S VARIATION

The cashews could be replaced with the same quantity of unsalted, roasted peanuts.

Chinese Beef

This dish is quick to cook, but benefits from a lengthy marinating, as this tenderizes and flavours the meat.

Serves 4

225 g/8 oz lean steak, cut into
2.5-cm/1-inch cubes

1 tbsp light soy sauce

1 tsp sesame oil

2 tsp Chinese rice wine or
dry sherry

1 tsp caster (superfine) sugar

2 tsp hoi-sin sauce

1 garlic clove, crushed

$^1/_2$ tsp cornflour (cornstarch)

green (bell) pepper matchsticks,
to garnish

rice or noodles, to serve

SAUCE

2 tbsp dark soy sauce

1 tsp caster (superfine) sugar

$^1/_2$ tsp cornflour (cornstarch)

3 tbsp oyster sauce

8 tbsp water

2 tbsp vegetable oil

3 garlic cloves, crushed

1-cm/$^1/_2$-inch piece fresh ginger
root, grated

8 baby corn cobs, halved lengthways

$^1/_2$ green (bell) pepper,
seeded and thinly sliced

25 g/1 oz canned bamboo shoots, drained

1 Put the steak in a shallow glass bowl. Mix together the soy sauce, sesame oil, rice wine or sherry, sugar, hoi-sin sauce, garlic and cornflour (cornstarch) and pour on the steak, turning it to coat completely. Cover and marinate for at least 1 hour.

2 Meanwhile, make the sauce. Mix the dark soy sauce with the sugar, cornflour (cornstarch), oyster sauce and water. Heat the oil in a preheated wok. Add the steak, together with the marinade, and stir-fry for about 2–3 minutes, until sealed.

3 Add the garlic, ginger, baby corn cobs, (bell) pepper and bamboo shoots. Stir in the oyster sauce mixture and bring to the boil, reduce the heat and cook for a further 2–3 minutes. Garnish with green (bell) pepper matchsticks and serve with rice or noodles.

COOK'S TIP

For a fuller flavour, marinate the beef in the refrigerator overnight.

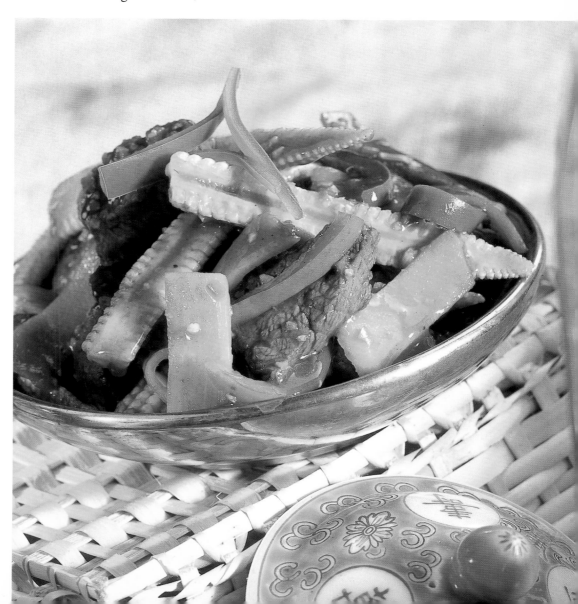

Crispy Shredded Beef

A very popular Szechuan dish served in most
Chinese restaurants all over the world.

Serves 4
275–350 g/9¹/₂–12 oz beef steak (such as topside or rump)
2 eggs
¹/₄ tsp salt
4–5 tbsp plain (all-purpose) flour
vegetable oil, for deep-frying
2 medium carrots, cut into matchstick strips
2 spring onions (scallions), finely shredded
1 garlic clove, finely chopped
2–3 small fresh green or red chillies, seeded and finely shredded
4 tbsp sugar
3 tbsp rice vinegar
1 tbsp light soy sauce
2–3 tbsp Chinese Stock (see page16) or water
1 tsp Cornflour (Cornstarch) Paste (see page 16)

1 Cut the steak across the grain into
thin strips. Beat the eggs in a bowl
with the salt and flour, adding a little
water if necessary. Add the steak and
mix until coated with the batter.

2 Heat the oil in a preheated wok until
smoking. Add the steak strips and
deep-fry for 4–5 minutes, stirring to
separate the shreds. Remove with a
slotted spoon and drain on kitchen
paper (paper towels).

3 Add the carrots to the wok and
deep-fry for about 1–1½ minutes,
then remove with a slotted spoon and
drain on kitchen paper (paper towels).

4 Pour off the excess oil, leaving
about 1 tablespoon in the wok. Add
the spring onions (scallions), garlic,
chillies and carrots, stir-fry for about
1 minute. Add the sugar, vinegar, soy
sauce and stock or water, blend well
and bring to the boil.

5 Stir in the cornflour (cornstarch)
paste and simmer for a few minutes to
thicken the sauce. Return the steak to
the wok and stir until the shreds of
meat are well coated with the sauce.
Transfer to a warm serving dish and
serve immediately.

Sweet & Sour Pork

This has to be the most popular Chinese dish all over the world.
To vary, replace pork with fish, prawns (shrimp), chicken or vegetables.

Serves 4
225–275 g/8–9¹/₂ oz lean pork
2 tsp brandy or whisky
vegetable oil, for deep-frying
1 egg, beaten
2 tbsp plain (all-purpose) flour
salt and pepper

SAUCE
1 tbsp vegetable oil
1 small onion, diced
1 small carrot, diced
¹/₂ small green (bell) pepper, seeded and diced
1 tbsp light soy sauce
3 tbsp sugar
3 tbsp wine vinegar
1 tbsp tomato purée (paste)
about 3–4 tbsp Chinese Stock (see page 16) or water
1 tbsp Cornflour (Cornstarch) Paste (see page 16)

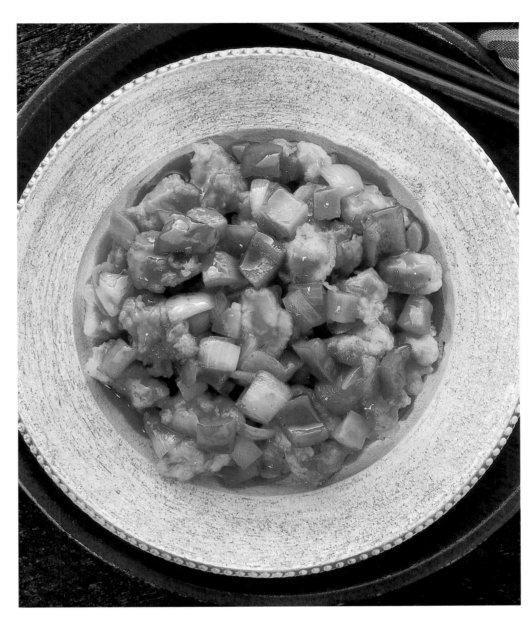

1 Cut the pork into bite-size cubes. Place in a dish with the salt, pepper and brandy or whisky and marinate for 15–20 minutes.

2 Heat the oil in a preheated wok or deep-fryer. Place the pork cubes in a bowl with the beaten egg and turn to coat. Sprinkle the flour over them and turn the pork cubes until they are well coated.

3 Deep-fry the pork cubes in batches for about 3–4 minutes, stirring gently to separate the pieces. Remove with a slotted spoon and drain on kitchen paper (paper towels). Reheat the oil and return the meat to the wok for 1–2 minutes, until golden brown. Remove with a slotted spoon and drain on kitchen paper (paper towels).

4 To make the sauce, heat the oil in a preheated wok, add the vegetables and stir-fry for about 1 minute. Add the seasonings and tomato purée (paste) with the stock or water, bring to the boil and thicken with the cornflour (cornstarch) paste.

5 Add the pork and blend well so that each piece of meat is coated with the sauce. Serve immediately.

Spare Ribs with Chilli

For the best results, chop the spare ribs into bite-size pieces
or ask your butcher to do this for you.

Serves 4
450 g/1 lb pork spare ribs
1 tsp caster (superfine) sugar
1 tbsp light soy sauce
1 tsp Chinese rice wine or dry sherry
1 tsp cornflour (cornstarch)
about 600 ml/1 pint/2^1/$_2$ cups vegetable oil
1 garlic clove, finely chopped
1 spring onion (scallion), cut into short sections
1 small fresh green or red chilli seeded and thinly sliced
2 tbsp black bean sauce
about 150 ml/^{1}/$_4$ pint/^{2}/$_3$ cup Chinese Stock (see page 16) or water
1 small onion, diced
1 green (bell) pepper, seeded and diced

1 Trim any excess fat from the ribs, and chop each one into 3–4 bite-size pieces. Place the ribs in a shallow dish with the sugar, soy sauce, rice wine or sherry and cornflour (cornstarch) and marinate for 35–45 minutes.

2 Heat the oil in a preheated wok. Add the spare ribs and deep-fry for 2–3 minutes, until light brown. Remove with a slotted spoon and drain on kitchen paper (paper towels).

3 Pour off the oil, leaving about 1 tablespoon in the wok. Add the garlic, spring onion (scallion), chilli and black bean sauce and stir-fry for 30–40 seconds.

4 Add the spare ribs, blend well, then add the stock or water. Bring to the boil, reduce the heat, cover and braise for 8–10 minutes, stirring occasionally.

5 Add the onion and green (bell) pepper. Increase the heat to high, and stir, uncovered, for about 2 minutes to reduce the sauce a little. Serve hot.

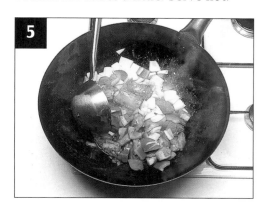

Deep-fried Pork with a Soy Dipping Sauce

Small pieces of pork are coated in a light batter and deep-fried in this recipe – the pork is delicious dipped in a soy and honey sauce.

Serves 4

450 g/1 lb pork fillet
(tenderloin)

2 tbsp peanut oil

200 g/7 oz/1¾ cups plain
(all-purpose) flour

2 tsp baking powder

1 egg, beaten

225 ml/8 fl oz/1 cup milk

pinch of chilli powder

vegetable oil, for deep-frying

chives, to garnish

SAUCE

2 tbsp dark soy sauce

3 tbsp clear honey

1 tbsp wine vinegar

1 tbsp chopped chives

1 tbsp tomato purée (paste)

1 Cut the pork into 2.5-cm/1-inch cubes. Heat the peanut oil in a preheated wok. Add the pork and stir-fry for 2–3 minutes, until sealed. Remove the meat with a slotted spoon and set aside.

2 Sift the flour and baking powder into a bowl and make a well in the centre. Beat in the egg, milk and chilli powder to make a thick batter.

3 Heat the oil for deep-frying in a wok until almost smoking, then reduce the heat slightly. Toss the pork pieces in the batter to coat thoroughly and deep-fry until golden brown. Remove from the wok with a slotted spoon and drain on absorbent kitchen paper (paper towels).

4 Meanwhile, make the sauce. Mix together the soy sauce, honey, vinegar chives and tomato purée (paste) and spoon into a small serving bowl.

5 Serve the sauce with the hot pork cubes, garnished with chives.

COOK'S TIP

Be careful when heating the oil for deep-frying. It must be heated so that it is almost smoking, then the heat must be reduced immediately.

Fish-flavoured Shredded Pork

'Fish-flavoured' (yu-xiang in Chinese) is a Szechuan cookery term meaning that the dish contains seasonings normally used in fish dishes.

Serves 4
about 2 tbsp dried wood (tree) ears
225–275 g/8–9½ oz pork fillet (tenderloin)
1 tsp salt
2 tsp Cornflour (Cornstarch) Paste (see page 16)
3 tbsp vegetable oil
1 garlic clove, finely chopped
½ tsp finely chopped ginger root
2 spring onions (scallions), finely chopped, with the white and green parts separated
2 celery sticks, thinly sliced
½ tsp sugar
1 tbsp light soy sauce
1 tbsp chilli bean sauce
2 tsp rice vinegar
1 tsp Chinese rice wine or dry sherry
a few drops of sesame oil

1 Soak the wood (tree) ears in warm water for 20 minutes, then rinse in cold water until the water is clear. Drain well, then cut into thin shreds.

2 Cut the pork into thin shreds and mix in a bowl with a pinch of the salt and about half the cornflour (cornstarch) paste until well coated.

3 Heat 1 tablespoon of oil in a preheated wok. Add the pork strips and stir-fry for about 1 minute, or until the colour changes. Remove with a slotted spoon.

4 Heat the remaining oil in the wok. Add the garlic, ginger, the white parts of the spring onions (scallions), the wood (tree) ears and celery. Stir-fry for about 1 minute. Return the pork strips to the wok, together with the sugar, soy sauce, chilli bean sauce, vinegar, rice wine or sherry and remaining salt. Continue stirring for another minute.

5 Finally add the green parts of the spring onions (scallions) and blend in the remaining cornflour (cornstarch) paste and sesame oil. Stir until the sauce has thickened. Transfer to a serving dish and serve immediately.

Red Spiced Beef

A spicy stir-fry flavoured with paprika, chilli and tomato,
with a crisp bite to it from the celery strips.

Serves 4
500 g/1 lb 2 oz sirloin or rump steak
2 tbsp paprika
2–3 tsp mild chilli powder
1/2 tsp salt
6 celery sticks
4 tomatoes, peeled, seeded and sliced
6 tbsp stock or water
2 tbsp tomato purée (paste)
2 tbsp clear honey
3 tbsp wine vinegar
1 tbsp Worcestershire sauce
2 tbsp sunflower oil
4 spring onions (scallions), thinly sliced diagonally
1–2 garlic cloves, crushed
celery leaves, to garnish (optional)
Chinese noodles, to serve

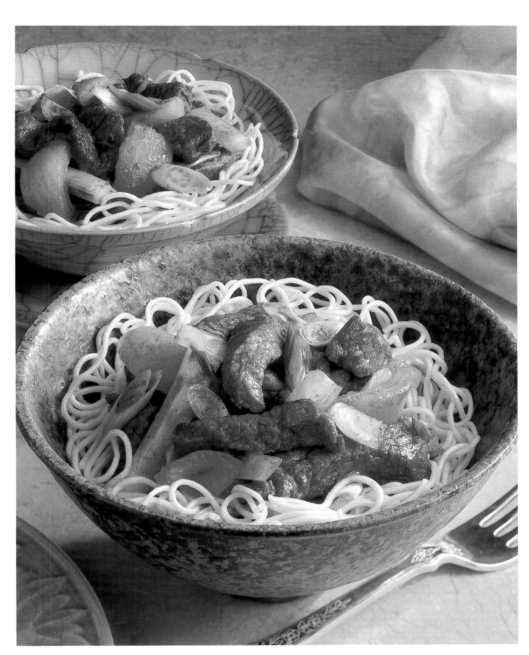

1 Cut the steak across the grain into narrow strips 1 cm/½ inch thick and place in a bowl.

2 Combine the paprika, chilli powder and salt. Add to the steak and mix thoroughly until the meat strips are evenly coated with the spice mixture. Cover and marinate in a cool place for a minimum of 30 minutes.

3 Cut the celery into 5-cm/2-inch lengths, then slice into strips about 5 mm/¼ inch thick. Combine the stock, tomato purée (paste), honey, vinegar and Worcestershire sauce.

4 Heat the oil in a preheated wok. Add the spring onions (scallions), celery, tomatoes and garlic, and stir-fry for about 1 minute, until the vegetables are beginning to soften. Then add the steak strips and stir-fry over a high heat for 3–4 minutes, until the meat is well sealed.

5 Add the sauce to the wok and continue to stir-fry briskly until thoroughly coated and sizzling.

6 Serve with noodles and garnish with celery leaves, if desired.

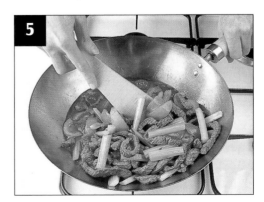

Pork with Plum Sauce

Plum sauce is often used in Chinese cooking with duck
or rich, fattier meat to counteract the flavour.

Serves 4
1 tbsp cornflour (cornstarch)
2 tbsp light soy sauce
2 tbsp Chinese rice wine or dry sherry
4 tsp light brown sugar
pinch of ground cinnamon
450 g/1 lb pork fillet (tenderloin), sliced
5 tsp vegetable oil
2 garlic cloves, crushed
2 spring onions (scallions) chopped
4 tbsp plum sauce
1 tbsp hoi-sin sauce
150 ml/¼ pint/⅔ cup water
dash of chilli sauce
fried plum quarters and spring onions (scallions), to garnish

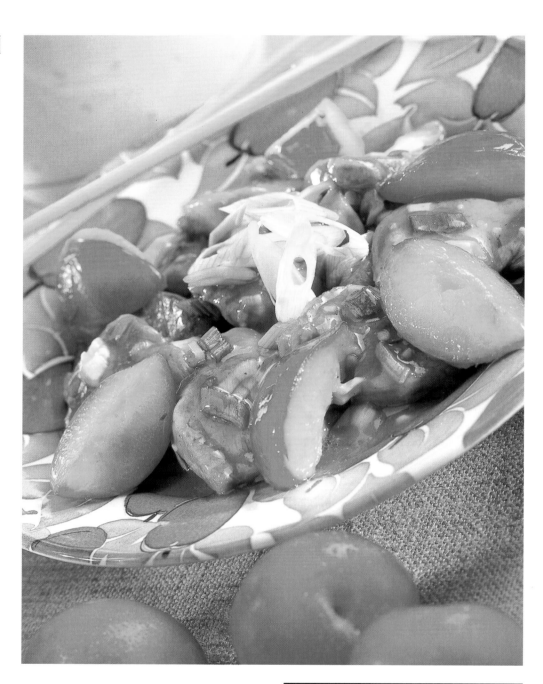

1 Mix the cornflour (cornstarch), soy sauce, Chinese rice wine or sherry, sugar and cinnamon together. Place the pork in a single layer in a shallow non-metallic dish and pour the marinade over it. Cover and marinate for a minimum of 30 minutes. Remove the pork from the dish, reserving the marinade.

2 Heat the oil in a preheated wok. Add the pork and stir-fry for 3–4 minutes, until lightly browned.

3 Stir in the garlic, spring onions (scallions), plum sauce, hoi-sin sauce, water and chilli sauce. Bring the sauce to the boil, cover, lower the heat and simmer for 8–10 minutes, or until the pork is cooked through.

4 Stir in the reserved marinade and cook for a further 5 minutes. Transfer to a serving dish, garnish with fried plum quarters and spring onions (scallions) and serve immediately.

VARIATION

Strips of boneless duck meat may be used instead of the pork.

Stir-fried Pork with Vegetables

This is another basic meat and vegetable recipe that can be varied with chicken, beef or lamb, and vegetables according to seasonal availability.

Serves 4
250 g/9 oz pork fillet (tenderloin)
1 tsp sugar
1 tbsp light soy sauce
1 tsp Chinese rice wine or dry sherry
1 tsp Cornflour (Cornstarch) Paste (see page 16)
1 small carrot
1 small green (bell) pepper, seeded
about 175 g/6 oz Chinese leaves (cabbage)
4 tbsp vegetable oil
1 spring onion (scallion), cut into short sections
a few small slices of peeled fresh ginger root
1 tsp salt
2–3 tbsp Chinese Stock (see page 16) or water
a few drops of sesame oil

4 Add the carrot, (bell) pepper, Chinese leaves (cabbage), spring onion (scallion) and ginger and stir-fry for about 2 minutes. Add the salt and remaining sugar. Return the pork to the wok and add the remaining soy sauce and the stock or water. Blend thoroughly and stir for a further 1–2 minutes, until hot. Sprinkle with the sesame oil. Transfer the pork and vegetables to a warm serving dish and serve immediately.

1 Thinly slice the pork fillet (tenderloin) into small pieces and place in a shallow dish. Add half the sugar, half the soy sauce, the Chinese rice wine or sherry and cornflour (cornstarch) paste. Set aside to marinate in the refrigerator for 10–15 minutes.

2 Cut the carrot, green (bell) pepper and Chinese leaves (cabbage) into thin slices roughly the same length and width as the pork pieces.

3 Heat the oil in a preheated wok and stir-fry the pork for about 1 minute to seal in the flavour. Remove with a slotted spoon and keep warm.

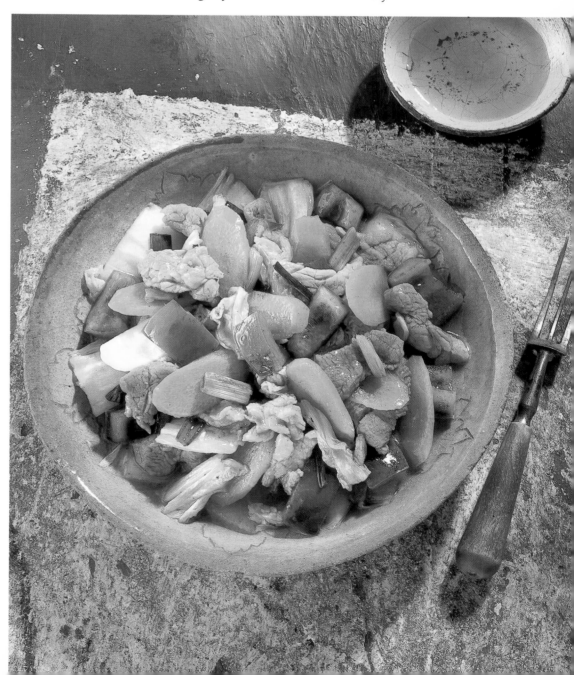

Braised Pork & Tofu (Bean Curd)

This is a typical example of the way Chinese cuisine harmonizes and contrasts flavours and textures.

Serves 4
3 cakes tofu (bean curd)
115 g/4 oz boneless pork
1 leek
1–2 spring onions (scallions), cut into short sections
a few small dried whole chillies, soaked
vegetable oil, for deep-frying
2 tbsp yellow bean sauce
1 tbsp light soy sauce
2 tsp Chinese rice wine or dry sherry
a few drops of sesame oil

Chinese rice wine or sherry and braise for 2–3 minutes, stirring very gently to blend everything well. Sprinkle on the sesame oil. Transfer to a warm serving dish and serve immediately.

VARIATION

The pork can be replaced by chicken or prawns (shrimp).

1 Split each cake of tofu (bean curd) into 3 slices crossways, then cut each slice diagonally into 2 triangles.

2 Cut the pork into shreds. Cut the leek into thin strips. Drain the chillies, remove the seeds using the tip of a knife, then cut the flesh into small shreds.

3 Heat the oil in a preheated wok until smoking. Deep-fry the tofu (bean curd) triangles for 2–3 minutes, or until golden brown all over. Remove with a slotted spoon and drain on kitchen paper (paper towels).

4 Pour off the hot oil, leaving about 1 tablespoon in the wok. Add the pork strips, spring onions (scallions) and chillies and stir-fry for 1 minute, or until the pork changes colour.

5 Add the leek, tofu (bean curd), yellow bean sauce, soy sauce and

Fish, Aubergine (Eggplant) & Pork

Like Fish-flavoured Shredded Pork (see page 152), there is no fish
involved in this dish, only flavourings normally used with fish.

Serves 4
450 g/1 lb aubergines (eggplants)
vegetable oil, for deep-frying
1 garlic clove, finely chopped
1/2 tsp finely chopped fresh ginger root
2 spring onions (scallions), chopped finely, with the white and green parts separated
175 g/6 oz pork, thinly shredded
1 tbsp light soy sauce
2 tsp Chinese rice wine or dry sherry
1 tbsp chilli bean sauce
1/2 tsp salt
1/2 tsp sugar
1 tbsp rice vinegar
2 tsp Cornflour (Cornstarch) Paste (see page 16)
a few drops of sesame oil

1 Cut the aubergines (eggplants) into
rounds and then into thin strips
about the size of potato chips – the
skin may either be peeled or left on.

2 Heat the oil in a preheated wok
until smoking. Add the aubergines
(eggplants) and deep-fry for about
3–4 minutes, or until soft. Remove
and drain thoroughly on kitchen
paper (paper towels).

3 Carefully pour off the excess hot
oil, leaving about 1 tablespoon in the
wok. Add the garlic, ginger and the
white parts of the spring onions
(scallions), followed by the pork. Stir-
fry for about 1 minute, or until the
colour of the meat changes, then add
the soy sauce, rice wine or sherry and
chilli bean sauce, blending well.

4 Return the aubergines (eggplants) to
the wok and add the salt, sugar and
vinegar. Stir for 1–2 minutes, then add
the cornflour (cornstarch) paste) and
stir until the sauce has thickened.

5 Add the green parts of the spring
onions (scallions) and sprinkle on the
sesame oil. Serve hot.

Vegetable Dishes

No Chinese meal can be regarded as complete without a freshly cooked, colourful vegetable dish on the table, quite separate from the vegetables included as an integral part of other dishes.

Flavour, texture, colour and nutrients are all preserved by such cooking techniques as steaming. stir-frying or brief braising. Vegetables should be as fresh as possible –

Chinese cooks buy them daily. Vegetables are washed just before cutting or slicing and cooked immediately

afterwards to minimize the loss of flavour, texture and nutrients.

Besides forming an essential part of a Chinese meal, many of the recipes in this chapter would provide a special and unusual accompaniment to a western-style grill (broil) or roast. Try Stir-fried Mixed Vegetables, Stir-fried Cucumber with Ginger and Chilli, Braised Chinese Leaves (Cabbage) or Garlic Spinach.

Vegetable Chop Suey

Make sure that the vegetables are all cut into pieces of a similar size in this recipe, so that they cook within the same amount of time.

Serves 4
1 yellow (bell) pepper, seeded
1 red (bell) pepper, seeded
1 carrot
1 courgette (zucchini)
1 fennel bulb
1 onion
50 g/1¾ oz mangetout (snow peas), sliced diagonally
2 tbsp peanut oil
3 garlic cloves, crushed
1 tsp grated fresh ginger root
115 g/4 oz/½ cup beansprouts
2 tsp light brown sugar
2 tbsp light soy sauce
125 ml/4 fl oz/½ cup vegetable stock

1 Cut the (bell) peppers, carrot, courgette (zucchini) and fennel into thin slices. Quarter the onion and then cut each piece in half. Slice the mangetouts (snow peas) diagonally.

2 Heat the oil in a preheated wok until almost smoking. Add the garlic and ginger and stir-fry for 30 seconds.

3 Add the onion and stir-fry for a further 30 seconds.

4 Add the (bell) peppers, carrot, courgette (zucchini), fennel and mangetout (snow peas) and stir-fry for 2 minutes.

5 Add the beansprouts and stir in the sugar, soy sauce and stock. Reduce the heat to low and simmer for a further 1–2 minutes, or until the vegetables are tender and thoroughly coated in the sauce.

6 Transfer the vegetable chop suey to a warm serving dish and serve immediately.

COOK'S TIP

Use any combination of colourful vegetables that you have to hand for this versatile dish.

Sweet & Sour Vegetables

Make your choice of vegetables from the suggested list, including spring onions (scallions) and garlic. For a hotter, spicier sauce add chilli sauce.

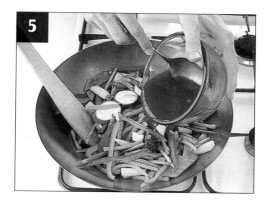

Serves 4
5–6 vegetables from the following:
1 (bell) pepper, seeded and sliced
115 g/4 oz French (green) beans, cut into 2–3 pieces
115 g/4 oz mangetout (snow peas), cut into 2–3 pieces
225 g/8 oz broccoli or cauliflower florets
225 g/8 oz courgettes (zucchini), cut into 5-cm/2-inch lengths
175 g/6 oz carrots, cut into julienne strips
115 g/4 oz baby corn cobs, sliced thinly
175 g/6 oz parsnip or celeriac (celery root), finely diced
13 celery sticks, thinly sliced crosswise
4 tomatoes, peeled, quartered and seeded
115 g/4 oz button mushrooms, sliced
7-cm/3-inch length of cucumber, diced
200 g/7 oz can water chestnuts or bamboo shoots, drained and sliced
400 g/14 oz can beansprouts, drained
4 spring onions (scallions), thinly sliced
1 garlic clove, crushed
2 tbsp sunflower oil

SWEET & SOUR SAUCE

2 tbsp wine vinegar
2 tbsp clear honey
1 tbsp tomato purée (paste)
2 tbsp soy sauce
2 tbsp Chinese rice wine or dry sherry
1–2 tsp sweet chilli sauce (optional)
2 tsp cornflour (cornstarch)

1 Prepare the selected vegetables, cutting them into uniform lengths.

2 Combine the sauce ingredients in a bowl, blending well together.

3 Heat the oil in a preheated wok. Add the spring onions (scallions) and garlic and stir-fry for 1 minute.

4 Add the prepared vegetables – the harder and firmer ones first – and stir-fry for 2 minutes. Then add the softer ones such as mushrooms, mangetouts (snow peas) and tomatoes and continue to stir-fry for 2 minutes.

5 Add the sauce to the wok. Bring to the boil, tossing until the vegetables are thoroughly coated. Serve hot.

Vegetable Casserole

This mixed vegetable casserole is very versatile and is delicious
with any combination of vegetables of your choice.

Serves 4

4 tbsp vegetable oil

2 medium carrots, sliced

1 courgette (zucchini), sliced

4 baby corn cobs,
halved lengthways

125 g/4¹/₂ oz cauliflower florets

1 leek, sliced

125 g/4¹/₂ oz canned water chestnuts,
drained and halved

225 g/8 oz tofu
(bean curd), diced

300 ml/¹/₂ pint/1¹/₄ cups
vegetable stock

1 tsp salt

2 tsp dark brown sugar

2 tsp dark soy sauce

2 tbsp Chinese rice wine or
dry sherry

1 tbsp cornflour (cornstarch)

2 tbsp water

1 tbsp chopped coriander
(cilantro)

1 Heat the oil in a preheated wok
until almost smoking. Lower the heat
slightly, add the carrots, courgette
(zucchini), corn cobs, cauliflower and
leek and stir-fry for 2–3 minutes.

2 Stir in the water chestnuts, tofu
(bean curd), stock, salt, sugar, soy and
wine or sherry and bring to the boil.

3 Reduce the heat to low, cover and
simmer the vegetables for 20 minutes.
Blend the cornflour (cornstarch) with
the water to form a paste. Remove the
lid from the wok and stir in the
cornflour (cornstarch) mixture. Bring

the sauce to the boil, stirring until it
thickens and clears. Sprinkle with

coriander (cilantro), transfer to a
serving dish and serve immediately.

Stir-fried Mixed Vegetables

The Chinese never mix ingredients indiscriminately – they are carefully selected
to achieve a harmonious balance of colours and textures.

Serves 4
50 g/1³/₄ oz mangetout (snow peas)
1 small carrot
115 g/4 oz Chinese leaves (cabbage)
115 g/4 oz/¹/₂ cup fresh beansprouts
50 g/1³/₄ oz black or white mushrooms
50 g/1³/₄ oz canned bamboo shoots, drained
3–4 tbsp vegetable oil
1 tsp salt
1 tsp sugar
1 tbsp oyster sauce or light soy sauce
a few drops of sesame oil (optional)
dipping sauce, to serve (optional)

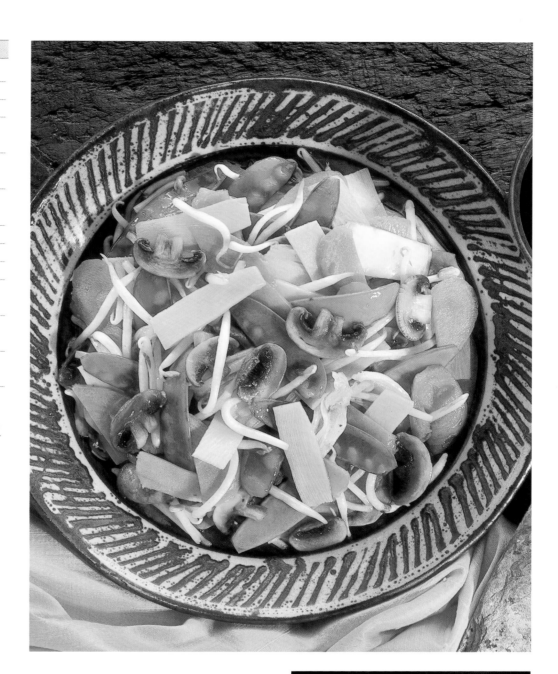

1 Prepare the vegetables. Top and tail the mangetout (snow peas), and cut the carrot, Chinese leaves (cabbage), mushrooms and bamboo shoots into roughly the same shape and size as the mangetouts (snow peas).

2 Heat the oil in a preheated wok, and add the carrot. Stir-fry for a few seconds, then add the mangetout (snow peas) and Chinese leaves (cabbage) and stir-fry for about 1 minute.

3 Add the beansprouts, mushrooms and bamboo shoots and stir-fry for another minute.

4 Add the salt and sugar, continue stirring for another minute, then add the oyster sauce or soy sauce. Blend well and sprinkle with sesame oil (if using). Transfer to a warm serving dish and serve immediately or let cool and serve cold, with a dipping sauce, if wished.

COOK'S TIP

Many ready–made sauces, both hotly spiced and mild, are available from Chinese supermarkets.

Braised Bamboo Shoots

This dish has a wonderfully strong ginger flavour which is integral to Chinese cooking.
The mixed (bell) peppers give the otherwise insipid bamboo shoots a burst of colour.

Serves 4
2 tbsp peanut oil
225 g/8 oz can bamboo shoots, drained
2.5-cm/1-inch piece fresh ginger root, finely chopped
1 small red (bell) pepper, seeded and thinly sliced
1 small green (bell) pepper, seeded and thinly sliced
1 small yellow (bell) pepper, seeded and thinly sliced
1 leek, sliced
125 ml/4 fl oz/^{1}/$_2$ cup vegetable stock
1 tbsp light soy sauce
2 tsp light brown sugar
2 tsp Chinese rice wine or dry sherry
1 tsp cornflour (cornstarch)
2 tsp water
1 tsp sesame oil

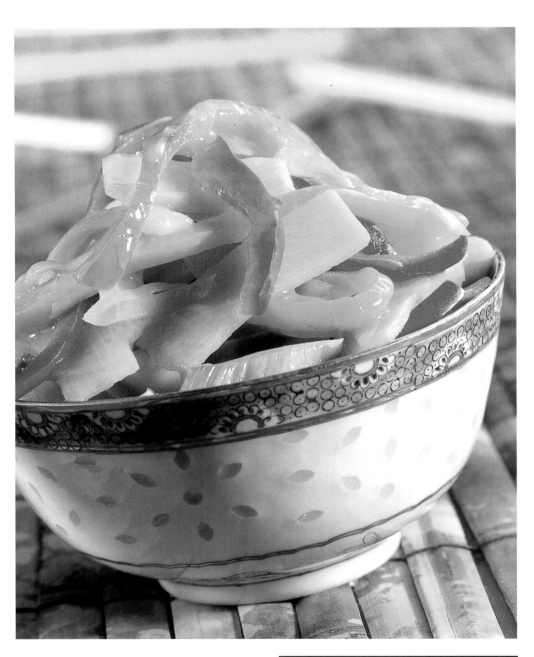

1 Heat the oil in a preheated wok. Add the bamboo shoots, ginger, (bell) peppers and leek and stir-fry for 2–3 minutes.

2 Stir in the stock, soy sauce, sugar and Chinese rice wine or sherry and bring to the boil, stirring constantly. Reduce the heat and simmer for 4–5 minutes, until the vegetables begin to soften.

3 Blend the cornflour (cornstarch) with the water to form a smooth paste and stir into the wok. Bring to the boil, stirring until the sauce thickens and clears.

4 Sprinkle the sesame oil over the vegetables and cook for 1 further minute.

5 Transfer to a warm serving dish and serve immediately.

COOK'S TIP

Add a chopped fresh red chilli or a few drops of chilli sauce for a spicier dish.

Golden Needles with Bamboo Shoots

Golden needles are the dried flower buds of the tiger lily. Available at specialist shops and Chinese supermarkets, they impart a unique musky flavour.

Serves 4
25 g/1 oz/¼ cup dried lily flowers
2 × 215 g/7½ oz cans bamboo shoots, drained
50 g/1¾ oz/¼ cup cornflour (cornstarch)
vegetable oil, for deep-frying
1 tbsp vegetable oil
450 ml/¾ pint/2 cups vegetable stock
1 tbsp dark soy sauce
1 tbsp Chinese rice wine or dry sherry
1 tsp sugar
1 large garlic clove, sliced
½ each red, green and yellow (bell) peppers, seeded and thinly sliced

1 Soak the lily flowers in hot water for 30 minutes.

2 Coat the bamboo shoots in cornflour (cornstarch). Heat the oil for deep-frying in a large heavy-based saucepan. Deep-fry the bamboo shoots, in batches, until just beginning to colour. Remove with a slotted spoon and drain on kitchen paper (paper towels).

3 Drain the lily flowers and trim off the hard ends. Heat the oil in a preheated wok or large frying pan (skillet). Add the lily flowers, bamboo shoots, stock, soy sauce, rice wine or sherry, sugar and garlic.

4 Add the (bell) peppers to the wok or pan (skillet). Bring to the boil, stirring constantly, then reduce the heat and simmer for 5 minutes. Add extra water or stock if necessary.

Bamboo Shoots with Green Vegetables

In this recipe, spinach is fried with spices and then braised in a soy-flavoured sauce with bamboo shoots for a rich, delicious dish.

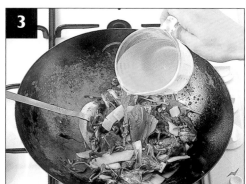

Serves 4

3 tbsp peanut oil

225 g/8 oz spinach, chopped

175 g/6 oz bamboo shoots

1 garlic clove, crushed

2 fresh red chillies, sliced

pinch of ground cinnamon

300 ml/½ pint/1¼ cups vegetable stock

pinch of sugar

pinch of salt

1 tbsp light soy sauce

1 Heat the oil in a preheated wok. Add the spinach and bamboo shoots and stir-fry for 1 minute.

2 Add the garlic, chilli and cinnamon and stir-fry for a further 30 seconds.

3 Stir in the stock, sugar, salt and soy sauce, cover and cook over a medium heat for 5 minutes, or until the vegetables are cooked through and the sauce reduced.

4 Transfer to a warm serving dish and serve immediately.

COOK'S TIP

If there is too much liquid after the final 5 minutes' cooking in step 3, blend a little cornflour (cornstarch) with double the quantity of cold water and stir into the sauce. Continue stirring until the sauce is thickened and clear.

Chinese Braised Vegetables

This colourful selection of braised vegetables makes
a splendid accompaniment to a main dish.

Serves 4-6
3 tbsp sunflower oil
1 garlic clove, crushed
1 head Chinese leave (cabbage), coarsely shredded
2 onions, cut into wedges
225 g/8 oz broccoli florets
2 large carrots, cut into julienne strips
12 baby corn cobs, halved if large
50 g/1¾ oz mangetout (snow peas), halved
75 g/2¾ oz Chinese or oyster mushrooms, sliced
1 tbsp grated fresh ginger root
175 ml/6 fl oz/¾ cup vegetable stock
2 tbsp light soy sauce
1 tbsp cornflour (cornstarch)
salt and pepper
½ tsp sugar

1 Heat the oil in a preheated wok or large, heavy-based frying pan (skillet). Add the garlic, Chinese leaves (cabbage), onions, broccoli, carrots, corn, mangetout (snow peas), mushrooms and ginger and stir-fry for 2 minutes.

2 Add the stock, cover and cook for a further 2–3 minutes.

3 Blend the soy sauce with the cornflour (cornstarch), and salt and pepper to taste.

4 Remove the braised vegetables from the pan with a slotted spoon and keep warm. Add the soy sauce mixture to the pan juices, mixing well. Bring to the boil, stirring constantly, until the mixture thickens slightly. Stir in the sugar.

5 Return the vegetables to the pan and toss in the slightly thickened sauce. Cook gently to heat through, transfer to a warm serving dish and serve immediately.

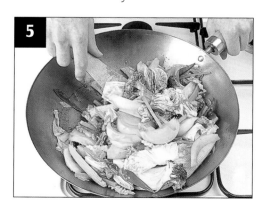

Stir-Fried Cucumber with Ginger & Chilli

Warm cucumbers are absolutely delicious, especially when combined with the heat of chilli and the flavour of ginger.

Serves 4
2 medium cucumbers
2 tsp salt
1 tbsp vegetable oil
2 garlic cloves, crushed
1-cm/$\frac{1}{2}$-inch fresh ginger root, grated
2 spring onions (scallions), chopped
2 fresh red chillies, chopped
1 tsp yellow bean sauce
1 tbsp clear honey
125 ml/4 fl oz/$\frac{1}{2}$ cup water
1 tsp sesame oil

1 Peel the cucumbers and cut them in half lengthways. Scrape the seeds from the centre, using a teaspoon, and discard.

2 Cut the cucumber into strips and sprinkle the salt over them. Place in a colander for 20 minutes. Rinse well under cold running water and pat dry with kitchen paper (paper towels).

3 Heat the oil in a preheated wok until almost smoking. Lower the heat slightly and add the garlic, ginger, chilli and spring onions (scallions) and stir-fry for 30 seconds.

4 Add the cucumbers to the wok, together with the yellow bean sauce and honey. Stir-fry for a further 30 seconds and add the water.

5 Cook over a high heat until most of the water has evaporated. Sprinkle in the sesame oil and serve immediately.

COOK'S VARIATION

You could use Asian squashes, such as dudi or tindoori, in this recipe.

COOK'S TIP

The cucumber is salted and left to stand to draw out the excess water.

Stir-Fried Beansprouts

Be sure to use fresh beansprouts, rather than the canned variety, for this crunchy-textured dish.

Serves 4
225 g/8 oz/1 cup fresh beansprouts
2–3 spring onions (scallions)
1 red chilli (optional)
3 tbsp vegetable oil
½ tsp salt
¹⁄ tsp sugar
1 tbsp light soy sauce
a few drops of sesame oil (optional)

1 Rinse the beansprouts in cold water, discarding any husks or small pieces that float to the top. Drain well on kitchen paper (paper towels).

2 Cut the spring onions (scallions) into short sections. Shred the chilli, if using, discarding the seeds.

3 Heat the oil in a preheated wok. Add the beansprouts, spring onions (scallions) and chilli, if using, and stir-fry for about 2 minutes.

4 Add the salt, sugar, soy sauce and sesame oil, if using. Stir well to blend. Serve hot or cold.

COOK'S TIP

Beansprouts are extremely easy to grow yourself and this ensures the freshest supply. You can grow them in a clean jar or a special sprouter.

Beansprouts with (Bell) Peppers

This dish is served cold as a salad or appetizer and is very easy
to make. It is a form of cold chop suey.

Serves 4
450 g/1 lb/2 cups beansprouts
2 fresh red chillies
1 red (bell) pepper, seeded and thinly sliced
1 green (bell) pepper, seeded and thinly sliced
50 g/1¾ oz canned water chestnuts, drained and quartered
1 celery stick, sliced
3 tbsp rice wine vinegar
2 tbsp light soy sauce
2 tbsp chopped chives
1 garlic clove, crushed
pinch of Chinese curry powder

1 Place the beansprouts, chilli, (bell) peppers, water chestnuts and celery in a bowl and mix well.

2 Mix together the rice wine vinegar, soy sauce, chives, garlic and Chinese curry powder and pour on top of the vegetables. Toss to mix thoroughly.

3 Cover the salad and chill for at least 3 hours. Drain the vegetables well, spoon into a serving dish and serve.

COOK'S TIP

If wished, top the salad with a
nest of crisp-fried Chinese
rice noodles for a more
substantial dish.

Stir-fried Seasonal Vegetables

When selecting different fresh vegetables for this dish, bear in mind that there should always be a contrast in colour as well as texture.

Serves 4
1 red (bell) pepper, seeded
115 g/4 oz courgettes (zucchini)
115 g/4 oz cauliflower
115 g/4 oz French (green) beans
3 tbsp vegetable oil
a few small slices fresh ginger root
1/2 tsp salt
1/2 tsp sugar
Chinese Stock (see page 16) or water
1 tbsp light soy sauce
a few drops of sesame oil (optional)

1 Cut the red (bell) pepper into small squares. Thinly slice the courgettes (zucchini). Trim the cauliflower and divide into small florets, discarding any thick stems. Make sure the vegetables are cut into roughly similar shapes and sizes to ensure even cooking. Top and tail the French (green) beans, then cut them in half.

2 Heat the oil in a preheated wok, add the vegetables and slices of ginger and stir-fry for about 2 minutes.

3 Add the salt and sugar, and continue to stir-fry for 1–2 minutes, adding a little Chinese stock or water if the vegetables appear to be too dry. Do not add liquid unless it really seems necessary.

4 Add the soy sauce and sesame oil, if using. Blend well to coat the vegetables. Transfer to a warm serving dish and serve immediately.

COOK'S TIP

This mixture could be used as a filling for ready-made Chinese pancakes.

COOK'S TIP

Do not overfill the wok, as it would be impossible to stir-fry without throwing ingredients everywhere.

Vegetables in Black Bean Sauce

This recipe, as the title suggests, is a colourful mixture of vegetables,
cooked in a black bean and soy sauce.

Serves 4
2 tbsp peanut oil
6 spring onions (scallions), sliced
3 garlic cloves, crushed
1 green (bell) pepper, seeded and diced
1 red (bell) pepper, seeded and diced
1 fresh red chilli, sliced
2 tbsp canned water chestnuts, drained and chopped
1 courgette (zucchini), chopped
125 g/4^1/$_2$ oz oyster mushrooms
3 tbsp black bean sauce
2 tsp Chinese rice wine or dry sherry
4 tbsp dark soy sauce
1 tsp dark brown sugar
2 tbsp water
1 tsp sesame oil

1 Heat the oil in a preheated wok until it is almost smoking. Lower the heat slightly, add the spring onions (scallions) and garlic and stir-fry for 30 seconds.

2 Add the (bell) peppers, chilli, water chestnuts and courgette (zucchini) and stir-fry for 2–3 minutes, until the vegetables begin to soften.

3 Add the mushrooms, black bean sauce, Chinese rice wine or sherry, soy sauce, sugar and water and stir-fry for a further 4 minutes. Sprinkle with sesame oil. Transfer to a warm serving dish and serve immediately.

COOK'S TIP

If you cannot obtain oyster mushrooms, use canned Chinese straw mushrooms instead.

VARIATION

Add 225 g/8 oz diced, marinated tofu (bean curd) to this recipe for a main meal for 4 people.

Vegetable & Nut Stir-Fry

A colourful selection of vegetables are stir-fried in a creamy peanut sauce
and sprinkled with nuts to serve.

Serves 4
3 tbsp crunchy peanut butter
150 ml/¼ pint/⅔ cup water
1 tbsp light soy sauce
1 tsp sugar
1 carrot
½ red onion
4 baby courgettes (zucchini)
1 red (bell) pepper, seeded
225 g/8 oz egg thread noodles
25g/1 oz/¼ cup peanuts, chopped roughly
2 tbsp vegetable oil
1 tsp sesame oil
1 small green chilli, seeded and thinly sliced
1 garlic clove, thinly sliced
200 g/7 oz can water chestnuts, drained and sliced
175 g/6 oz/¾ cup beansprouts
salt

1 In a small bowl, gradually blend the peanut butter with the water. Stir in the soy sauce and sugar.

2 Cut the carrot into thin matchsticks and slice the onion. Slice the courgettes (zucchini) on the diagonal and cut the (bell) pepper into chunks.

3 Bring a large pan of water to the boil and add the egg noodles. Remove from the heat immediately and set aside for 4 minutes, stirring occasionally to divide the noodles.

4 Heat a wok or large frying pan (skillet), add the peanuts and dry-fry until they are beginning to brown. Remove and set aside.

5 Heat the oils in the wok or pan. Add the carrot, onion, courgette (zucchini), (bell) pepper, chilli and garlic and stir-fry for 2–3 minutes. Add the water chestnuts, beansprouts and peanut sauce. Bring to the boil and heat thoroughly. Season to taste. Drain the noodles and serve with the stir-fry, sprinkled with the peanuts.

Chinese Green Bean Stir-fry

These beans are simply cooked in a spicy, hot sauce
for a tasty and easy recipe.

Serves 4
2 tbsp peanut oil
450 g/1 lb thin green beans, cut in half
2 fresh red chillies, sliced
$\frac{1}{2}$ tsp ground star anise
1 garlic clove crushed
2 tbsp light soy sauce
2 tsp clear honey
$\frac{1}{2}$ tsp sesame oil

1 Heat the oil in a preheated wok until almost smoking. Lower the heat slightly, add the beans and stir-fry for 1 minute.

2 Add the chillies, star anise and garlic and stir-fry for a further 30 seconds.

3 Mix together the soy sauce, honey and sesame oil and stir into the wok. Cook for 2 minutes, tossing the beans in the sauce to coat.

4 Transfer to a warm serving dish and serve immediately.

COOK'S TIP

This dish makes a great accompaniment to fish or lightly cooked meats with a mild flavour.

Stir-fried Greens

The basis of this recipe is pak choi, sometimes known as bok choy or Chinese greens.
If unavailable, use Swiss chard or Savoy cabbage in its place.

Serves 4
2 tbsp peanut oil
2 garlic cloves, crushed
1/2 tsp ground star anise
1 tsp salt
350 g/12 oz pak choi, roughly shredded
225 g/8 oz baby spinach
25 g/1 oz mangetout (snow peas)
1 celery stick, sliced
1 green (bell) pepper, seeded and sliced
50 ml/2 fl oz/1/4 cup vegetable stock
1 tsp sesame oil

1 Heat the oil in a preheated wok. Add the garlic and stir-fry for 30 seconds. Stir in the salt, pak choi, spinach, mangetout (snow peas), celery and (bell) pepper and stir-fry for 3–4 minutes.

2 Add the stock, cover and cook for 3–4 minutes.

3 Remove the lid from the wok and stir in the sesame oil. Mix well, transfer to a warm serving dish and serve immediately.

COOK'S TIP

Serve this dish as part of a vegetarian meal or with roast meats for non–vegetarians.

Ma-Po Tofu (Bean Curd)

Ma-Po, the wife of a Szechuan chef, created this dish in the nineteenth century.
Replace the beef with dried mushrooms to make a vegetarian meal.

Serves 4
3 cakes tofu (bean curd)
3 tbsp vegetable oil
115 g/4 oz coarsely minced (ground) beef
½ tsp finely chopped garlic
1 leek, cut into short sections
½ tsp salt
1 tbsp black bean sauce
1 tbsp light soy sauce
1 tsp chilli bean sauce
3–4 tbsp Chinese Stock (see page 16) or water
2 tsp Cornflour (Cornstarch) Paste (see page 16)
a few drops of sesame oil
black pepper
finely chopped spring onions (scallions), to garnish

1 Cut the tofu (bean curd) into 1-cm/½-inch cubes, handling it carefully. Bring some water to the boil in a small pan or a wok, add the tofu (bean curd) and blanch for 2–3 minutes to harden. Remove and drain well.

2 Heat the oil in a preheated wok. Add the minced (ground) beef and garlic and stir-fry for about 1 minute, or until the beef is just beginning to colour. Add the leek, salt, black bean sauce, soy sauce and chilli bean sauce and blend well.

3 Add the stock or water and the tofu (bean curd). Bring to the boil and braise gently for 2–3 minutes.

4 Add the cornflour (cornstarch) paste and stir until the sauce has thickened. Sprinkle with sesame oil and black pepper, garnish with spring onions (scallions) and serve immediately.

COOK'S TIP

If using dried mushrooms, soak them in warm water for 30 minutes.

Tofu (Bean Curd) & Vegetables with Black Bean Sauce

Chunks of smoked tofu (bean curd) are stir-fried with a delicious mixture of vegetables and black bean sauce.

Serves 4
275 g/9½ oz smoked tofu (bean curd), cubed
2 tbsp soy sauce
1 tbsp Chinese rice wine or dry sherry
1 tsp sesame oil
4 dried Chinese mushrooms, soaked in warm water for 30 minutes
2 tbsp peanut oil
1 carrot, cut into thin sticks
1 celery stalk, cut into thin sticks
115 g/4 oz (16–18) baby corn cobs, halved lengthways
1 courgette (zucchini), sliced
4 spring onions (scallions), chopped
115 g/4 oz mangetout (snow peas), each cut into 3 pieces
2 tbsp black bean sauce
1 tsp cornflour (cornstarch)
salt and pepper
1 tbsp toasted sesame seeds, to garnish
egg noodles, to serve

1 Marinate the tofu (bean curd) in the soy sauce, Chinese rice wine or sherry and sesame oil for 30 minutes.

2 Drain the mushrooms, reserving 1 tbsp of the liquid. Squeeze out excess water from the mushrooms and discard the hard stalks. Thinly slice the caps.

3 Heat the oil in a preheated wok. Add the carrot, celery and corn and stir-fry for 2 minutes. Alternatively, place in a large bowl, cover and microwave on HIGH power for 1 minute.

4 Add the mushrooms, courgette (zucchini), spring onions (scallions) and mangetout (snow peas) and stir-fry for 4–5 minutes, until just tender. Or, cover and microwave on HIGH power for 4 minutes, stirring every minute.

5 Add the black bean sauce. Mix the cornflour (cornstarch) with the reserved mushroom water and stir it into the vegetables, together with the tofu (bean curd) and marinade. Stir-fry or cover and microwave on HIGH power for 2–3 minutes, until heated through and the sauce has thickened slightly. Season. Garnish and serve.

Sweet & Sour Tofu (Bean Curd) with Vegetables

Sweet-and-sour sauce was one of the first Chinese sauces introduced to Western diets, and remains one of the most popular. It is ideal with meat, fish or vegetables, as in this recipe.

Serves 4

2 tbsp vegetable oil

2 garlic cloves, crushed

2 celery sticks, sliced

1 carrot, cut into
thin strips

1 green (bell) pepper,
seeded and diced

75 g/2³/₄ oz mangetout
(snow peas), cut in half
diagonally

8 baby corn cobs

115 g/4 oz/¹/₂ cup beansprouts

450 g/1 lb tofu
(bean curd), cubed

boiled rice or noodles,
to serve

SAUCE

2 tbsp light brown sugar

2 tbsp wine vinegar

225 ml/8 fl oz/1 cup vegetable stock

1 tsp tomato puree (paste)

1 tbsp cornflour (cornstarch)

1 Heat the oil in a preheated wok until almost smoking. Reduce the heat slightly, add the garlic, celery, carrot, (bell) pepper, mangetout (snow peas) and corn cobs and stir-fry for 3–4 minutes.

2 Add the beansprouts and tofu (bean curd) to the wok and cook for a further 2 minutes, stirring well.

3 Mix together the brown sugar, vinegar, stock, tomato purée (paste) and cornflour (cornstarch) to make a smooth paste. Stir the mixture into

the wok. Bring to the boil, stirring until the sauce thickens and clears. Continue to cook for 1 minute. Transfer to a warm serving dish and serve with boiled rice or noodles.

COOK'S TIP

Be careful not to break up the tofu (bean curd) when stirring.

Vegetable & Tofu (Bean Curd) Casserole

This colourful Chinese-style casserole is made with tofu
(bean curd), vegetables and black bean sauce.

Serves 4
6 Chinese dried mushrooms, soaked in warm water for 30 minutes
275 g/9¾ oz tofu (bean curd)
3 tbsp vegetable oil
1 carrot, cut into thin strips
115 g/4 oz mangetout (snow peas)
115 g/4 oz baby corn cobs, halved lengthways
200 g/7 oz can bamboo shoots, drained and sliced
1 red (bell) pepper, seeded and diced
115 g/4 oz Chinese leaves (cabbage), shredded
1 tbsp soy sauce
1 tbsp black bean sauce
1 tsp sugar
1 tsp cornflour (cornstarch)
vegetable oil for deep-frying
225 g/8 oz Chinese rice noodles
salt

1 Drain the mushrooms, reserving the liquid. Squeeze out the excess. Remove the stems and slice the caps.

2 Cut the tofu (bean curd) into cubes. Boil in lightly salted water for 2–3 minutes to firm up. Drain well.

3 Heat half the oil in a large saucepan. Add the tofu (bean curd) and fry until lightly browned all over. Remove with a slotted spoon and drain on kitchen paper (paper towels).

4 Add the remaining oil and stir-fry the mushrooms, carrot, mangetout (snow peas), corn, bamboo shoots and (bell) pepper for 2–3 minutes. Add the Chinese leaves (cabbage) and tofu (bean curd), and stir-fry for 2 minutes.

5 Stir in the soy sauce, black bean sauce and sugar and season with salt. Add 6 tablespoons of the reserved mushroom liquid mixed with the cornflour (cornstarch). Bring to the boil, reduce the heat, cover and braise for 2–3 minutes until thickened.

6 Heat the oil for deep-frying in a large saucepan. Add the noodles in batches and deep-fry until puffed up and lightly golden. Drain and serve with the casserole.

Vegetable Stir-fry with Tofu (Bean Curd)

Tofu (bean curd) is the perfect ingredient for absorbing all the
other flavours contained in this dish. If a marinated tofu (bean curd) is used,
it will add a flavour of its own.

Serves 4
450 g/1 lb tofu (bean curd)
2 tbsp peanut oil
8 spring onions (scallions), cut into batons
2 celery sticks, sliced
125 g/4^1/$_2$ oz broccoli florets
125 g/4^1/$_2$ oz courgettes (zucchini), sliced
2 garlic cloves, thinly sliced
450 g/1 lb baby spinach

SAUCE

425 ml/^{3}/$_4$ pint/2 cups vegetable stock
2 tbsp light soy sauce
3 tbsp hoi-sin sauce
^{1}/$_2$ tsp chilli powder
1 tbsp sesame oil
boiled rice, to serve

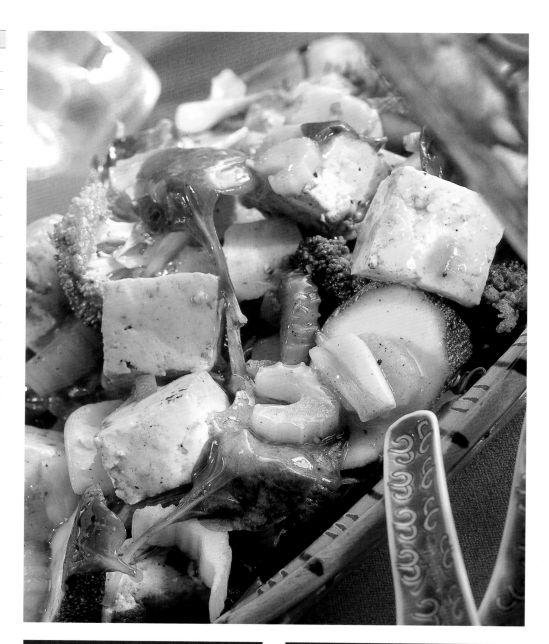

1 Cut the tofu (bean curd) into 2.5-cm/1-inch cubes and set aside.

2 Heat the peanut oil in a preheated wok. Add the spring onions (scallions), celery, broccoli, courgettes (zucchini), garlic, spinach and tofu (bean curd) and stir-fry for 3–4 minutes.

3 Put the stock, soy sauce, hoi-sin sauce, chilli powder and sesame oil in a flameproof casserole and bring the sauce to the boil. Add the vegetables and tofu (bean curd) from the wok, reduce the heat, cover and simmer for 10 minutes. Transfer to a warm serving dish and serve immediately with boiled rice.

COOK'S TIP

For extra flavour, add 2 finely chopped, soaked and drained dried Chinese mushrooms to the wok with the other vegetables in step 2.

COOK'S TIP

This recipe has a green vegetable theme, but alter the colour and flavour by adding your favourite vegetables.

Stir-Fried Mushrooms, Cucumber & Smoked Tofu (Bean Curd)

Chunks of cucumber and smoked tofu (bean curd) are stir-fried with straw mushrooms, mangetouts (snow peas) and corn in a yellow bean sauce.

Serves 4
1 large cucumber
1 tsp salt
225 g/8 oz smoked tofu (bean curd)
2 tbsp vegetable oil
50 g/1¾ oz mangetout (snow peas)
115 g/4 oz baby corn cobs, halved if large
1 celery stick, sliced diagonally
400 g/14 oz can straw mushrooms, drained
2 spring onions (scallions), cut into strips
1-cm/½-inch piece fresh ginger root, chopped
1 tbsp yellow bean sauce
1 tbsp light soy sauce
1 tbsp Chinese rice wine or dry sherry

1 Cut the cucumber in half lengthways. Remove the seeds, using a teaspoon, and discard. Cut the flesh into cubes, place in a colander and sprinkle with the salt. set aside to drain for 10 minutes. Rinse thoroughly in cold water to remove the salt and drain thoroughly.

2 Cut the smoked tofu (bean curd) into 2.5-cm/1-inch cubes. Heat the oil in a preheated wok or large heavy-based frying pan (skillet). Add the tofu (bean curd), mangetout (snow peas), baby corn cobs and celery. Stir-fry until the tofu (bean curd) is lightly browned.

3 Add the straw mushrooms, spring onions (scallions) and ginger, and stir-fry for a further minute. Stir in the cucumber, yellow bean sauce, soy sauce, Chinese rice wine or sherry and 2 tablespoons of water. Stir-fry for 1 further minute.

4 Transfer to a warm serving dish and serve immediately.

Deep-Fried Tofu (Bean Curd) with Chinese Five Spice

A marinated tofu (bean curd) is ideal in this recipe for added flavour,
although the spicy coating is very tasty with plain tofu (bean curd).

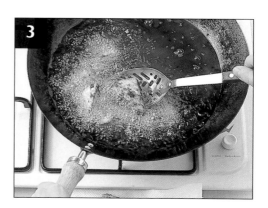

Serves 4
1 tbsp sea salt
4½ tsp Chinese five-spice powder
3 tbsp light brown sugar
2 garlic cloves, crushed
1 tsp grated fresh ginger root
2 x 225 g/8 oz cakes tofu (bean curd)
vegetable oil, for deep-frying
2 leeks, shredded and halved
fresh shredded leek, to garnish

5 Arrange the leeks on a warm serving plate and place the fried tofu (bean curd) triangles on top.

6 Garnish the triangles with the fresh shredded leek and serve immediately.

COOK'S TIP

Fry the tofu (bean curd) in batches and keep each batch warm until all of the tofu (bean curd) has been fried and is ready to serve.

1 Mix the salt, Chinese five-spice, sugar, garlic and ginger in a bowl and then spread the mixture out on a plate. Cut the tofu (bean curd) cakes in half diagonally to form two triangles. Cut each triangle in half and then in half again to form a total of 16 triangles.

2 Gently roll the tofu (bean curd) triangles in the spice mixture, turning to coat thoroughly. Set aside to marinate for 1 hour.

3 Heat the oil for deep-frying in a preheated wok until almost smoking. Reduce the heat slightly, add the tofu (bean curd) triangles and fry for 5 minutes, until golden brown. Remove from the wok with a slotted spoon and keep warm.

4 Add the leeks to the wok and stir-fry for 1 minute. Remove with a slotted spoon and drain on absorbent kitchen paper (paper towels).

Braised Vegetables with Tofu (Bean Curd)

Also called Lo Han Zhai or Buddha's Delight, the original recipe uses 18 vegetables to represent the 18 Buddhas (Lo Han) – but nowadays 6–8 are acceptable.

Serves 4
5 g/¹/₄ oz dried wood (tree) ears
1 cake tofu (bean curd)
50 g/1³/₄ oz mangetout (snow peas)
115 g/4 oz Chinese leaves (cabbage)
1 small carrot
75 g/2³/₄ oz canned baby corn cobs, drained
75 g/2³/₄ oz canned straw mushrooms, drained
50 g/1³/₄ oz canned water chestnuts, drained
300 ml/¹/₂ pint/1¹/₄ cups vegetable oil
1 tsp salt
¹/₂ tsp sugar
1 tbsp light soy sauce or oyster sauce
2–3 tbsp Chinese Stock (see page 16) or water
a few drops of sesame oil

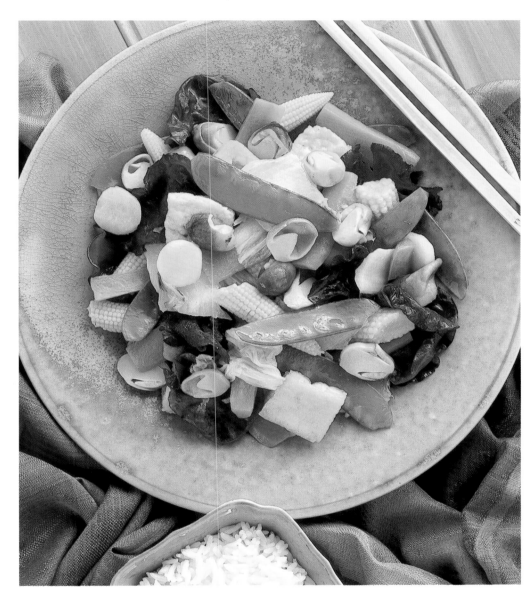

1 Put the wood (tree) ears in a bowl and cover with warm water. Soak for 25–30 minutes, then rinse thoroughly in cold water and drain, discarding any hard stalks and dry on kitchen paper (paper towels).

2 Cut the cake of tofu (bean curd) into about 18 small pieces. Top and tail the mangetouts (snow peas). Cut the Chinese leaves (cabbage) and the carrot into slices roughly the same size and shape as the mangetout (snow peas). Cut the baby corn, the straw mushrooms and the water chestnuts in half.

3 Heat the oil in a preheated wok. Add the tofu (bean curd) and deep-fry for about 2 minutes, until it turns slightly golden. Remove with a slotted spoon and drain thoroughly.

4 Pour off the excess oil, leaving about 2 tablespoons in the wok. Add the carrot, Chinese leaves (cabbage) and mangetouts (snow peas) and stir-fry for about 1 minute.

5 Add the corn, mushrooms and water chestnuts. Stir for 2 minutes, then add the salt, sugar, soy sauce and stock or water. Bring to the boil and cook for 1 more minute. Sprinkle with sesame oil and serve hot or cold.

Aubergine (Eggplant) in Chilli Sauce

Strips of aubergine (eggplant) are deep-fried, then served in a fragrant
chilli sauce with carrot matchsticks and spring onions (scallions).

Serves 4
1 large aubergine (eggplant)
vegetable oil, for deep–frying
2 carrots
4 spring onions (scallions)
2 large garlic cloves
1 tbsp vegetable oil
2 tsp chilli sauce
1 tbsp soy sauce
1 tbsp Chinese rice wine or dry sherry

1 Slice the aubergine (eggplant) and then cut into strips about the size of potato chips (French fries).

2 Heat enough oil in a wok or large heavy-based saucepan to deep-fry the aubergine (eggplant) in batches until just browned. Remove the strips with a slotted spoon and drain on kitchen paper (paper towels).

3 Cut the carrots into thin matchsticks. Trim and slice the spring onions (scallions) diagonally. Slice the garlic cloves thinly.

4 Heat 1 tablespoon of oil in a wok or large frying pan (skillet). Add the carrot matchsticks and stir-fry for 1 minute. Add the chopped spring onions (scallions) and garlic and stir-fry for 1 further minute.

5 Stir in the chilli sauce, soy sauce and wine or sherry, then stir in the drained aubergine (eggplant). Stir well until the vegetables are thoroughly heated through before serving.

Spicy Aubergines (Eggplants)

Try to obtain the smaller Chinese aubergines (eggplants) for this dish, as they have a slightly sweeter taste, but the recipe is delicious with the larger variety as well.

Serves 4
450 g/1 lb aubergines (eggplants), washed
2 tsp salt
3 tbsp vegetable oil
2 garlic cloves, crushed
2.5-cm/1-inch piece fresh ginger root, chopped
1 onion, halved and sliced
1 fresh red chilli, sliced
2 tbsp dark soy sauce
1 tbsp hoi-sin sauce
$\frac{1}{2}$ tsp chilli sauce
1 tbsp dark brown sugar
1 tbsp wine vinegar
1 tsp ground Szechuan pepper
300 ml/$\frac{1}{2}$ pint/1$\frac{1}{4}$ cups vegetable stock

Increase the heat to high and bring to the boil. Cook until the the sauce has thickened slightly and is coating the aubergines (eggplants) completely.

4 Transfer the spicy aubergines (eggplants) to a warm serving dish and serve immediately.

COOK'S TIP

Sprinkling the aubergines (eggplant) with salt and letting them stand removes the bitter juices, which would otherwise taint the flavour of the dish.

1 Cut the aubergines (eggplants) into cubes if you are using the larger variety, or cut the smaller type in half. Place the aubergines (eggplants) in a colander and sprinkle with the salt. Let stand for 30 minutes. Rinse the aubergines (eggplants) under cold running water and pat dry with kitchen paper (paper towels).

2 Heat the oil in a preheated wok and add the garlic, ginger, onion and fresh chilli. Stir-fry for 30 seconds and add the aubergines (eggplants). Continue to cook for 1–2 minutes.

3 Add the remaining ingredients to the wok, reduce the heat and simmer, uncovered, for 10 minutes, until the aubergines (eggplants) are cooked.

Aubergine (Eggplant) in Black Bean Sauce

Stir-fried aubergine (eggplant) is served in a black bean sauce with garlic and spring onions (scallions). This is good served with plain boiled rice.

Serves 4
50 g/1³/₄ oz/¹/₃ cup dried black beans
425 ml/³/₄ pint/2 cups vegetable stock
1 tbsp malt vinegar
1 tbsp Chinese rice wine or dry sherry
1 tbsp soy sauce
1 tbsp sugar
1¹/₂ tsp cornflour (cornstarch)
1 red chilli, seeded and chopped
1-cm/¹/₂-inch piece fresh ginger root, chopped
2 aubergines (eggplants)
2 tsp salt
3 tbsp vegetable oil
2 garlic cloves, sliced
4 spring onions (scallions), sliced diagonally
shredded radishes, to garnish

1 Soak the beans overnight in plenty of cold water. Drain and place in a saucepan. Cover with cold water, bring to the boil and boil rapidly, uncovered, for 10 minutes. Drain. Return the beans to the saucepan with the stock and bring to the boil.

2 Blend together the vinegar, rice wine or sherry, soy sauce, sugar, cornflour (cornstarch), chilli and ginger in a small bowl. Add to the beans, then cover and simmer for 40 minutes, or until the beans are tender and the sauce has thickened. Stir occasionally.

3 Cut the aubergines (eggplants) into chunks and place in a colander.

Sprinkle with the salt and let drain for 30 minutes. Rinse well and dry on kitchen paper (paper towels).

4 Heat the oil in a preheated wok or large frying pan (skillet). Add the aubergine (eggplant) and garlic. Stir-fry for 3–4 minutes until the aubergine (eggplant) has started to brown.

5 Add the sauce to the aubergine (eggplant), with the spring onions (scallions). Heat thoroughly and garnish with radish shreds.

Spicy Mushrooms

A mixture of mushrooms common in Western cooking,
have been used in this recipe for a richly flavoured dish.
If Chinese dried mushrooms are available, add a small quantity.

Serves 4

2 tbsp peanut oil

2 garlic cloves, crushed

3 spring onions
(scallions), chopped

300 g/10¹⁄₂ oz button
mushrooms

2 large open-cap mushrooms,
thinly sliced

115 g/4 oz oyster mushrooms, torn
into pieces or
fresh shiitake mushrooms,
finely chopped

1 tsp chilli sauce

1 tbsp dark soy sauce

1 tbsp hoi-sin sauce

1 tbsp wine vinegar

¹⁄₂ tsp ground
Szechuan pepper

1 tbsp dark brown sugar

1 tsp sesame oil

chopped parsley, to garnish

1 Heat the oil in a preheated wok until almost smoking. Reduce the heat slightly, add the garlic and spring onions (scallions) and stir-fry for 30 seconds.

2 Add the button, open-cap and oyster or shiitake mushrooms, chilli sauce, soy sauce, hoi-sin sauce, wine vinegar, pepper and brown sugar and stir-fry for 4–5 minutes, until the mushrooms are cooked.

3 Sprinkle the sesame oil on top. Transfer to a warm serving dish and serve immediately, garnished with the fresh parsley.

COOK'S TIP

Follow the lines of the gills when tearing oyster mushrooms.

COOK'S TIP

This dish is ideal served with rich meat or fish dishes.

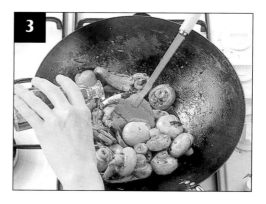

Money Bags

These steamed dumplings are filled with mushroom and sweetcorn (corn). Try dipping them in a mixture of soy sauce, Chinese rice wine or dry sherry and slivers of fresh ginger root.

Serves 4
3 Chinese dried mushrooms or thinly sliced open-cup mushrooms
225 g/8 oz/2 cups plain (all-purpose) flour
1 egg, beaten
75 ml/3 fl oz/$^1/_3$ cup water
1 tsp baking powder
$^3/_4$ tsp salt
2 tbsp vegetable oil
2 spring onions (scallions), chopped
75 g/2$^3/_4$ oz/$^1/_2$ cup sweetcorn (corn) kernels
$^1/_2$ red chilli, seeded and chopped
1 tbsp brown bean sauce

1 Place the dried mushrooms in a small bowl, cover with warm water and soak for 20–25 minutes.

2 To make the wrappers, sift the flour into a bowl. Add the egg and mix lightly. Stir in the water, baking powder and salt. Mix to a soft dough. Knead lightly until smooth on a floured board. Cover with a damp cloth and set aside for 5–6 minutes. This allows the baking powder time to activate, so that the dumplings swell when they are steamed.

3 Drain the mushrooms, squeezing them dry. Remove the tough stalks and chop the caps.

4 Heat the oil in a wok or large heavy-based frying pan (skillet). Add the

mushrooms, spring onions (scallions), sweetcorn (corn) and chilli and stir-fry for 2 minutes. Stir in the brown bean sauce and remove the wok or pan (skillet) from the heat.

5 Roll the dough out on a lightly floured surface into a large sausage and cut into 24 even-size pieces.

6 Roll each piece out into a thin round and place a teaspoonful of the filling in the centre. Gather up the edges, pinch together and twist to seal.

7 Stand the dumplings in an oiled steaming basket. Place over a saucepan of simmering water, cover and steam for 12–14 minutes before serving.

Steamed Vegetable Cabbage Rolls

In this recipe a mixed vegetable stuffing is wrapped in Chinese leaves (cabbage) and steamed until tender. Serve with chilli or soy sauce for a really tasty meal.

Serves 4
8 large Chinese leaves (Chinese cabbage leaves)
FILLING
2 baby corn cobs, sliced
1 carrot, finely chopped
1 celery stick, chopped
4 spring onions (scallions), chopped
4 water chestnuts, chopped
2 tbsp chopped unsalted cashew nuts
1 garlic clove, chopped
1 tsp grated fresh ginger root
25 g/1 oz canned bamboo shoots, drained and chopped
1 tsp sesame oil
2 tsp soy sauce

1 Put the Chinese leaves (cabbage) in a large bowl and pour boiling water over them to soften the leaves. Leave for 1 minute and drain well.

2 Make the filling. Mix together the corn, carrot, celery, spring onions (scallions), water chestnuts, cashews, garlic, ginger, bamboo shoots, sesame oil and soy sauce in a bowl. Spread out the Chinese leaves (cabbage) on a board and spoon an equal quantity of the filling mixture on to each one.

3 Roll the leaves up, folding in the sides, and secure with cocktail sticks (toothpicks).

4 Place the filled rolls in a small heatproof dish in a steamer, cover and cook for 15–20 minutes, until the parcels are cooked through.

5 Transfer the filled rolls to a warm serving dish and serve immediately with chilli or soy sauce, according to your choice.

COOK'S TIP

Make the parcels in advance, cover and store in the refrigerator until required and then steam as in step 4.

Braised Chinese Leaves (Cabbage)

Almost any kind of western or Chinese cabbage can be used
for this dish. White cabbage works particularly well.

Serves 4
450 g/1 lb Chinese leaves (cabbage) or firm white cabbage
3 tbsp vegetable oil
$^1/_2$ tsp Szechuan peppercorns
5–6 small dried red chillies, seeded and chopped
$^1/_2$ tsp salt
1 tbsp sugar
1 tbsp light soy sauce
1 tbsp rice vinegar
a few drops of sesame oil (optional)

1 Shred the Chinese leaves (cabbage) crossways into thin strips. If using firm-packed white cabbage, cut out the thick core before shredding.

2 Heat the oil in a preheated wok, add the Szechuan peppercorns and the dried chillies and stir-fry for a few seconds.

3 Add the Chinese leaves (cabbage) or white cabbage to the peppercorns and chillies, stir-fry for about 1 minute, then add salt and continue stirring for another minute.

4 Add the sugar, soy sauce and vinegar, blend well and stir-fry for 1 further minute. Sprinkle with the sesame oil, if using. Transfer to a warm serving plate and serve immediately. Alternatively, transfer to a plate, cool and serve cold.

Creamy Cabbage & Leeks

This dish is very quick to make. The Chinese leaves (cabbage) complement the leek perfectly.
A dash of cream is added to the sauce, but this may be omitted if preferred.

Serves 4
450 g/1 lb Chinese leaves (cabbage), shredded
2 tbsp peanut oil
2 leeks, shredded
4 garlic cloves, crushed
300 ml/$\frac{1}{2}$ pint/1$\frac{1}{4}$ cups vegetable stock
1 tbsp light soy sauce
2 tsp cornflour (cornstarch)
4 tsp water
2 tbsp single (light) cream or natural (unsweetened) yogurt
1 tbsp chopped fresh coriander (cilantro), to garnish

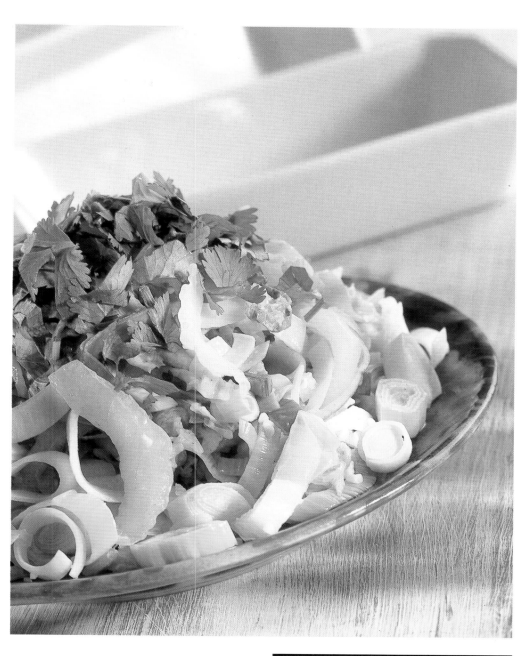

1 Blanch the Chinese leaves (cabbage) in boiling water for 30 seconds, then drain well, rinse under cold water and drain again. Heat the peanut oil in a preheated wok and add the Chinese leaves (cabbage), leeks and garlic. Stir-fry for 2–3 minutes.

2 Add the stock and soy sauce to the wok, reduce the heat to low, cover and simmer for 10 minutes, or until the vegetables are tender.

3 Remove the vegetables with a slotted spoon, set aside and keep warm. Bring the stock to the boil and boil vigorously to reduce by half. Blend the cornflour (cornstarch) with the water and stir it into the stock. Bring to the boil, stirring until thickened and clear.

4 Reduce the heat and return the vegetables to the wok. Add the cream or yogurt. Cook over a gentle heat for 1 minute.

5 Transfer to a warm serving dish, sprinkle with the chopped coriander (cilantro) to garnish and serve.

COOK'S TIP

Do not boil the sauce once the cream or yogurt has been added, as it will separate on boiling.

Lemon Chinese Leaves

Stir-fried Chinese leaves (cabbage) are served with a tangy sauce
made of grated lemon rind, lemon juice and fresh ginger.

Serves 4
450 g/1 lb Chinese leaves (cabbage)
3 tbsp vegetable oil
1-cm/^{1}/$_2$-inch piece fresh ginger root, grated
1 tsp salt
1 tsp sugar
125 ml/4 fl oz/^{1}/$_2$ cup water or vegetable stock
1 tsp grated lemon rind
1 tbsp cornflour (cornstarch)
1 tbsp lemon juice

1 Separate the Chinese leaves (cabbage), wash and drain thoroughly. Pat dry with kitchen paper (paper towels). With a sharp knife, cut into 5-cm/2-inch wide slices.

2 Heat the oil in a preheated wok or frying pan (skillet). Add the ginger and Chinese leaves (cabbage) and stir-fry for 2–3 minutes, or until the leaves begin to wilt. Add the salt and sugar, and mix well until the leaves soften. Remove with a slotted spoon and set aside.

3 Add the water or vegetable stock and grated lemon zest and bring to the boil. Meanwhile, mix the cornflour (cornstarch) to a smooth paste with the lemon juice, then add to the water or stock in the pan. Simmer, stirring constantly, for about 1 minute to make a smooth sauce.

4 Return the cooked leaves to the pan and mix thoroughly. Arrange on a serving plate and serve immediately.

Rice Dishes

Rice is a staple food throughout much of China and is served with most meals. Plain boiled rice is the usual everyday accompaniment to family meals, but it can easily be enlivened by steaming or frying it with other ingredients, such as (bell) peppers, peas, spring onions (scallions) or mushrooms. While rice has a fairly bland flavour, it provides a complementary

texture to many other ingredients and absorbs the stronger flavours of other dishes, as well as providing the essential bulk

required for satisfying the appetite.

Some of the recipes in this chapter could be adapted to make a quick and easy main meal. Try Special Fried Rice with Prawns (Shrimp), Chicken & Rice Casserole, Rice with Crab & Mussels or Fried Rice with Pork, Tomatoes, Peas & Mushrooms.

White long-grain rice is most frequently served with savoury dishes, although brown long-grain rice may also be used.

Chinese Fried Rice

The rice for this dish may be cooked in the wok or in a saucepan,
but it is essential to use cold, dry rice with separate grains for success.

Serves 4
700 ml/1¼ pints/3 cups water
½ tsp salt
300 g/10½ oz/1½ cups long-grain rice
2 eggs
4 tsp cold water
3 tbsp sunflower oil
4 spring onions (scallions), sliced diagonally
1 red, green or yellow (bell) pepper, seeded and thinly sliced
3–4 lean bacon slices, cut into strips
200 g/7 oz/1 cup beansprouts
115 g/4 oz/1 cup frozen peas, thawed
2 tbsp light soy sauce (optional)
salt and pepper

1 Bring the water to the boil with the salt in a wok. Rinse the rice under cold water until it runs clear, drain and add to the wok. Stir, cover tightly and simmer gently for 12–13 minutes. (Do not remove the lid during cooking or the steam will escape and the rice will not be cooked.)

2 Stir the rice and spread out on a large plate or baking sheet (cookie sheet) to cool and dry.

3 Beat each egg separately with salt and pepper and 2 teaspoons cold water. Heat 1 tablespoon of oil in a preheated wok. Pour in 1 egg, swirl it around and cook until set. Remove to a board and cook the second egg. Cut the omelettes into thin slices.

4 Heat the remaining oil in the wok. When it is hot, add the spring onions

(scallions) and (bell) pepper slices and stir-fry for 1–2 minutes. Add the bacon and continue to stir-fry for a further 1–2 minutes. Add the beansprouts and peas and toss together thoroughly. Stir in the soy sauce if using.

5 Add the rice and season to taste with salt and pepper. Stir-fry for 1–2 minutes. Add the strips of omelette and continue to stir for about 2 minutes, or until the rice is piping hot. Transfer to a warm serving dish and serve at once.

Vegetable Fried Rice

This dish can be served as part of a substantial meal for a number of people or as a vegetarian meal in itself for four.

Serves 4
150 g/5 oz/²/₃ cup long-grain white rice
3 tbsp peanut oil
2 garlic cloves, crushed
¹/₂ tsp Chinese five-spice powder
50 g/1³/₄ oz/¹/₃ cup green beans
1 green (bell) pepper, seeded and chopped
4 baby corn cobs, sliced
25 g/1 oz canned bamboo shoots drained and chopped
3 tomatoes, peeled, seeded and chopped
50 g/1³/₄ oz/¹/₂ cup cooked peas
1 tsp sesame oil

1 Cook the rice in lightly salted boiling water for 15 minutes. Drain, rinse under cold running water and drain well again.

2 Heat the peanut oil in a preheated wok. Add the garlic and Chinese five-spice powder and stir-fry for 30 seconds.

3 Add the green beans, (bell) pepper and corn cobs and stir-fry for about 2 minutes.

4 Stir in the bamboo shoots, tomatoes, peas and rice and stir-fry for 1 further minute. Sprinkle with sesame oil.

5 Transfer to a warm serving dish and serve immediately.

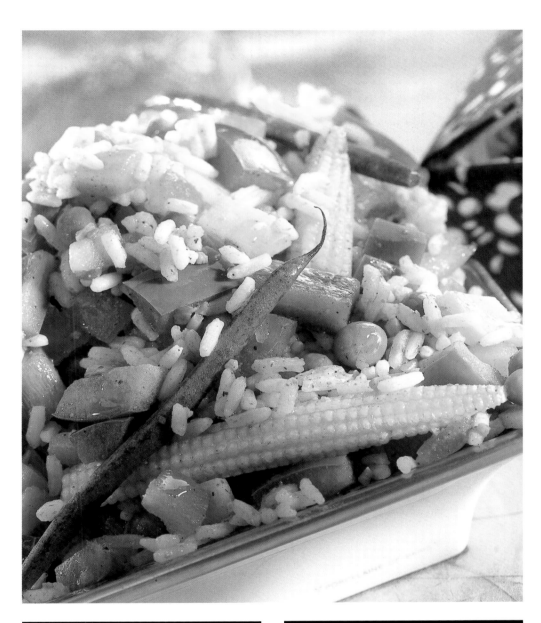

COOK'S TIP

When cooking rice by the non-absorption method, as here, stir it once only. Stirring more frequently will break up the grains and the cooked rice will be sticky.

COOK'S TIP

Use a selection of vegetables of your choice in this recipe, cutting them to a similar size in order to ensure that they cook in the same amount of time.

Fragrant Steamed Rice in Lotus Leaves

The fragrance of the lotus leaves flavours the rice. Lotus leaves are available from Chinese foodstores, but cabbage or spinach leaves can be substituted.

Serves 4
2 lotus leaves
4 Chinese dried mushrooms
175 g/6 oz/^{3}/$_4$ cup long-grain rice
1 cinnamon stick
6 cardamom pods
4 cloves
1 tsp salt
2 eggs
1 tbsp vegetable oil
2 spring onions (scallions), chopped
1 tbsp light soy sauce
2 tbsp Chinese rice wine or dry sherry
1 tsp sugar
1 tsp sesame oil

1 Unfold the lotus leaves and cut along the fold to divide each leaf in half. Lay on a large baking sheet (cookie sheet) and pour over enough hot water to cover. Soak for about 30 minutes, or until softened.

2 Place the mushrooms in a small bowl and cover with warm water. Soak for 20–25 minutes.

3 Cook the rice in boiling water with the cinnamon stick, cardamom pods, cloves and salt for about 10 minutes, until partially cooked. Drain and remove the cinnamon stick.

4 Beat the eggs lightly. Heat the oil in a preheated wok or heavy-based frying pan (skillet). Add the eggs and cook quickly, stirring constantly until set. Remove from the wok or pan (skillet) and set aside.

5 Drain the mushrooms, squeezing out the excess water. Remove the stalks and chop the caps. Place the rice in a bowl. Stir in the mushrooms, eggs, spring onions (scallions), soy sauce, rice wine or sherry, sugar and sesame oil. Season with salt to taste.

6 Drain the lotus leaves and divide the rice mixture into 4 portions. Place a portion in the centre of each leaf and fold up to form a parcel. Place in a steamer, cover and steam for 20 minutes. To serve, cut the tops of the leaves open to expose the filling.

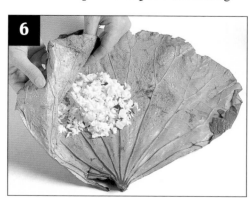

Green Fried Rice with Spinach

Spinach is used in this recipe to give the rice a wonderful green colouring.
Tossed with the carrot strips, it is a really appealing dish.

Serves 4
150 g/5^{1}/$_{2}$ oz/^{2}/$_{3}$ cup long-grain rice
2 tbsp vegetable oil
2 garlic cloves, crushed
1 tsp grated fresh ginger root
1 carrot, cut into matchsticks
1 courgette (zucchini), diced
225 g/8 oz baby spinach
2 tsp light soy sauce
2 tsp light brown sugar
salt

1 Cook the rice in lightly salted
boiling water for 15 minutes. Drain,
rinse under cold running water and
rinse thoroughly again.

2 Heat the oil in a preheated wok.
Add the garlic and ginger and stir-fry
for 30 seconds. Add the carrot and
courgette (zucchini) and stir-fry for
2 minutes.

3 Stir in the baby spinach and stir-fry
for 1 minute, until wilted. Add the
rice, soy sauce and sugar and mix
well. Transfer to a warm serving dish
and serve immediately.

VARIATION

Chinese leaves (cabbage) may be
used in place of the spinach, giving
a lighter green colour to the dish.

Egg Fried Rice with Chilli

This version of fried rice is given extra punch with hot red chillies,
spring onions (scallions) and fish sauce.

Serves 4
225 g/8 oz/1 cup basmati rice
3 tbsp sunflower oil
1 hot red chilli, seeded and finely chopped
2 tsp fish sauce
3 spring onions (scallions), chopped
1 large egg, beaten
1 tbsp chopped fresh parsley or coriander (cilantro)
1 tbsp light soy sauce
1 tsp sugar
salt and pepper

1 Cook the rice in lightly salted
boiling water for about 10 minutes,
until tender. Drain, rinse with boiling
water and drain again thoroughly.
Spread out on a large plate or baking
sheet (cookie sheet) to dry.

2 Heat the oil in a preheated wok or
large, heavy-based frying pan (skillet).
Add the chilli, fish sauce and spring
onions (scallions) and stir-fry for
1–2 minutes.

3 Add the beaten egg and stir-fry
quickly so that the egg scrambles into
small fluffy pieces.

4 Fork through the rice to separate
the grains, then add to the wok or pan
(skillet) and stir-fry for about
1 minute to mix thoroughly and to
heat through.

5 Sprinkle a little of the chopped
parsley or coriander (cilantro) over the

rice. Mix the soy sauce with the sugar
and remaining chopped parsley or
coriander (cilantro) and stir into the
rice mixture, tossing well to mix.

6 Transfer to a warm serving dish and
serve immediately.

COOK'S TIP

It is often difficult to identify
chillies. As a general rule, sharply
pointed, thin chillies tend to be
hotter than short, blunt ones.

Egg Fried Rice

The rice used for frying should not be too soft.
Ideally, the rice should have been slightly undercooked
and thoroughly cooled before frying.

Serves 4
3 eggs
1 tsp salt
2 spring onions (scallions), finely chopped
2–3 tbsp vegetable oil
450 g/1 lb/3 cups cooked rice, well drained and cooled
115 g/4 oz/1 cup cooked peas

1 Lightly beat the eggs with a pinch of salt and 1 tablespoon of the spring onions (scallions).

2 Heat the oil in a preheated wok, add the eggs and stir until lightly scrambled. (The eggs should be cooked only until they start to set, so that they are still moist.)

3 Add the cold rice and stir to make sure that each grain is separated. Make sure the oil is really hot, otherwise the rice will become heavy and greasy.

4 Add the remaining salt, spring onions (scallions) and peas. Blend well and serve hot or cold.

Egg Fu Yong with Rice

Cooked rice mixed with scrambled eggs, Chinese mushrooms, bamboo shoots
and water chestnuts – a great way of using up leftover cooked rice.

Serves 2-4

175 g/6 oz/³/₄ cup
long grain rice

2 Chinese dried mushrooms
(or thinly sliced
open-cup mushrooms)

3 eggs

3 tbsp vegetable oil

4 spring onions
(scallions), sliced

¹/₂ green (bell) pepper,
seeded and chopped

50 g/1³/₄ oz/¹/₃ cup canned bamboo
shoots, drained

50 g/1³/₄ oz/¹/₃ cup canned water
chestnuts, drained and sliced

115 g/4 oz/¹/₂ cup beansprouts

2 tbsp light soy sauce

2 tbsp Chinese rice wine or
dry sherry

2 tsp sesame oil

salt and pepper

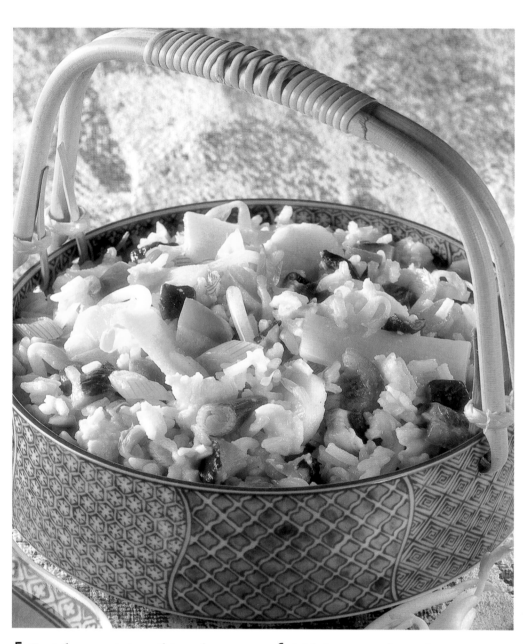

1 Cook the rice in lightly salted
boiling water for about 10 minutes,
until almost tender. Drain, rinse,
drain again and set aside to cool.

2 Place the dried mushrooms in a
small bowl, cover with warm water
and soak for 20–25 minutes.

3 Beat the eggs with a little salt. Heat
1 tablespoon of the oil in a wok or
frying pan (skillet). Add the eggs and
stir until set. Remove and set aside.

4 Drain the mushrooms and squeeze
out the excess water. Remove the tough
stalks and chop the caps.

5 Heat the remaining oil in a clean
wok or frying pan (skillet). Add the
mushrooms, spring onions (scallions)
and green (bell) pepper, and stir-fry
for 2 minutes. Add the bamboo
shoots, water chestnuts and
beansprouts. Stir-fry for 1 minute.

6 Add the rice to the wok or pan
(skillet), together with the soy sauce,
Chinese rice wine or sherry and
sesame oil. Mix well, heating the rice
thoroughly. Season to taste with salt
and pepper. Stir in the reserved eggs,
transfer to a serving dish and serve.

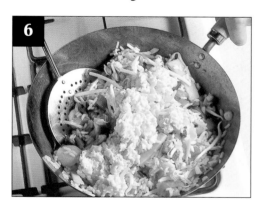

Special Fried Rice

This dish is a popular choice in Chinese restaurants. Ham and prawns (shrimp) are mixed with vegetables in a soy-flavoured rice.

Serves 4

150 g/5½ oz/⅔ cup
long-grain rice

2 tbsp vegetable oil

2 eggs, beaten

2 garlic cloves, crushed

1 tsp grated fresh ginger root

3 spring onions
(scallions), sliced

75 g/2¾ oz/¾ cup cooked peas

150 g/5½ oz/⅔ cup
beansprouts

225 g/8 oz/1⅓ cups
shredded ham

150 g/5½ oz peeled,
cooked prawns (shrimp)

2 tbsp light soy sauce

salt

1 Cook the rice in lightly salted boiling water for 15 minutes. Drain, rinse under cold water and drain thoroughly again.

2 Heat 1 tbsp of the oil in a preheated wok and add the beaten eggs and a further 1 teaspoon of oil. Tilt the wok so that the egg covers the base to make a thin omelette. Cook until lightly browned on the underside, flip the omelette and cook on the other side for 1 minute. Remove from the wok and let cool.

3 Heat the remaining oil in the wok. Add the garlic and ginger and stir-fry for 30 seconds. Add the spring onions (scallions), peas, beansprouts, ham and prawns (shrimp) and stir-fry for 2 minutes.

4 Stir in the soy sauce and rice and cook for a further 2 minutes. Slice the omelette very thinly and sprinkle it on to the dish. Transfer the special fried rice to a warm serving dish and serve immediately.

COOK'S TIP

As this recipe contains meat and fish, it is ideal served with simpler vegetable dishes.

Fried Rice with Prawns (Shrimp)

Use either large peeled prawns (shrimp)
or tiger prawns (jumbo shrimp) for this rice dish.

Serves 4

275 g/9½ oz/1½ cups
long-grain rice

2 eggs

4 tsp cold water

3 tbsp sunflower oil

4 spring onions (scallions),
thinly sliced diagonally

1 garlic clove, crushed

115 g/4 oz closed-cup or button
mushrooms, thinly sliced

2 tbsp oyster or anchovy sauce

200g/7 oz can water chestnuts,
drained and sliced

225 g/8 oz peeled prawns (shrimp),
thawed if frozen

½ bunch of watercress,
roughly chopped

salt and pepper

watercress sprigs,
to garnish (optional)

1 Cook the rice in lightly salted boiling water, following the instructions given in Chinese Fried Rice (see page 204) and keep warm.

2 Beat each egg separately with 2 teaspoons of cold water and salt and pepper to taste. Heat 2 teaspoons of oil in a preheated wok. Pour in the first egg, swirl it around, and cook undisturbed until set. Remove to a plate or board and repeat with the second egg. Cut the omelettes into 2.5-cm/1-inch squares.

3 Heat the remaining oil in the wok and when really hot add the spring onions (scallions) and garlic, and stir-

fry for 1 minute. Add the mushrooms and continue to cook for a further 2 minutes.

4 Stir in the oyster or anchovy sauce and seasoning. Add the water chestnuts and prawns (shrimp) and stir-fry for 2 minutes.

5 Stir in the cooked rice and stir-fry for 1 minute. Add the watercress and omelette squares and stir-fry for a further 1–2 minutes, until piping hot.

6 Transfer to a warm serving dish, garnish with sprigs of watercress, if using, and serve immediately.

Special Fried Rice with Prawns (Shrimp)

Special Fried Rice, sometimes called Yangchow Fried Rice, is almost a meal in itself.
Use completely dry and cold cooked rice for success.

Serves 4

50 g/1³/4 oz peeled cooked
prawns (shrimp)

50 g/1³/4 oz cooked chicken,
pork or ham

115 g/4 oz/1 cup peas

3 eggs

1 tsp salt

2 spring onions (scallions),
finely chopped

4 tbsp vegetable oil

1 tbsp light soy sauce

1 tsp Chinese rice wine
or dry sherry (optional)

450 g/1 lb/4 cups
cold cooked rice

1 Dry the prawns (shrimp) on kitchen paper (paper towels). Cut the meat into small dice about the same size as the peas.

2 In a bowl, lightly beat the eggs with a pinch of salt and a few pieces of the spring onions (scallions).

3 Heat 2 tablespoons of the oil in a preheated wok. Add the peas, prawns (shrimp) and meat and stir-fry for about 1 minute. Stir in the soy sauce and Chinese rice wine or sherry, then remove and keep warm.

4 Heat the remaining oil and add the eggs. Stir to scramble lightly. Add the rice and stir to separate the grains. Add the remaining salt and spring onions (scallions), the prawns (shrimp), meat and peas. Blend well and serve hot or cold.

Chicken & Rice Casserole

This is a spicy casserole of rice, chicken, vegetables and chilli in a soy and ginger flavoured sauce.
Although called a casserole, it requires only approximately 30 minutes cooking time.

Serves 4
150 g/5¹/₂ oz/²/₃ cup long grain rice
2 tsp salt
1 tbsp Chinese rice wine or dry sherry
2 tbsp light soy sauce
2 tbsp dark soy sauce
2 tsp dark brown sugar
1 tsp sesame oil
900 g/2 lb skinless, boneless chicken meat, diced
850 ml/1¹/₂ pints/3³/₄ cups chicken stock
2 open-cap mushrooms, thinly sliced
50 g/1³/₄ oz canned water chestnuts, drained and halved
75 g/2³/₄ oz broccoli florets
1 yellow (bell) pepper, seeded and sliced
4 tsp grated fresh ginger root
chopped chives, to garnish

1 Cook the rice in lightly salted boiling water for 15 minutes. Drain, rinse under cold water and drain again thoroughly.

2 Mix together the Chinese rice wine or sherry, soy sauces, sugar and sesame oil in a large bowl. Season to taste with salt. Stir the chicken into the mixture, turning to coat well, and marinate for 30 minutes.

3 Bring the stock to the boil, add the chicken, together with the marinade, mushrooms, water chestnuts, broccoli, (bell) pepper and ginger.

4 Stir in the rice, reduce the heat, cover and cook for 25–30 minutes, until the chicken and vegetables are cooked through.

5 Transfer to a warm serving dish and serve as a meal in itself.

VARIATION

This dish would work equally well with beef or pork. Chinese dried mushrooms may be used instead of the open-cap mushrooms.

Special Fried Rice with Cashew Nuts

In this simple recipe, cooked rice is fried with vegetables and cashew nuts.
It can be eaten on its own or served as an accompaniment.

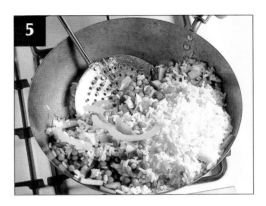

Serves 2–4

175 g/6 oz/³/₄ cup
long grain rice

50 g/1³/₄ oz/¹/₂ cup cashew nuts

1 carrot

¹/₂ cucumber

1 yellow (bell) pepper

2 spring onions (scallions)

2 tbsp vegetable oil

1 garlic clove, crushed

115 g/4 oz/³/₄ cup frozen
peas, thawed

1 tbsp light soy sauce

1 tsp salt

coriander (cilantro) leaves,
to garnish

1 Bring a large pan of lightly salted water to the boil. Add the rice and simmer for 15 minutes. Strain and rinse, drain thoroughly and set aside to cool.

2 Heat a wok or large frying pan (skillet), add the cashew nuts and dry-fry until lightly browned. Remove and set aside.

3 Cut the carrot in half along the length, then slice thinly into semi-circles. Halve the cucumber, remove the seeds, using a teaspoon, and discard. Dice the flesh. Seed and slice the (bell) pepper and chop the spring onions (scallions).

4 Heat the oil in a preheated wok or large frying pan (skillet). Add the prepared vegetables and the garlic. Stir-fry for 3 minutes.

5 Add the rice, peas, soy sauce and salt. Continue to stir-fry until well-mixed and thoroughly heated. Stir in the reserved cashew nuts. Transfer the special fried rice to a serving dish and serve garnished with coriander (cilantro) leaves.

VARIATION

You could substitute blanched almonds or pine nuts for the cashews in this recipe, if wished.

Fried Rice & Prawns (Shrimp)

When you've got one eye on the clock and a meal to make, try this!
Quickly made yet simply stunning to look at, its taste belies its simplicity.

Serves 4
50 g/1¾ oz/¼ cup butter
3 tbsp vegetable oil
450 g/1 lb/3 cups cold cooked basmati rice
6 spring onions (scallions), sliced finely
115 g/4 oz mangetout (snow peas), halved
1 carrot, cut into julienne strips
115 g/4 oz canned water chestnuts, drained and sliced
1 small crisp lettuce, shredded
350 g/12 oz peeled cooked tiger prawns (jumbo shrimp)
1 large red chilli, seeded and sliced diagonally
3 egg yolks
4 tsp sesame oil
salt and pepper

1 Heat the butter and the oil in a wok or large, heavy-based frying pan (skillet). Add the cooked rice and stir-fry for 2 minutes.

2 Add the spring onions (scallions), mangetout (snow peas), carrot and water chestnuts and season to taste with salt and pepper. Mix thoroughly. Stir-fry over a medium heat for a further 2 minutes.

3 Add the shredded lettuce, prawns (shrimp) and chilli and stir-fry for a further 2 minutes.

4 Beat the egg yolks with the sesame oil and stir into the wok or pan

(skillet), coating the rice and vegetable mixture. Cook for about 2 minutes to set the egg mixture.

5 Transfer to a large serving dish and serve at once.

COOK'S VARIATION

You could substitute pak choi for the lettuce and a thinly sliced red (bell) pepper for the carrot.

Crab Fried Rice

Canned crabmeat is used in this recipe for convenience, but fresh white crabmeat could be used – quite deliciously – in its place.

Serves 4
150 g/5^1/$_2$ oz/^{2}/$_3$ cup long-grain rice
2 tbsp peanut oil
125 g/4^1/$_2$ oz canned white crabmeat, drained
150 g/5^1/$_2$ oz/^{2}/$_3$ cup beansprouts
1 leek, sliced
1 tbsp light soy sauce
2 tsp lime juice
2 eggs, beaten
1 tsp sesame oil
sliced lime, to garnish

1 Cook the rice in boiling salted water for 15 minutes. Drain, rinse under cold running water and drain again.

2 Heat the oil in a preheated wok. Add the crabmeat, beansprouts and leek and stir-fry for 2–3 minutes. Remove from the wok with a slotted spoon and set aside.

3 Add the eggs to the wok and cook, stirring, for 2–3 minutes, until they begin to set.

4 Stir the rice and crabmeat mixture into the wok, mixing well, and add the soy sauce and lime juice. Cook for 1 minute and sprinkle with the sesame oil. Transfer to a warm serving dish, garnish with the sliced lime and serve immediately.

COOK'S VARIATION

Cooked lobster may be used in place of the crab for a really special dish.

COOK'S TIP

The juice of citrus fruits can be squeezed more easily if they are slightly warm.

Rice with Crab & Mussels

Shellfish makes an ideal partner for rice. Mussels and crab add flavour
and texture to this spicy dish.

Serves 4
275 g/9¹/₂ oz/1¹/₂ cups long-grain rice
175 g/6 oz crabmeat, fresh, canned or frozen (thawed if frozen), or 8 crab sticks, thawed if frozen
2 tbsp sesame or sunflower oil
2.5-cm/1-inch pieced fresh ginger root, grated
4 spring onions (scallions), thinly sliced diagonally
115 g/4 oz mangetout (snow peas), cut into 2–3 pieces
¹/₂ tsp turmeric
1 tsp ground cumin
2 x 200g/7 oz jars mussels, well drained, or 350 g/12 oz frozen mussels, thawed
400 g/14 oz can beansprouts, well drained
salt and pepper

TO GARNISH

crab claws or legs (optional)
8 mangetout (snow peas), blanched

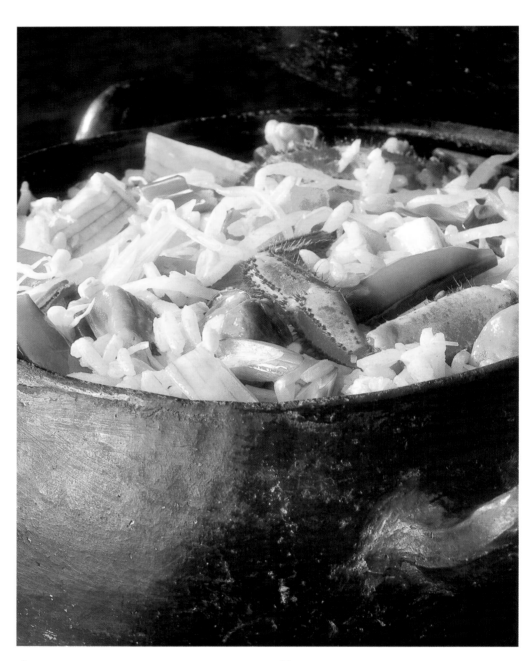

1 Cook the rice in boiling salted water, following the instructions given in Chinese Fried Rice (see page 204).

2 Meanwhile, flake the fresh crabmeat, if using. If using crab sticks, cut them into 3 or 4 pieces.

3 Heat the oil in a preheated wok. Add the ginger and spring onions (scallions) and stir-fry for 1–2 minutes. Add the mangetout (snow peas) and continue to cook for a further minute.

4 Sprinkle the turmeric and cumin over the vegetables and mix thoroughly. Season to taste with salt and pepper. Add the crabmeat or crab sticks and mussels and stir-fry for 1 minute.

5 Stir in the cooked rice and beansprouts and stir-fry for 2 minutes, or until really hot and well mixed.

6 Serve very hot, garnished with crab claws and mangetout (snow peas).

Fried Rice with Pork, Tomatoes, Peas & Mushrooms

This dish is a meal in itself, containing pieces of pork,
fried with rice, peas, tomatoes and mushrooms.

Serves 4
150 g/5½ oz/⅔ cup long-grain rice
3 tbsp peanut oil
1 large onion, cut into eight
225 g/8 oz pork fillet (tenderloin), thinly sliced
2 open-cap mushrooms, sliced
2 garlic cloves, crushed
1 tbsp light soy sauce
1 tsp light brown sugar
2 tomatoes, peeled, seeded and chopped
50 g/1¾ oz/½ cup cooked peas
2 eggs, beaten
salt

1 Cook the rice in lightly salted boiling water for 15 minutes, until tender, but not soft. Drain, rinse under cold running water and drain again thoroughly.

2 Heat the oil in a preheated wok. Add the onion and pork and stir-fry for 3–4 minutes, until the meat is beginning to colour.

3 Add the mushrooms and garlic and stir-fry for 1 minute. Add the soy sauce and sugar and stir-fry for a further 2 minutes

4 Stir in the rice, tomatoes and peas, mixing well. Transfer to a warmed dish and keep warm.

5 Stir the eggs into the wok and cook, stirring, for 2–3 minutes, until beginning to set.

6 Return the rice mixture to the wok and mix well. Heat through.

7 Transfer to a warm serving dish and serve immediately.

COOK'S TIP

Cook the rice in advance and chill or freeze until required.

Transparent (Cellophane) Noodles with Yellow Bean Sauce

Transparent (cellophane) or thread noodles are excellent re-heated, unlike most other noodles which must be served as soon as they are ready.

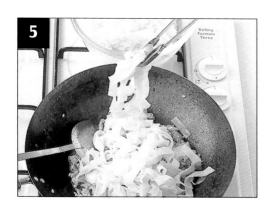

Serves 4
175 g/6 oz transparent (cellophane) noodles
1 tbsp peanut oil
1 leek, sliced
2 garlic cloves, crushed
450 g/1 lb minced (ground) chicken
450 ml/16 fl oz/2 cups chicken stock
1 tsp chilli sauce
2 tbsp yellow bean sauce
4 tbsp light soy sauce
1 tsp sesame oil
chopped chives, to garnish

COOK'S TIP

Chilli sauce is made from chillies, vinegar, sugar and salt. Tabasco sauce can be substituted.

COOK'S TIP

Cellophane noodles are available from many supermarkets and all Chinese supermarkets.

1 Put the noodles in a bowl, cover with boiling water and soak for 15 minutes. Drain and cut into short lengths with a pair of kitchen scissors.

2 Heat the oil in a preheated wok. Add the leek and garlic and stir-fry for 30 seconds.

3 Add the chicken and stir-fry for 4–5 minutes, until cooked.

4 Add the chicken stock, chilli sauce, yellow bean sauce and soy sauce and cook for 3–4 minutes.

5 Add the drained noodles and sesame oil and cook for 4–5 minutes, until heated through.

6 Spoon into warm bowls, sprinkle with chopped chives and serve immediately.

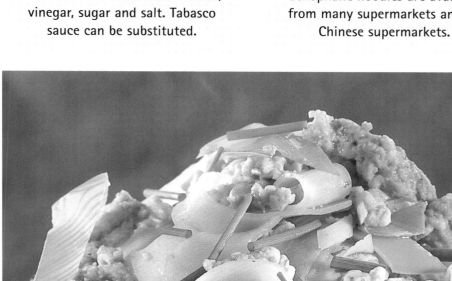

Homemade Noodles with Stir-Fried Vegetables

These noodles are simple to make; you do not need a pasta-making machine, as they are rolled out by hand.

Serves 4
NOODLES
115 g/4 oz/1 cup plain (all-purpose) flour
2 tbsp cornflour (cornstarch)
1/2 tsp salt
125 ml/4 fl oz/1/2 cup boiling water
5 tbsp vegetable oil
STIR-FRY
1 courgette (zucchini), cut into matchsticks
1 celery stick, cut into matchsticks
1 carrot, cut into matchsticks
115 g/4 oz open-cup mushrooms, thinly sliced
1 leek, thinly sliced
115 g/4 oz broccoli, divided into florets and stalks thinly sliced
115 g/4 oz/1/2 cup fresh beansprouts
1 tbsp soy sauce
2 tsp rice wine vinegar
1/2 tsp sugar

1 Sift the flour, cornflour (cornstarch) and salt into a bowl. Make a well in the centre and pour in the boiling water and 1 teaspoon of the oil. Mix quickly with a wooden spoon, to make a soft dough. Cover and leave for 5–6 minutes.

2 Make the noodles by rolling small balls of dough across a very lightly oiled work surface (counter) with the palm of your hand to form thin noodles. Do not worry if some of the noodles break. Set aside.

3 Heat 3 tablespoons of oil in a preheated wok. Add the noodles and fry over a high heat for 1 minute. Reduce the heat and cook for a further 2 minutes. Remove and drain on kitchen paper (paper towels).

4 Heat the remaining oil. Stir-fry the courgette (zucchini), celery and carrot for 1 minute. Add the mushrooms, broccoli and leek, and stir-fry for 1 minute. Stir in the remaining ingredients, heat through and serve.

Transparent (Cellophane) Noodles with Prawns (Shrimp)

In this recipe tiger prawns (jumbo shrimp) are cooked with orange juice, (bell) peppers, soy and vinegar and served on a bed of transparent (cellophane) noodles for an truly wonderful dish.

Serves 4
175 g/6 oz transparent (cellophane) noodles
1 tbsp vegetable oil
1 garlic clove, crushed
2 tsp grated fresh ginger root
24 raw tiger prawns (jumbo shrimp), peeled and deveined
1 red (bell) pepper, seeded and thinly sliced
1 green (bell) pepper, seeded and thinly sliced
1 onion, chopped
2 tbsp light soy sauce
juice of 1 orange
2 tsp wine vinegar
pinch of brown sugar
150 ml/¼ pint/⅔ cup fish stock
1 tbsp cornflour (cornstarch)
2 tsp water
coriander (cilantro) sprigs and orange rind, to garnish

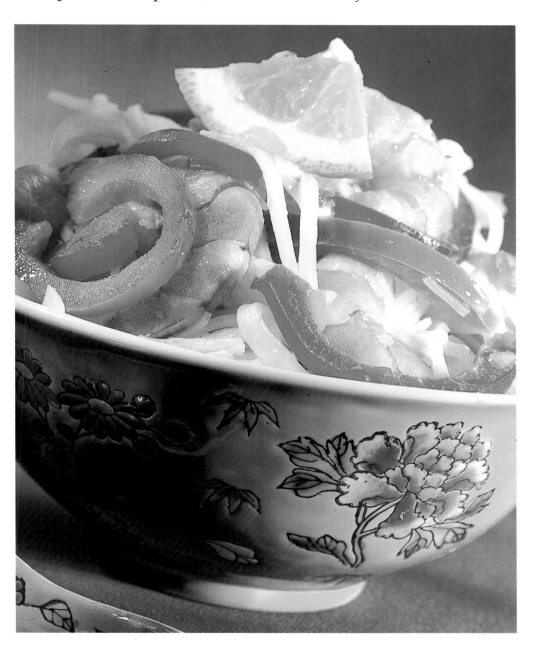

1 Cook the noodles in boiling water for 1 minute. Drain, rinse under cold water and drain thoroughly again.

2 Heat the oil in a preheated wok. Add the garlic and ginger and stir-fry for 30 seconds. Add the prawns (shrimp) and stir-fry for 2 minutes. Remove the prawns (shrimp) with a slotted spoon and keep warm.

3 Add the (bell) peppers and onion and stir-fry for 2 minutes. Stir in the soy sauce, orange juice, vinegar, sugar and stock. Return the prawns (shrimp) to the wok and cook for 8-10 minutes, until cooked through.

4 Blend the cornflour (cornstarch) with the water and add to the wok. Bring to the boil. Add the noodles and cook for 1–2 minutes. Serve garnished with coriander (cilantro) sprigs and orange rind.

VARIATION

Lime or lemon juice and rind may be used instead of the orange. Use 3–5½ teaspoons of these juices.

Seafood Chow Mein

Use whatever seafood is available for this delicious
noodle dish – mussels or crab would be suitable.

Serves 4
75 g/2³/₄ oz squid, cleaned
3–4 fresh scallops
75 g/2³/₄ oz raw prawns (shrimp), peeled and deveined
¹/₂ egg white, beaten lightly
1 tbsp Cornflour (Cornstarch) Paste (see page 16)
275 g/9¹/₂ oz egg noodles
5–6 tbsp vegetable oil
2 tbsp light soy sauce
50 g/1³/₄ oz mangetout (snow peas)
¹/₂ tsp salt
¹/₂ tsp sugar
1 tsp Chinese rice wine or dry sherry
2 spring onions (scallions), finely shredded
a few drops of sesame oil

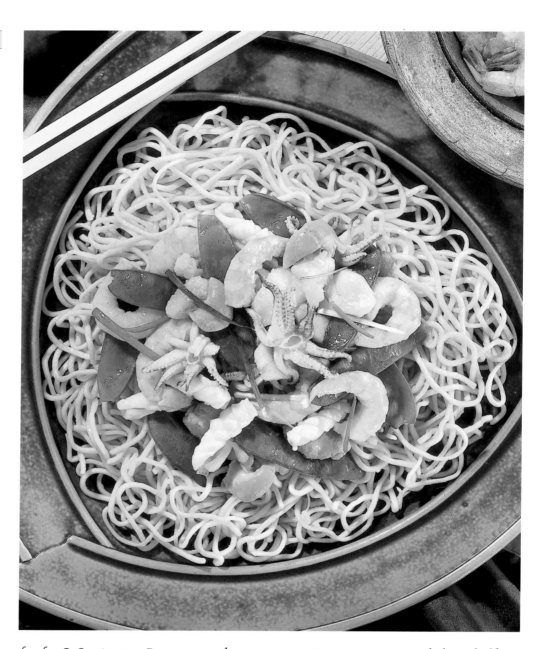

1 Open up the squid and score the inside in a criss-cross pattern. Cut into small pieces. Soak the squid in boiling water until all the pieces curl up. Rinse in cold water and drain.

2 Cut each scallop into 3–4 slices. Cut the prawns (shrimp) in half lengthways if large. Mix the scallops and prawns with the egg white and cornflour (cornstarch) paste.

3 Cook the noodles in boiling water according to the instructions on the packet, then drain and rinse under cold water. Drain well, then toss with 1 tablespoon of oil.

4 Heat 3 tablespoons of oil in a preheated wok. Add the noodles and 1 tablespoon of the soy sauce and stir-fry for 2–3 minutes. Remove to a large warm serving dish.

5 Heat the remaining oil and stir-fry the mangetout (snow peas) and seafood for 2 minutes. Stir in the salt, sugar, Chinese rice wine or sherry, the remaining soy sauce and about half the spring onions (scallions).

6 Pour the seafood mixture on top of the noodles and sprinkle with sesame oil. Garnish with the remaining spring onions (scallions) and serve.

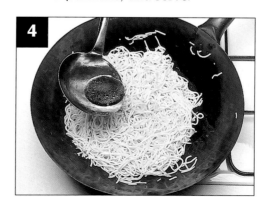

Curried Prawn (Shrimp) Noodles

These noodles have a fairly strong flavour and are almost a meal in themselves.
If served as an accompaniment, they are ideal with plain vegetable or fish dishes.

Serves 4

225 g/8 oz rice noodles

4 tbsp vegetable oil

1 onion, sliced

2 ham slices, shredded

2 tbsp Chinese curry powder

150 ml/¼ pint/⅔ cups
fish stock

225 g/8 oz peeled and deveined, raw
prawns (shrimp)

2 garlic cloves, crushed

6 spring onions
(scallions), chopped

1 tbsp light soy sauce

2 tbsp hoi–sin sauce

1 tbsp Chinese rice wine or
dry sherry

2 tsp lime juice

snipped chives, to garnish

1 Cook the rice noodles in boiling
water for 3–4 minutes. Drain, rinse
under cold water and drain
thoroughly again.

2 Heat 2 tablespoons of the oil in a
preheated wok. Add the onion and
ham and stir-fry for 1 minute. Add
the curry powder and stir-fry for a
further 30 seconds.

3 Stir the noodles and fish stock into
the wok and cook for 2–3 minutes.
Remove from the wok, set aside and
keep warm.

4 Heat the remaining oil in the wok
and add the prawns (shrimp), garlic
and spring onions (scallions). Stir-fry
for 1 minute, then add the soy sauce,

hoi-sin sauce, Chinese rice wine or
sherry and lime juice and heat
through. Pour this mixture over the
noodles.

5 Serve immediately, garnished with
freshly snipped chives.

COOK'S TIP

If cooked prawns (shrimp) are used,
toss them into the mixture at the
last minute, just long enough for
them to heat right through.

Noodles with Prawns (Shrimp)

This is a simple dish using egg noodles and large prawns (shrimp),
which give the dish a wonderful flavour, texture and colour.

Serves 4

225 g/8 oz thin egg noodles

2 tbsp peanut oil

1 garlic clove, crushed

$\frac{1}{2}$ tsp ground star anise

1 bunch spring onions (scallions),
cut into 5-cm/2-inch pieces

24 raw tiger prawns
(jumbo shrimp),
peeled with tails intact

2 tbsp light soy sauce

2 tsp lime juice

zest of 1 lime, to garnish

1 Blanch the noodles in boiling water
for 2 minutes. Drain, rinse under cold
water and drain thoroughly again.

2 Heat the oil in a preheated wok
until almost smoking. Add the garlic
and star anise and stir-fry for
30 seconds. Add the spring onions
(scallions) and prawns (shrimp) and
stir-fry for 2–3 minutes, until the
prawns (shrimp) change colour.

3 Stir in the soy sauce, lime juice and
noodles and mix well. Cook for
1 minute, then spoon into a warm
serving dish. Sprinkle with lime zest
to garnish and serve.

COOK'S TIP

This dish is just as tasty made with
smaller prawns (shrimp), but it does
not look quite so appealing.

Singapore-Style Rice Noodles

Rice noodles, or vermicelli, are also known as rice sticks.
Egg noodles can be used for this dish, but it will not taste quite the same.

Serves 4
200 g/7 oz rice vermicelli
115 g/4 oz boneless cooked chicken or pork
50 g/1³/₄ oz peeled cooked prawns (shrimp), thawed if frozen
4 tbsp vegetable oil
1 onion, thinly sliced
115 g/4 oz/¹/₂ cup fresh beansprouts
1 tsp salt
1 tbsp mild curry powder
2 tbsp light soy sauce
2 spring onions (scallions), thinly shredded
1–2 small fresh green or red chillies, seeded and thinly shredded

1 Soak the rice vermicelli in boiling water for 8–10 minutes, then rinse in cold water and drain well.

2 Thinly slice the cooked meat. Dry the prawns (shrimp) on kitchen paper (paper towels).

3 Heat the oil in a preheated wok. Add the onion and stir-fry until translucent. Add the beansprouts and stir-fry for 1 minute.

4 Add the noodles, together with the meat and prawns (shrimp), and continue stirring for another minute.

5 Blend in the salt, curry powder and soy sauce, followed by the spring onions (scallions) and chillies. Stir-fry for 1 more minute. Transfer to a serving dish and serve immediately.

Cantonese Fried Noodles

This dish is usually served as a snack or light meal.
It may also be served as an accompaniment to plain meat and fish dishes.

Serves 4
350 g/12 oz egg noodles
675 g/1¹/₂ lb lean steak, cut into thin strips
3 tbsp vegetable oil
75 g/2³/₄ oz canned bamboo shoots, drained and sliced
6 spring onions (scallions), sliced
25 g/1 oz green beans, cut in half
115 g/4 oz green cabbage, shredded
1 tbsp dark soy sauce
2 tbsp beef stock
1 tbsp Chinese rice wine or dry sherry
1 tbsp light brown sugar
2 tbsp chopped parsley, to garnish

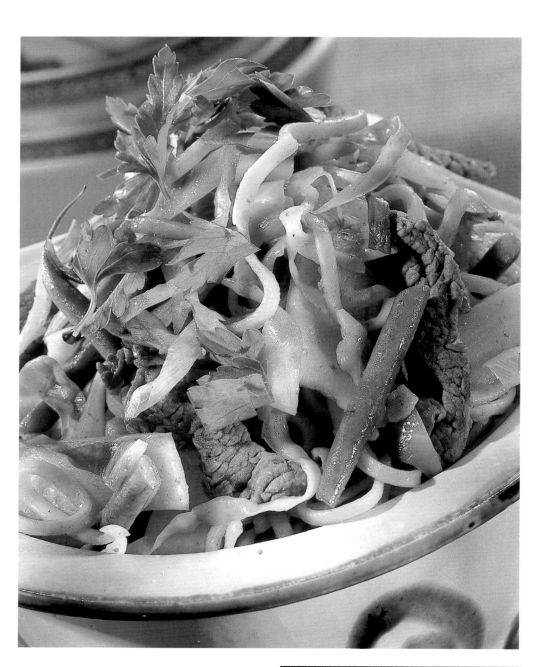

1 Cook the noodles in boiling water for 2–3 minutes. Drain, rinse under cold running water and drain thoroughly again.

2 Heat 1 tablespoon of the oil in a preheated wok. Add the noodles and stir-fry for 1–2 minutes. Drain and set aside.

3 Heat the remaining oil in the wok. Add the steak and stir-fry for 2–3 minutes. Add the bamboo shoots, spring onions (scallions), beans and cabbage and stir-fry for 1–2 minutes.

4 Add the soy sauce, stock, Chinese rice wine or sherry and sugar to the wok, mixing well.

5 Stir the noodles into the wok, mixing. Heat through for 1–2 minutes.

6 Transfer to a warm serving dish and serve immediately, sprinkled with chopped parsley.

VARIATION

Use lean pork or chicken instead of the steak in this recipe and alter the stock accordingly.

Chicken Noodles

Rice noodles are used in this recipe. They are available
in some supermarkets or Chinese supermarkets. If unavailable,
egg noodles may be used in their place.

Serves 4
225 g/8 oz rice noodles
2 tbsp peanut oil
225 g/8 oz skinless, boneless chicken breast, sliced
2 garlic cloves, crushed
1 tsp grated fresh ginger root
1 tsp Chinese curry powder
1 red (bell) pepper, seeded and thinly sliced
75 g/1¾ oz mangetout (snow peas), shredded
1 tbsp light soy sauce
2 tsp Chinese rice wine or dry sherry
2 tbsp chicken stock
1 tsp sesame oil
1 tbsp chopped fresh coriander (cilantro)

1 Soak the rice noodles for 4 minutes
in warm water. Drain thoroughly and
set aside.

2 Heat the oil in a preheated wok.
Add the chicken and stir-fry for
2–3 minutes.

3 Add the garlic, ginger and curry
powder and stir-fry for a further
30 seconds. Add the (bell) pepper and
mangetout (snow peas) and stir-fry
for 2–3 minutes.

4 Add the noodles, soy sauce,
Chinese rice wine or sherry and
chicken stock to the wok, mix
thoroughly and cook, stirring
constantly, for 1 minute.

5 Sprinkle the sesame oil and
coriander (cilantro) over the dish.

6 Transfer to a warm serving dish and
serve immediately.

VARIATION

Use pork or duck in this recipe
instead of the chicken.

Chicken on Crispy Noodles

Blanched noodles are fried in the wok until crisp and brown, and then topped
with a shredded chicken sauce for a delightfully tasty dish.

Serves 4
225 g/8 oz skinless, boneless chicken breasts, shredded
1 egg white
5 tsp cornflour (cornstarch)
225 g/8 oz thin egg noodles
325 ml/11 fl oz/1⅓ cups vegetable oil
600 ml/1 pint/2½ cups chicken stock
2 tbsp Chinese rice wine or dry sherry
2 tbsp oyster sauce
1 tbsp light soy sauce
1 tbsp hoi-sin sauce
1 red (bell) pepper, seeded and thinly sliced
2 tbsp water
3 spring onions (scallions), chopped

1 Mix the chicken, egg white and
2 teaspoons of the cornflour
(cornstarch) in a bowl. Let stand for
at least 30 minutes.

2 Blanch the noodles in boiling water
for 2 minutes, then drain. Heat the
vegetable oil in a preheated wok. Add
the noodles, spreading them to cover
the base. Cook over a low heat for
5 minutes, until browned on the
underside. Flip them over and brown
the other side. Remove from the wok
and keep warm. Drain the oil from
the wok.

3 Add 300 ml/½ pint/1¼ cups of the
stock to the wok, remove from the
heat and stir in the chicken. Return to
the heat and cook for 2 minutes.
Drain, discarding the stock.

4 Wipe the wok with kitchen paper
(paper towels) and return to the heat.

5 Add the wine or sherry, sauces,
(bell) pepper and the remaining
chicken stock. Bring to the boil. Blend
the remaining cornflour (cornstarch)
with the water to form a paste and stir
it into the mixture.

6 Return the chicken to the wok and
cook over a low heat for 2 minutes.

7 Put the noodles on top and sprinkle
with spring onions (scallions) and
serve immediately.

Pork Chow Mein

When time is short, serve this quick-and-easy dish with a green salad
for a delicious light lunch.

Serves 4
225 g/8 oz egg noodles
4–5 tbsp vegetable oil
225 g/8 oz cooked pork fillet (tenderloin)
115 g/4 oz French (green) beans
2 tbsp light soy sauce
1 tsp salt
1/2 tsp sugar
1 tbsp Chinese rice wine or dry sherry
2 spring onions (scallions), finely shredded
a few drops of sesame oil
chilli sauce, to serve (optional)

1 Cook the noodles in boiling water according to the instructions on the packet. Drain and rinse under cold water. Drain again then toss with 1 tablespoon of the oil.

2 Slice the pork into thin shreds. Top and tail the beans.

3 Heat 3 tablespoons of the vegetable oil in a preheated wok. Add the noodles and stir-fry for 2–3 minutes, together with 1 tablespoon of the soy sauce. Remove to a warm serving dish. Keep warm.

4 Heat the remaining vegetable oil in the wok. Add the beans and the pork and stir-fry for approximately 2 minutes. Add the salt, sugar, Chinese rice wine or sherry, the remaining soy sauce and about half the spring onions (scallions).

5 Blend the mixture thoroughly and add a little stock if necessary. Pour the mixture on top of the noodles and sprinkle with sesame oil and the remaining spring onions (scallions).

6 Serve immediately with chilli sauce, if using.

VARIATION

This chow mein can also be made with 225 g/8 oz shredded cooked chicken or turkey breast. It is especially tasty served cold as a salad.

Chilli Pork Noodles

This is quite a spicy dish, with a peanut flavour.
Alter the amount of chilli to your liking.

Serves 4
350 g/12 oz minced (ground) pork
1 tbsp light soy sauce
1 tbsp Chinese rice wine or dry sherry
350 g/12 oz egg noodles
2 tsp sesame oil
2 tbsp vegetable oil
2 garlic cloves, crushed
2 tsp grated fresh ginger root
2 fresh red chillies, sliced
1 red (bell) pepper, seeded and finely sliced
25 g/1 oz/$^1/_4$ cup unsalted peanuts
3 tbsp peanut butter
3 tbsp dark soy sauce
dash of chilli oil
300 ml/$^1/_2$ pint/1$^1/_4$ cups pork stock or Chinese Stock (see page 16)

1 Mix together the pork, light soy sauce and Chinese rice wine or sherry in a bowl. Cover and marinate for 30 minutes.

2 Meanwhile, cook the noodles in boiling water for 4 minutes. Drain and rinse in cold water. Drain well again and toss in the sesame oil.

3 Heat the oil in a preheated wok. Add the garlic, ginger, chillies and red (bell) pepper and stir-fry for about 30 seconds. Add the pork, together with the marinade. Continue cooking for 1 minute, stirring until the pork is sealed and lightly browned.

4 Add the peanuts, peanut butter, soy sauce, chilli oil and stock and cook for 2–3 minutes. Toss the noodles into the mixture and heat through. Transfer to a warm serving dish and serve immediately.

VARIATION

Minced (ground) chicken or lamb would also be excellent in this recipe instead of the pork.

Beef Chow Mein

Wafer-thin strips of lean steak are cooked with a colourful selection of vegetables and served with noodles in a rich sauce.

Serves 4

450 g/1 lb egg noodles
4 tbsp peanut oil
450 g/1 lb lean steak, cut into thin strips
2 garlic cloves, crushed
1 tsp grated fresh ginger root
1 green (bell) pepper, seeded and thinly sliced
1 carrot, thinly sliced
2 celery sticks, sliced
8 spring onions (scallions)
1 tsp dark brown sugar
1 tbsp Chinese rice wine or dry sherry
2 tbsp dark soy sauce
few drops chilli sauce

1 Cook the noodles in boiling salted water for 4–5 minutes. Drain, rinse under cold running water and drain thoroughly again. Toss them in 1 tablespoon of the oil.

2 Heat the remaining oil in a preheated wok. Add the strips of steak and stir-fry for 3–4 minutes, until browned and sealed. Add the garlic and ginger and stir-fry for a further 30 seconds.

3 Add the (bell) pepper, carrot, celery and spring onions (scallions) and stir-fry for 2 minutes.

4 Add the sugar, Chinese rice wine or sherry, soy sauce and the chilli sauce to taste and cook, stirring constantly, for 1 minute.

5 Stir in the noodles, mixing well, and cook until warmed through.

6 Transfer to a warm serving dish and serve immediately.

COOK'S VARIATION

Add drained canned straw mushrooms for extra texture.

Fried Noodles with Mushrooms & Pork

This dish benefits from the use of coloured oyster mushrooms.
If these are unavailable, plain grey mushrooms will suffice.

Serves 4
450 g/1 lb thin egg noodles
2 tbsp peanut oil
350 g/12 oz pork fillet (tenderloin), sliced
2 garlic cloves, crushed
1 onion, quartered
225 g/8 oz oyster mushrooms, torn into pieces
4 tomatoes, peeled, seeded and thinly sliced
2 tbsp light soy sauce
50 ml/2 fl oz/¼ cup pork stock or Chinese Stock (see page 16)
1 tbsp chopped fresh coriander (cilantro)

1 Cook the noodles in boiling water for 2–3 minutes. Drain, rinse under cold running water and drain thoroughly again.

2 Heat 1 tablespoon of the oil in a preheated wok. Add the noodles and stir-fry for 2 minutes. Remove from the wok with a slotted spoon and set aside.

3 Heat the remaining oil in the wok. Add the pork and stir-fry for about 4–5 minutes, until lightly coloured and sealed.

4 Stir the garlic and onion into the wok and stir-fry for a further 2–3 minutes.

5 Add the mushrooms, tomatoes, soy sauce and pork or Chinese stock.

6 Return the noodles to the wok. Stir well and cook for 1–2 minutes until heated through.

7 Transfer to a warm serving dish, sprinkle with coriander (cilantro) and serve immediately.

COOK'S TIP

For crisper noodles, fry them in 2 tablespoons oil for 5–6 minutes, spreading them thinly in the wok and turning half way through.

Lamb with Transparent (Cellophane) Noodles

Lamb is quick fried, coated in a soy sauce and served on a bed of transparent (cellophane) noodles for a richly flavoured dish.

Serves 4

150 g/5½ oz transparent (cellophane) noodles

450 g/1 lb boneless lean lamb, thinly sliced

2 tbsp peanut oil

2 garlic cloves, crushed

2 leeks, sliced

3 tbsp dark soy sauce

250 ml/9 fl oz/1 cup lamb stock

dash of chilli sauce

1 Bring a large pan of water to the boil. Add the noodles and cook for 1 minute. Drain well, rinse under cold running water and drain well again.

2 Heat the oil in a preheated wok. Add the lamb and stir-fry for 2 minutes. Add the garlic and leeks to the wok and stir-fry for a further 2 minutes.

3 Stir in the soy sauce, stock and chilli sauce and cook for 3–4 minutes, until the meat is cooked through.

4 Add the noodles and cook for 1 minute, until heated through. Serve immediately.

COOK'S TIP

Transparent (cellophane) noodles are available in Chinese foodstores. If they are unavailable, use egg noodles instead, and cook them according to the packet instructions.

Desserts

Family meals in China usually end with fresh fruit. Desserts are served only at banquets and on very special occasions, although sweet snacks are often nibbled between meal times. Nevertheless, when Chinese cooks do prepare a dish for the sweet-toothed, at the New Year festival, for example, there are no half measures.

Just as northern China is well known

for wontons and dumplings containing a melt-in-the mouth savoury filling, it is also famous for wonderfully self-indulgent parcels of sweetly spiced dried or fresh fruit. Rice, too, is used for preparing desserts, often pressed into a mould and concealing a delicious surprise in the centre. Cutting the first slice from Sweet Rice is truly a revelation. However, fruit reigns supreme and, with such a vast choice available, this is hardly surprising. Try Mango Mousse or Ginger Lychees with Orange Sorbet.

Sweet Fruit Wontons

Sweet wontons are very adaptable and may be filled with whole, small fruits or a spicy chopped mixture, as in this recipe.

Serves 4
12 wonton wrappers
oil, for deep-frying
2 tbsp clear honey

FILLING

175 g/6 oz/1 cup chopped. dried, stoned (pitted) dates
2 tsp dark brown sugar
¹/₂ tsp ground cinnamon
2 tsp cornflour (cornstarch)
6 tsp cold water

1 First start making the filling. Mix together the chopped dates, sugar and cinnamon in a bowl.

2 Spread out the wonton wrappers on a chopping board and spoon a little of the filling into the centre of each wrapper.

3 Mix together the cornflour (cornstarch) and water and brush this around the edges of the wrappers.

4 Fold the wrappers over the filling, bringing the edges together, then bring the two corners together, sealing with the cornflour (cornstarch) mixture.

5 Heat the oil for deep-frying in a wok to 180°C/350°F, or until a cube of stale bread browns in 30 seconds. Fry the wontons, in batches, for about 2–3 minutes, until golden. Remove from the oil with a slotted spoon and drain on absorbent kitchen paper (paper towels).

6 Place the honey in a bowl and stand it in warm water until it has become quite runny.

7 Drizzle the honey over the wontons, transfer to a serving dish and serve immediately.

COOK'S TIP

Wonton wrappers may be found in Chinese supermarkets. Alternatively, make the dough as described for Wonton Soup (see page 60).

Banana Pastries

These pastries require a little time to prepare, but are well worth the effort.
A sweet banana filling is wrapped in dough and baked.

Serves 4
DOUGH
450 g/1 lb/4 cups plain (all-purpose) flour
50 g/1³⁄₄ oz/4 tbsp lard (shortening)
50 g/1³⁄₄ oz/4 tbsp unsalted (sweet) butter
125 ml/4 fl oz/¹⁄₂ cup water
FILLING
2 large bananas
75 g/2³⁄₄ oz/¹⁄₃ cup finely chopped no-need-to-soak dried apricots
pinch of nutmeg
dash of orange juice
1 egg yolk, beaten
icing (confectioner's) sugar, for dusting

Pinch the edges together and seal by pressing with the prongs of a fork.

4 Arrange the pastries on a non-stick baking sheet (cookie sheet) and brush with the beaten egg. Cut a small slit in each pastry and cook in a preheated oven at 180°C/350°F/Gas 4 for 25 minutes, or until golden brown.

5 Dust with icing (confectioner's) sugar and serve with cream or ice cream.

1 First make the dough. Sift the flour into a large mixing bowl. Add the lard (shortening) and butter and rub into the flour with the fingertips until the mixture resembles breadcrumbs. Gradually blend in the water to make a soft dough. Wrap in clear film (plastic wrap) and chill in the refrigerator for 30 minutes.

2 Mash the bananas in a bowl with a fork and stir in the apricots, nutmeg and orange juice, mixing well.

3 Roll the dough out on a lightly floured surface and cut out 16 x 10-cm/4-inch rounds. Spoon a little of the banana filling on to one half of each round and fold the dough over the filling to make semi-circles.

Mango Dumplings

Fresh mango and canned lychees fill these small steamed dumplings,
making a really colourful and tasty treat.

Serves 4
DOUGH
150 ml/¼ pint/⅔ cup milk
150 ml/¼ pint/⅔ cup water
2 tsp baking powder
1 tbsp caster (superfine) sugar
400 g/14 oz/3¼ cups plain (all-purpose) flour
1 small mango
115 g/4 oz can lychees, drained
1 tbsp ground almonds
4 tbsp orange juice
ground cinnamon and icing (confectioners') sugar, for dusting

1 Mix together the water and milk
and stir into the baking powder and
sugar in a mixing bowl. Gradually stir
in the flour to make a soft dough. Set
aside in a warm place for 1 hour.

2 Peel the mango and cut the flesh
from the stone (pit). Roughly chop
and reserve half. Chop the lychees
and add to half the chopped mango,
together with the ground almonds.
Let stand for 20 minutes.

3 Meanwhile, blend the remaining
mango, together with the orange
juice, in a food processor until
smooth. Press through a plastic
strainer to make a smooth sauce.

4 Divide the dough into 16 equal
pieces. Roll each piece out on a lightly
floured surface into 7.5-cm/ 3-inch
rounds. Spoon a little of the mango
and lychee mixture on to the centre
of each round and bring the dough up

around the fruit to the top, and pinch
together to make "purses".

5 Place the mango and lychee
dumplings in a single layer on a
heatproof plate in a steamer, cover

and steam for about 20–25 minutes,
until cooked through.

6 Remove from the steamer, dust
with cinnamon and sugar and serve
with the mango sauce.

Sweet Rice

This dessert is served at banquets and celebratory meals
in China, as it looks wonderful when sliced.

Serves 4
175 g/6 oz/³/₄ cup pudding rice
25 g/1 oz/2 tbsp unsalted (sweet) butter
1 tbsp caster (superfine) sugar
8 dried dates, pitted and chopped
1 tbsp raisins
5 walnut halves
5 glacé (candied) cherries, halved
5 pieces angelica, chopped
115 g/4 oz/¹/₂ cup canned chestnut purée

SYRUP

4¹/₂ tsp light brown sugar
150 ml/¹/₄ pint/²/₃ cup water
2 tbsp orange juice
1¹/₂ tsp cornflour (cornstarch)

1 Put the rice in a saucepan and cover with cold water. Bring to the boil, cover and simmer for 15 minutes, until the water has been absorbed. Stir in the butter and sugar.

2 Lightly grease a 600-ml/1-pint/2½-cup pudding basin (ovenproof bowl). Cover the base and sides with a thin layer of the rice, pressing it on with the back of a spoon.

3 Mix the fruit and nuts together and press them into the rice, again using the back of a spoon.

4 Spread a thicker layer of rice over this and fill the centre with the chestnut purée. Cover with the remaining rice, pressing it down.

5 Cover the basin (bowl) with pleated greaseproof (wax) paper and foil.

Secure with string. Place in a steamer or stand it in a pan and add hot water until it reaches halfway up the sides. Cover and steam for 45 minutes. Let stand for 10 minutes.

6 Before serving, dissolve the sugar for the syrup in the water and orange juice over a gentle heat. Bring to the boil. Blend the cornflour (cornstarch) to a smooth paste with 1 tbsp of cold water and stir into the boiling syrup. Cook for 1 minute until thickened.

7 Turn out the pudding. Pour the syrup over the top and serve.

Honeyed Rice Puddings

These small rice puddings are quite sweet, but have a wonderful flavour because of the combination of ginger, honey and cinnamon.

Serves 4
300 g/10¹/₂ oz/1¹/₂ cups pudding rice
2 tbsp clear honey
large pinch of ground cinnamon
3 pieces stem (preserved) ginger, drained and chopped
15 no-need to soak dried apricots, chopped
honey, for drizzling

1 Put the rice in a saucepan and add just enough cold water to cover. Bring to the boil, reduce the heat, cover and cook for 15 minutes, or until the water has been absorbed.

2 Stir the honey and cinnamon into the rice.

3 Lightly grease 4 x 150-ml/¹/₄-pint/²/₃-cup ramekin dishes.

4 Put the apricots and ginger in a food processor and process to make a paste. Divide the paste into 4 equal portions and shape each into a flat round to fit into the circumference of the ramekin dishes.

5 Divide half the rice among the ramekins and place the apricot paste on top.

6 Cover the apricot mixture with the remaining rice. Cover the ramekins with greaseproof (wax) paper and foil. Place the ramekins in a steamer and steam for 30 minutes, or until set.

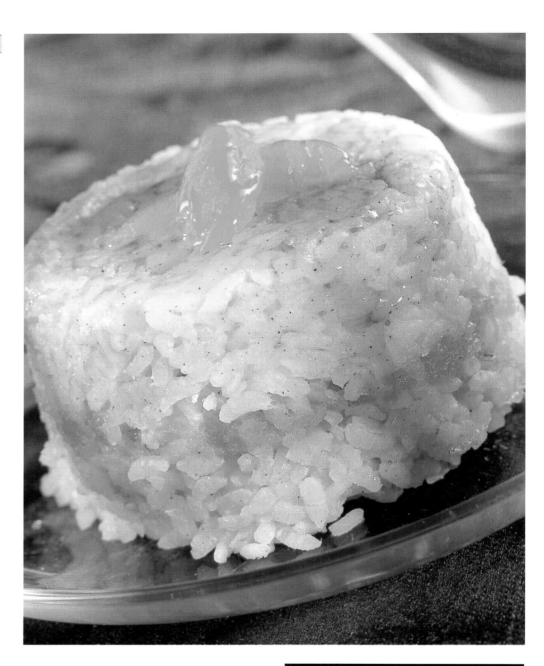

7 Remove the ramekins from the steamer and let stand for 5 minutes.

8 Turn the puddings out on to warm serving plates and drizzle with clear honey. Serve immediately.

COOK'S TIP

The puddings may be chilled in their dishes, turned out and served with ice cream or cream.

Mango Mousse

This is a light, softly set and tangy mousse, which is perfect
for clearing the palate after a meal of mixed flavours.

Serves 4

400 g/14 oz can mangoes in syrup
2 pieces stem (preserved) ginger, chopped
200 ml/7 fl oz/1 cup double (heavy) cream
20 g/³/₄ oz/4 tsp powdered gelatine
2 tbsp water
2 egg whites
1¹/₂ tbsp light brown sugar
chopped mango and stem (preserved) ginger, to decorate

6 Beat the sugar into the egg whites
and then gently fold into the mango
and cream mixture with a metal spoon.

7 Spoon the mousse into individual
serving dishes and decorate with
chopped mango and stem (preserved)
ginger. Serve immediately.

COOK'S TIP

The gelatine must be stirred into
the mango mixture in a gentle
stream to prevent it from setting in
lumps when it comes into contact
with the cold mixture.

1 Drain the mangoes, reserving the
syrup. Put the mango pieces and
ginger in a food processor or blender
and process for 30 seconds, or until a
smooth purée. Measure the quantity
of purée and make up to 300 ml/
¹/₂ pint/1¹/₄ cups with the reserved
mango syrup. Place the mango
mixture in a measuring jug.

2 In a separate bowl, whip the cream
until it forms soft peaks.

3 Carefully fold the mango mixture
into the whipped cream until fully
combined.

4 Dissolve the gelatine in the water,
cool slightly and pour it into the
mango and cream mixture in a steady
stream, stirring constantly. Leave to
chill in the refrigerator for about 30
minutes, until almost set.

5 Beat the egg whites in a clean bowl
until they form peaks.

Poached Allspice Pears

These pears are moist and delicious after poaching in a sugar and allspice mixture.
They are wonderful served hot or cold.

Serves 4
4 large, ripe pears
300 ml/^{1}/$_2$ pint/1^1/$_4$ cups orange juice
2 tsp ground allspice
50 g/1^3/$_4$ oz/^{1}/$_3$ cup raisins
2 tbsp light brown sugar

1 Peel, core and halve the pears.

2 Place the pear halves in a wok, together with the orange juice, allspice, raisins and sugar. Heat gently to dissolve the sugar.

3 Once the sugar has dissolved, bring the mixture to the boil for 1 minute.

4 Reduce the heat to low and simmer for 10 minutes, until the pears are cooked, but still fairly firm – test by inserting the tip of a knife.

5 Serve the pears hot with the syrup or cool and chill in the refrigerator before serving cold.

VARIATION

Use cinnamon instead of the allspice and decorate with cinnamon sticks and mint sprigs.

Chinese Custard Tarts

These small tarts are irresistible – a custard is baked in a rich, sweet pastry.
The tarts may be served warm or cold.

Makes 15

DOUGH

175 g/6 oz/1^1/$_2$ cups plain
(all-purpose) flour

3 tbsp caster (superfine) sugar

50 g/1^3/$_4$ oz/4 tbsp unsalted
(sweet) butter

25 g/1 oz/2 tbsp lard
(shortening)

2 tbsp water

CUSTARD

2 small eggs, separated

50 g/1^3/$_4$ oz/^{1}/$_4$ cup caster
(superfine) sugar

175 ml/6 fl oz/^{3}/$_4$ cup pint milk

^{1}/$_2$ tsp ground nutmeg

nutmeg, for sprinkling

cream, to serve

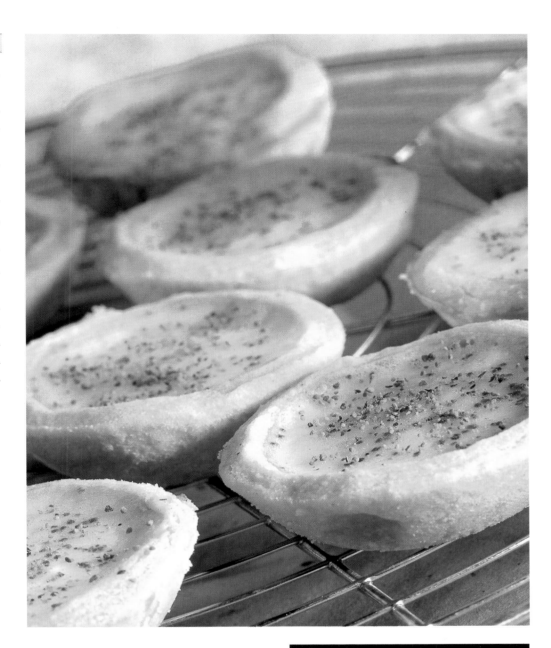

1 First make the pastry. Sift the flour into a bowl, add the sugar and rub in the butter and lard (shortening) until the mixture resembles breadcrumbs. Mix in the water to make a firm dough.

2 Transfer the dough to a lightly floured surface and knead for 5 minutes, until smooth. Cover with clear film (plastic wrap) and chill in the refrigerator while you are preparing the filling.

3 Beat the eggs and sugar together and gradually beat in the milk. Add the nutmeg.

4 Separate the dough into 15 even-size pieces. Flatten into rounds and press into shallow patty tins (pans).

5 Spoon the custard into the pastry cases (tart shells) and cook in a preheated oven at 150°C/300°F/Gas 2 for 25–30 minutes. Cool slightly before removing from the tins (pans). Transfer to a wire rack and sprinkle with nutmeg. Serve with cream.

COOK'S TIP

Make the dough in advance, cover and chill in the refrigerator until required. Make the custard filling and continue from step 5.

Ginger Lychees With Orange Sorbet

This dish is truly delicious. The fresh flavour of the sorbet
perfectly complements the spicy lychees.

Serves 4
SORBET
225 g/8 oz/¼ cups caster (superfine) sugar
450 ml/16 fl oz/2 cups cold water
350 g/12 oz can mandarins in natural juice
2 tbsp lemon juice
STUFFED LYCHEES
425 g/15 oz can lychees, drained
50 g/1¾ oz stem (preserved) ginger, drained
lime zest, cut into diamond shapes, to decorate

1 First make the sorbet. Place the sugar and water in a saucepan. Using a wooden spoon, stir over a low heat until the sugar has dissolved. Bring to the boil and boil vigorously for 2–3 minutes.

2 Meanwhile, process the mandarins in a food processor or blender until smooth, or press through a plastic strainer to make a smooth paste. Stir into the syrup, together with the lemon juice. Set aside to cool.

3 Pour the mixture into a rigid, plastic container suitable for the freezer and freeze until set, stirring from time to time.

4 Meanwhile, drain the lychees on absorbent kitchen paper (paper towels). Finely chop the ginger and

spoon into the centre of the lychees to stuff them.

5 Arrange the lychees on to serving plates and serve with scoops of the orange sorbet, decorated with lime zest.

COOK'S TIP

Let the sorbet stand in the refrigerator for 10 minutes before scooping to serve.

Chinese Fruit Salad

The syrup for this colourful dish is filled with
Chinese flavours for a refreshing dessert.

Serves 4
75 ml/3 fl oz Chinese rice wine or dry sherry
rind and juice of 1 lemon
850 ml/1½ pints water
225 g/8 oz caster (superfine) sugar
2 cloves
2.5-cm/1-inch piece cinnamon stick, bruised
1 vanilla pod (bean)
pinch of mixed (apple pie) spice
1 star anise pod
2.5-cm/1-inch piece fresh ginger root, sliced
50 g/1¾ oz unsalted cashew nuts
2 kiwi fruits, halved and sliced
1 star fruit, sliced
400 g/14 oz can lychees in syrup, drained
115 g/4 oz strawberries, hulled and sliced
1 piece stem (preserved) ginger, drained and sliced
chopped mint, to decorate

1 Put the Chinese rice wine or sherry,
lemon rind and juice and water in a
saucepan. Add the sugar, cloves,
cinnamon, vanilla pod (bean), mixed
(apple pie) spice, star anise and fresh
ginger root.

2 Heat gently, stirring constantly,
until the sugar has dissolved and then
bring to the boil. Reduce the heat and
simmer for 5 minutes. Set aside to
cool completely.

3 Strain the syrup, discarding the
flavourings. Stir in the cashew nuts,
cover and chill.

4 Prepare the fruits and spoon into a
dish. Pour the syrup over them,
decorate with chopped mint and serve.

COOK'S TIP

Make the syrup in advance, cover
and chill in the refrigerator
overnight before straining, for a
fuller flavour.

Index

A

alcoholic drinks 19
allspice pears, poached 248
almonds:
  broccoli, (bell) pepper &
    almond salad 53
  chicken soup with almonds 77
  crisp fried pak choi &
    almonds 195
appetizers 21-43
aromatic & crispy duck 127
aubergines (eggplants):
  aubergine in black bean
    sauce 186
  aubergine in chilli sauce 184
  fish, aubergine & pork 157
  spicy aubergines 185

B

bacon
  Chinese fried rice 204
baked crab with ginger 102
bamboo shoots 12
  bamboo shoots with
    green vegetables 166
  braised bamboo shoots 164
  golden needles with
    bamboo shoots 165
  noodles in soup 63
  pork dim sum 36
  pot sticker dumplings 40
banana pastries 243
bang-bang chicken 119
barbecue pork (char siu) 39
barbecue spare ribs 37
basil 12
bean curd see tofu
bean sauce 12
beansprouts 12
  beansprouts with
    (bell) peppers 170
  chicken chop suey 122
  chicken with beansprouts 109
  Chinese chicken salad 108
  Chinese fried rice 204
  Chinese hot salad 48
  chow mein 222
  crab fried rice 217
  cucumber & beansprout salad 52
  egg fu yong with rice 210
  Oriental salad 49
  rice with crab & mussels 218
  Singapore-style rice noodles 231
  special fried rice 211
  spring rolls 25
  stir-fried beansprouts 169

vegetable chop suey 160
beef 133
  beef & chilli black bean
    sauce 144
  beef & green beans 145
  beef & pak choi 142
  beef & vegetable noodle soup 62
  beef chow mein 237
  (bell) peppered beef cashew 146
  Cantonese fried noodles 232
  Chinese beef 147
  crispy shredded beef 148
  Ma-Po tofu (bean curd) 176
  oyster sauce beef 141
  red spiced beef 153
  spicy beef & broccoli stir-fry 143
bell peppers see peppers
black bean sauce:
  aubergine (eggplant) in
    black bean sauce 186
  beef & chilli black bean
    sauce 144
  fish with black bean sauce 83
  fried squid flowers 104
  spare ribs with chilli 150
  tofu (bean curd) & vegetables
    with black bean sauce 177
  vegetables in black bean
    sauce 172
black beans 12
bok choy see pak choi
braised bamboo shoots 164
braised chicken 115
braised Chinese leaves
  (cabbage) 190
braised fish fillets 85
braised pork & tofu (bean curd) 156
braised vegetables with tofu
  (bean curd) 183
braising 15
bread:
  sesame prawn (shrimp) toasts 33
broccoli:
  broccoli, (bell) pepper & almond
    salad 53
  broccoli in oyster sauce 198
  broccoli with ginger &
    orange 196
  clear chicken & egg soup 76
  fried prawns (shrimp) with
    cashews 101
  gingered broccoli 197
  peanut sesame chicken 114
  spicy beef & broccoli stir-fry 143
  stir-fried duck with broccoli &
    (bell) peppers 126
butterfly prawns (shrimp) 32

C

cabbage:
  Cantonese fried noodles 232
  steamed cabbage rolls 28
  see also Chinese leaves
Cantonese cooking 10
Cantonese fried noodles 232
Cantonese prawns (shrimp) 99
cardamom 12
carp:
  fish in Szechuan hot sauce 87
carrots:
  Chinese hot salad 48
  flowers 17
  (small) shrimp fu yong 97
cashew nuts 12
  (bell) peppered beef cashew 146
  chicken with cashew nuts &
    vegetables 111
  chicken with celery &
    cashew nuts 125
  fried prawns (shrimp) with
    cashews 101
  Kung Po chicken with cashew
    nuts 110
  sizzled chilli prawns (shrimp) 95
  special fried rice with cashew
    nuts 215
casseroles:
  chicken & rice casserole 214
  vegetable & tofu (bean curd)
    casserole 179
  vegetable casserole 162
cauliflower:
  duck in spicy sauce 128
celery:
  chicken with celery & cashew
    nuts 125
  red spiced beef 153
cellophane noodles see noodles
char siu 39
Chekiang cooking 10
chestnut purée:
  sweet rice 245
chicken 107
  bang-bang chicken 119
  braised chicken 115
  chicken & rice casserole 214
  chicken & sweetcorn (corn)
    soup 75
  chicken chop suey 122
  chicken fu yong 118
  chicken noodles 233
  chicken on crispy noodles 234
  chicken soup with almonds 77
  chicken with beansprouts 109
  chicken with (bell) pepper 116

chicken with cashew nuts &
    vegetables 111
  chicken with celery & cashew
    nuts 125
  chicken with mushrooms 123
  chicken with yellow bean
    sauce 113
  chilli chicken 120
  Chinese chicken salad 108
  Chinese omelette 42
  Chinese stock 16
  clear chicken & egg soup 76
  crispy chicken 124
  curried chicken & sweetcorn
    (corn) soup 71
  honeyed chicken wings 43
  Kung Po chicken with cashew
    nuts 110
  lemon chicken 112
  noodles in soup 63
  peanut sesame chicken 114
  pot sticker dumplings 40
  Singapore-style rice noodles 231
  spicy peanut chicken 117
  steamed cabbage rolls 28
  Szechuan chilli chicken 121
  three-flavour soup 70
  transparent (cellophane) noodles
    with yellow bean sauce 225
chilli bean paste 12
chilli oil 12
  pork with chilli & garlic sauce 35
chilli powder:
  red spiced beef 153
chilli sauce 12
  aubergine (eggplant) in chilli
    sauce 184
  sweet & sour prawns (shrimp)
    with chilli 98
chillies 12
  bamboo shoots with green
    vegetables 166
  beansprouts with (bell)
    peppers 170
  beef & chilli black bean
    sauce 144
  braised Chinese leaves
    (cabbage) 190
  braised pork & tofu
    (bean curd) 156
  chicken with (bell) pepper 116
  chilli chicken 120
  chilli pork noodles 236
  Chinese green bean stir-fry 174
  Chinese potato sticks 201
  crispy fish with chillies 84
  crispy shredded beef 148
  egg fried rice with chilli 208

flowers 17
  hot & sour duck salad 51
  hot lamb 135
  Kung Po chicken with cashew
    nuts 110
  Singapore-style rice noodles 231
  sizzled chilli prawns (shrimp) 95
  spare ribs with chilli 150
  spicy peanut chicken 117
  stir-fried cucumber with ginger &
    chilli 168
  Szechuan chilli chicken 121
  Szechuan prawns (shrimp) 94
Chinese beef 147
Chinese braised vegetables 167
Chinese cabbage
  see Chinese leaves
Chinese chicken salad 108
Chinese custard tarts 249
Chinese five-spice powder 12
  deep-fried tofu (bean curd) with
    Chinese five spice 182
  five-spiced lamb 138
Chinese fried rice 204
Chinese fruit salad 251
Chinese green bean stir-fry 174
Chinese greens see pak choi
Chinese hot salad 48
Chinese leaves (cabbage) 12
  braised Chinese leaves 190
  Chinese cabbage soup 59
  Chinese leaves stir-fried in soy
    & honey 193
  Chinese ravioli 30
  creamy cabbage and leeks 191
  lamb meatballs in soy sauce 134
  lemon Chinese leaves 192
  Oriental salad 49
  Peking duck soup 74
  steamed vegetable cabbage
    rolls 189
  pork pancake rolls 26
Chinese omelette 42
Chinese pancakes 12
Chinese potato sticks 201
Chinese ravioli 30
Chinese stock 16
chives:
  Chinese omelette 42
chop suey 109
  chicken 122
  vegetable 160
chopping 15
chopsticks 14
chow mein 222
  beef 237
  mixed vegetable 224
  pork 235
  seafood 228
cilantro 12
clear chicken & egg soup 76
cleavers 14
cloud ears see wood ears
collard greens see spring greens
cooking techniques 15
coriander (cilantro) 12
corn cobs 12
  beef & pak choi 142

Chinese beef 147
curried chicken & sweetcorn
  (corn) soup 71
peanut sesame chicken 114
  see also sweetcorn
cornflour (cornstarch) paste 16
courgettes (zucchini):
  Chinese hot salad 48
crabmeat:
  baked crab with ginger 102
  Chinese ravioli 30
  crab & ginger soup 69
  crab fried rice 217
  rice with crab & mussels 218
  sweetcorn (corn) & crabmeat
    soup 73
creamy cabbage and leeks 191
crisp fried pak choi & almonds 195
crispy chicken 124
crispy fish with chillies 84
crispy seaweed 23
crispy shredded beef 148
crispy wontons with piquant
  dipping sauce 22
cucumber:
  bang-bang chicken 119
  cucumber & beansprout salad 52
  fans 17
  mushroom & cucumber noodle
    soup 64
  pickled cucumber 50
  prawn (shrimp) stir-fry with
    lemon grass 96
  stir-fried cucumber with ginger
    & chilli 168
  stir-fried mushrooms,
    cucumber & smoked tofu
    (bean curd) 181
  sweet & sour cucumber 47
curries:
  curried chicken & sweetcorn
    (corn) soup 71
  curried prawn (shrimp)
    noodles 229
custard tarts, Chinese 249

D

dates:
  sweet fruit wontons 242
  sweet rice 245
deep-fried pork with a soy dipping
  sauce 151
deep-fried prawns (shrimp) 31
deep-fried spare ribs 34
deep-fried tofu (bean curd) with
  Chinese five spice 182
deep-frying 15
desserts 241-51
dim sum, pork 36
dipping sauces 17
drinks:
  alcoholic 19
  tea 18
duck 107
  aromatic & crispy duck 127
  duck in spicy sauce 128
  duck with mangoes 131

duck with pineapple 130
honey & soy glazed duck 129
hot & sour duck salad 51
Peking duck soup 74
steamed duck buns 41
stir-fried duck with broccoli &
  (bell) peppers 126
dumplings:
  mango dumplings 244
  money bags 188
  pot sticker dumplings 40
  (small) shrimp dumpling
    soup 67
  steamed duck buns 41

E

Eastern Chinese cooking 10
egg noodles see noodles
eggplants see aubergines
eggs:
  Cantonese prawns (shrimp) 99
  chicken fu yong 118
  Chinese fried rice 204
  Chinese omelette 42
  clear chicken & egg soup 76
  egg fried rice 209
  egg fried rice with chilli 208
  egg fu yong with rice 210
  (small) shrimp fu yong 97
equipment 14

F

fennel:
  hot lamb 135
fish & seafood 81-105
  braised fish fillets 85
  crispy fish with chillies 84
  fish & ginger stir-fry 105
  fish & vegetable soup 68
  fish in Szechuan hot sauce 87
  fish soup with wontons 65
  fish with black bean sauce 83
  mullet with ginger 86
  seafood combination 93
  steamed snapper with fruit &
    ginger stuffing 88
  trout with pineapple 82
fish, aubergine (eggplant) &
  pork 157
fish-flavoured shredded pork 152
fish sauce:
  hot & sour duck salad 51
five-spiced lamb 138
flowers, vegetable garnishes 17
fragrant steamed rice in lotus
  leaves 206
French (green) beans:
  beef & green beans 145
  Chinese green bean stir-fry 174
  Chinese hot salad 48
  five-spiced lamb 138
fried noodles with mushrooms
  & pork 238
fried prawns (shrimp) with
  cashews 101
fried rice & prawns (shrimp) 216

fried rice with pork, tomatoes,
  peas & mushrooms 219
fried rice with prawns
  (shrimp) 212
fried squid flowers 104
fried vegetable noodles 223
fruit:
  Chinese fruit salad 251
  see also lychees, mangoes etc
fu yong:
  chicken 118
  egg with rice 210
  (small) shrimp 97
Fukien cooking 10

G

garlic 12
  Cantonese prawns (shrimp) 99
  creamy cabbage and leeks 191
  garlic spinach 199
  lamb in garlic sauce 140
  lamb in mushroom sauce 139
  lamb meatballs in soy sauce 134
  pork with chilli & garlic sauce 35
garnishes 17
ginger 12
  baked crab with ginger 102
  braised bamboo shoots 164
  broccoli with ginger &
    orange 196
  crab & ginger soup 69
  fish & ginger stir-fry 105
  ginger lychees with orange
    sorbet 250
  gingered broccoli 197
  honeyed rice puddings 246
  lamb & ginger stir-fry 136
  mullet with ginger 86
  scallops in ginger sauce 89
  steamed snapper with fruit &
    ginger stuffing 88
  stir-fried cucumber with ginger
    & chilli 168
golden needles with bamboo
  shoots 165
green beans see French beans
green fried rice with spinach 207

H

ham:
  special fried rice 211
  three-flavour soup 70
hoi-sin sauce 13
  spicy spare ribs 38
homemade noodles with stir-fried
  vegetables 226
Honan cooking 10
honey:
  Chinese leaves (cabbage)
    stir-fried in soy & honey 193
  crispy chicken 124
  deep-fried pork with a soy
    dipping sauce 151
  honey & soy glazed duck 129
  honeyed chicken wings 43
  honeyed rice puddings 246

sweet & sour cucumber 47
hot & sour duck salad 51
hot & sour soup 57
    vegetarian hot & sour soup 58
hot lamb 135

I

ingredients 12-13

K

Kiangsu cooking 10
Kung Po chicken with cashew
    nuts 110

L

lamb 133
    five-spiced lamb 138
    hot lamb 135
    lamb & ginger stir-fry 136
    lamb & rice soup 78
    lamb in garlic sauce 140
    lamb in mushroom sauce 139
    lamb meatballs in soy sauce 134
    lamb with transparent
        (cellophane) noodles 239
    stir-fried lamb with sesame
        seeds 137
leeks:
    creamy cabbage and leeks 191
    deep-fried tofu (bean curd) with
        Chinese five spice 182
    lamb with transparent
        (cellophane) noodles 239
lemon:
    lemon chicken 112
    lemon Chinese leaves 192
lemon grass 13
    prawn (shrimp) stir-fry with
        lemon grass 96
lentil balls with sweet &
    sour sauce 194
lettuce-wrapped minced (ground)
    meat 27
lily buds 13
lotus leaves 13
    fragrant steamed rice in lotus
        leaves 206
lychees:
    ginger lychees with orange
        sorbet 250
    mango dumplings 244

M

Ma-Po tofu (bean curd) 176
mandarins:
    ginger lychees with orange
        sorbet 250
mangetout (snow peas) 13
    beef & pak choi 142
    lamb & ginger stir-fry 136
    Oriental salad 49
    spiced scallops 90
mangoes:
    duck with mangoes 131

mango dumplings 244
mango mousse 247
Mao Tai 19
marmalade:
    sweet & sour sauce 17
meals 11
meat 133-57
    see also beef, pork etc
meatballs:
    lamb meatballs in soy sauce 134
    spinach meatballs 24
mixed pickled vegetables 50
mixed vegetable chow mein 224
mixed vegetable soup 56
money bags 188
mousse, mango 247
mullet with ginger 86
mushrooms 13
    chicken with mushrooms 123
    fried noodles with mushrooms
        & pork 238
    fried rice with pork, tomatoes,
        peas & mushrooms 219
    fried rice with prawns
        (shrimp) 212
    lamb & ginger stir-fry 136
    lamb in mushroom sauce 139
    money bags 188
    mushroom & cucumber noodle
        soup 64
    prawn (shrimp) stir-fry with
        lemon grass 96
    spiced scallops 90
    spicy mushrooms 187
    spinach with straw
        mushrooms 200
    stir-fried mushrooms,
        cucumber & smoked tofu
        (bean curd) 181
mussels:
    rice with crab & mussels 218

N

noodles 13, 221-39
    beef & vegetable noodle soup 62
    beef chow mein 237
    Cantonese fried noodles 232
    chicken noodles 233
    chicken on crispy noodles 234
    chilli pork noodles 236
    chow mein 222
    curried prawn (shrimp)
        noodles 229
    fried noodles with mushrooms &
        pork 238
    fried vegetable noodles 223
    homemade noodles with
        stir-fried vegetables 226
    lamb with transparent
        (cellophane) noodles 239
    mixed vegetable chow mein 224
    mushroom & cucumber noodle
        soup 64
    noodles in soup 63
    noodles with prawns
        (shrimp) 230
    pork chow mein 235

seafood chow mein 228
    Singapore-style rice noodles 231
    transparent (cellophane) noodles
        with prawns (shrimp) 227
    transparent (cellophane) noodles
        with yellow bean sauce 225
    vegetable & nut stir-fry 173
    vegetable & tofu (bean curd)
        casserole 179
Northern Chinese cooking 10

O

omelette, Chinese 42
orange:
    broccoli with ginger &
        orange 196
    Chinese leaves (cabbage)
        stir-fried in soy & honey 193
    ginger lychees with orange
        sorbet 250
    Oriental salad 49
    peanut sesame chicken 114
    poached allspice pears 248
    steamed snapper with fruit &
        ginger stuffing 88
    transparent (cellophane) noodles
        with prawns (shrimp) 227
Oriental salad 49
oyster sauce 13
    broccoli in oyster sauce 198
    chicken on crispy noodles 234
    oyster sauce beef 141
    squid in oyster sauce &
        vegetables 103

P

pak choi 13
    beef & pak choi 142
    crisp fried pak choi &
        almonds 195
    stir-fried greens 175
pancakes:
    aromatic & crispy duck 127
    pork pancake rolls 26
paprika:
    red spiced beef 153
pastries, banana 243
peanut butter:
    vegetable & nut stir-fry 173
peanuts:
    peanut sesame chicken 114
    spicy peanut chicken 117
    vegetable & nut stir-fry 173
pears:
    poached allspice pears 248
peas:
    chicken fu yong 118
    Chinese fried rice 204
    egg fried rice 209
    fried rice with pork, tomatoes,
        peas & mushrooms 219
    special fried rice with prawns
        (shrimp) 213
Peking duck soup 74
peppercorns
    see Szechuan peppercorns

peppers (bell):
    beansprouts with peppers 170
    beef & pak choi 142
    (bell) peppered beef cashew 146
    braised bamboo shoots 164
    broccoli, pepper & almond
        salad 53
    chicken on crispy noodles 234
    chicken with pepper 116
    chilli chicken 120
    Chinese chicken salad 108
    Chinese fried rice 204
    Chinese hot salad 48
    Chinese ravioli 30
    five-spiced lamb 138
    fried prawns (shrimp) with
        cashews 101
    fried squid flowers 104
    golden needles with bamboo
        shoots 165
    lentil balls with sweet & sour
        sauce 194
    peanut sesame chicken 114
    pot sticker dumplings 40
    seafood combination 93
    spicy peanut chicken 117
    stir-fried duck with broccoli &
        peppers 126
    transparent (cellophane) noodles
        with prawns (shrimp) 227
pickles 45
    mixed pickled vegetables 50
    pickled cucumber 50
pine nuts:
    spinach with straw
        mushrooms 200
pineapple:
    duck with pineapple 130
    lentil balls with sweet & sour
        sauce 194
    trout with pineapple 82
piquant dipping sauce 22
plum sauce 13
    pork with plum sauce 154
poached allspice pears 248
pork 133
    barbecue pork (char siu) 39
    barbecue spare ribs 37
    braised pork & tofu
        (bean curd) 156
    Cantonese prawns (shrimp) 99
    chilli pork noodles 236
    Chinese stock 16
    deep-fried pork with a soy
        dipping sauce 151
    deep-fried spare ribs 34
    fish, aubergine (eggplant) &
        pork 157
    fish-flavoured shredded
        pork 152
    fried noodles with mushrooms &
        pork 238
    fried rice with pork, tomatoes,
        peas & mushrooms 219
    hot & sour soup 57
    lettuce-wrapped minced
        (ground) meat 27
    pork & Szechuan vegetable

soup 79
pork chow mein 235
pork dim sum 36
pork pancake rolls 26
pork with chilli & garlic sauce 35
pork with plum sauce 154
(small) shrimp dumpling
soup 67
spare ribs with chilli 150
spicy spare ribs 38
spinach meatballs 24
stir-fried pork with
vegetables 155
sweet & sour pork 149
pot sticker dumplings 40
potatoes:
Chinese potato sticks 201
poultry 107-31
prawns (shrimp):
butterfly prawns 32
Cantonese prawns 99
Chinese omelette 42
curried prawn noodles 229
deep-fried prawns 31
fish soup with wontons 65
fried prawns with cashews 101
fried rice with prawns 212, 216
noodles with prawns 230
prawn crackers 17
prawn soup 72
prawn stir-fry with lemon
grass 96
rice paper parcels 29
seafood combination 93
sesame prawn toasts 33
Singapore-style rice noodles 231
sizzled chilli prawns 95
special fried rice 211
special fried rice with
prawns 213
steamed cabbage rolls 28
stir-fried prawns 92
stir-fried prawns & vegetables 91
sweet & sour prawns 100
sweet & sour prawns with
chilli 98
Szechuan prawns 94
three-flavour soup 70
transparent (cellophane)
noodles with prawns 227

R
radishes:
flowers 17
roses 17
ravioli, Chinese 30
red spiced beef 153
rice 13, 203-19
chicken & rice casserole 214
Chinese fried rice 204
crab fried rice 217
egg fried rice 209
egg fried rice with chilli 208
egg fu yong with rice 210
fragrant steamed rice in lotus
leaves 206
fried rice & prawns (shrimp) 216

fried rice with pork,
tomatoes, peas &
mushrooms 219
fried rice with prawns
(shrimp) 212
green fried rice with
spinach 207
honeyed rice puddings 246
lamb & rice soup 78
plain rice 16
rice with crab & mussels 218
special fried rice 211
special fried rice with cashew
nuts 215
special fried rice with prawns
(shrimp) 213
sweet rice 245
vegetable fried rice 205
rice noodles see noodles
rice paper parcels 29
rice vinegar 13
hot & sour soup 57
sweet & sour cucumber 47
rice wine 13, 19
roasting 15
roses, vegetable garnishes 17

S
salads 45-53
broccoli, (bell) pepper & almond
salad 53
Chinese chicken salad 108
Chinese hot salad 48
cucumber & beansprout salad 52
hot & sour duck salad 51
Oriental salad 49
sweet & sour cucumber 47
sweet & sour tofu (bean curd)
salad 46
salt & pepper sauce 17
sauces:
chilli & garlic 35
lemon 112
piquant dipping 22
salt & pepper 17
spring onion 17
sweet & sour 17, 161
Szechuan hot 87
scallions see spring onions
scallops:
scallops in ginger sauce 89
spiced scallops 90
sea bass:
fish with black bean sauce 83
seafood & fish 81-105
seafood & tofu (bean curd)
soup 66
seafood chow mein 228
seafood combination 93
see also crabmeat, prawns etc
seaweed, crispy 23
sesame oil 13
sesame seeds 13
peanut sesame chicken 114
sesame prawn (shrimp)
toasts 33
stir-fried lamb with sesame

seeds 137
shallots 13
Shantung cooking 10
shrimp (small):
shrimp dumpling soup 67
shrimp fu yong 97
see also prawns
Singapore-style rice noodles 231
sizzled chilli prawns (shrimp) 95
snapper:
steamed snapper with fruit &
ginger stuffing 88
snow peas see mangetout
sorbet, orange 250
soups 55-79
beef & vegetable noodle soup 62
chicken & sweetcorn (corn)
soup 75
chicken soup with almonds 77
Chinese cabbage soup 59
clear chicken & egg soup 76
crab & ginger soup 69
curried chicken & sweetcorn
(corn) soup 71
fish & vegetable soup 68
fish soup with wontons 65
hot & sour soup 57
lamb & rice soup 78
mixed vegetable soup 56
mushroom & cucumber noodle
soup 64
noodles in soup 63
Peking duck soup 74
pork & Szechuan vegetable
soup 79
prawn (shrimp) soup 72
seafood & tofu (bean curd)
soup 66
(small) shrimp dumpling
soup 67
spinach & tofu (bean curd)
soup 61
sweetcorn (corn) & crabmeat
soup 73
three-flavour soup 70
vegetarian hot & sour soup 58
wonton soup 60
Southern Chinese cooking 10
soy sauce 13
barbecue spare ribs 37
chicken chop suey 122
Chinese leaves (cabbage)
stir-fried in soy & honey 193
deep-fried pork with a soy
dipping sauce 151
honey & soy glazed duck 129
lamb meatballs in soy sauce 134
spicy spare ribs 38
spare ribs:
barbecue spare ribs 37
deep-fried spare ribs 34
spare ribs with chilli 150
spicy spare ribs 38
special fried rice 211
special fried rice with cashew
nuts 215
special fried rice with prawns
(shrimp) 213

spiced scallops 90
spicy aubergines (eggplants) 185
spicy beef & broccoli stir-fry 143
spicy mushrooms 187
spicy peanut chicken 117
spicy spare ribs 38
spinach:
bamboo shoots with green
vegetables 166
garlic spinach 199
green fried rice with
spinach 207
noodles in soup 63
spinach & tofu (bean curd)
soup 61
spinach meatballs 24
spinach with straw
mushrooms 200
steamed snapper with fruit &
ginger stuffing 88
stir-fried greens 175
wonton soup 60
spirits 19
spring (collard) greens:
crispy seaweed 23
spring onions (scallions) 13
chicken with celery & cashew
nuts 125
Chinese fried rice 204
lamb & ginger stir-fry 136
pork dim sum 36
pot sticker dumplings 40
prawn (shrimp) stir-fry with
lemon grass 96
rice paper parcels 29
sizzled chilli prawns (shrimp) 95
spring onion sauce 17
spring roll skins 13
pork pancake rolls 26
spring rolls 25
squid:
fried squid flowers 104
seafood combination 93
squid in oyster sauce &
vegetables 103
steamed cabbage rolls 28
steamed duck buns 41
steamed snapper with fruit &
ginger stuffing 88
steamed vegetable cabbage
rolls 189
steamers 14
steaming 15
stir-fried beansprouts 169
stir-fried cucumber with ginger &
chilli 168
stir-fried duck with broccoli &
(bell) peppers 126
stir-fried greens 175
stir-fried lamb with sesame
seeds 137
stir-fried mixed vegetables 163
stir-fried mushrooms, cucumber &
smoked tofu (bean curd) 181
stir-fried pork with vegetables 155
stir-fried prawns (shrimp) 92
stir-fried prawns (shrimp) &
vegetables 91

stir-fried seasonal vegetables *171*
stir-frying *15*
stock, Chinese *16*
strainers *14*
straw mushrooms, spinach
    with *200*
sweet & sour cucumber *47*
sweet & sour pork *149*
sweet & sour prawns (shrimp) *100*
sweet & sour prawns (shrimp) with
    chilli *98*
sweet & sour sauce *17*
    lentil balls with sweet & sour
        sauce *194*
sweet & sour tofu (bean curd) salad
    46
sweet & sour tofu (bean curd) with
    vegetables *178*
sweet & sour vegetables *161*
sweet fruit wontons *242*
sweet rice *245*
sweetcorn (corn):
    chicken & sweetcorn soup *75*
    curried chicken & sweetcorn
        soup *71*
    money bags *188*
    sweetcorn & crabmeat soup *73*
    see also corn cobs
Szechuan chilli chicken *121*
Szechuan cooking *10*
Szechuan hot sauce *87*
Szechuan peppercorns *13*
    salt & pepper sauce *17*
Szechuan prawns (shrimp) *94*
Szechuan preserved vegetable *13*
    pork & Szechuan vegetable
        soup *79*

T

tarts, Chinese custard *249*
tea *18*
techniques *15*
three-flavour soup *70*
toasts, sesame prawn (shrimp) *33*
tofu (bean curd) *13*
    braised pork & tofu *156*
    braised vegetables with tofu *183*
    deep-fried tofu with Chinese five
        spice *182*
    hot & sour soup *57*
    Ma-Po tofu *176*
    seafood & tofu soup *66*
    spinach & tofu soup *61*
    stir-fried mushrooms, cucumber
        & smoked tofu *181*
    sweet & sour tofu salad *46*
    sweet & sour tofu with
        vegetables *178*
    tofu & vegetables with black
        bean sauce *177*
    vegetable & tofu casserole *179*
    vegetable stir-fry with tofu *180*
    vegetarian hot & sour soup *58*
tomatoes:
    fried noodles with mushrooms
        & pork *238*
    fried rice with pork, tomatoes,

peas & mushrooms *219*
red spiced beef *153*
roses *17*
transparent (cellophane) noodles
    with prawns (shrimp) *227*
transparent (cellophane) noodles
    with yellow bean sauce *225*
tree ears *see* wood ears
trout with pineapple *82*

V

vegetables *159-201*
    beef & vegetable noodle soup *62*
    braised fish fillets *85*
    braised vegetables with tofu
        (bean curd) *183*
    chicken with cashew nuts &
        vegetables *111*
    Chinese braised vegetables *167*
    fish & vegetable soup *68*
    fried vegetable noodles *223*
    homemade noodles with
        stir-fried vegetables *226*
    mixed pickled vegetables *50*
    mixed vegetable chow mein *224*
    mixed vegetable soup *56*
    oyster sauce beef *141*
    special fried rice with cashew
        nuts *215*
    spring rolls *25*
    steamed vegetable cabbage
        rolls *189*
    stir-fried mixed vegetables *163*
    stir-fried pork with
        vegetables *155*
    stir-fried prawns (shrimp) &
        vegetables *91*
    stir-fried seasonal vegetables *171*
    sweet & sour tofu (bean curd)
        with vegetables *178*
    sweet & sour vegetables *161*
    tofu (bean curd) & vegetables
        with black bean sauce *177*
    vegetable & nut stir-fry *173*
    vegetable & tofu (bean curd)
        casserole *179*
    vegetable casserole *162*
    vegetable chop suey *160*
    vegetable fried rice *205*
    vegetable stir-fry with tofu
        (bean curd) *180*
    vegetables in black bean
        sauce *172*
    see also Szechuan preserved
        vegetable; salads *and*
            individual vegetables
vegetarian hot & sour soup *58*
vermicelli:
    Oriental salad *49*
vinegar *see* rice vinegar;
    wine vinegar

W

water chestnuts *13*
    fried rice with prawns
        (shrimp) *212*

hot & sour duck salad *51*
    sweet & sour prawns (shrimp)
        with chilli *98*
Western Chinese cooking *10*
wine *19*
wine vinegar:
    vegetarian hot & sour soup *58*
woks *14*
wonton wrappers *13*
    Chinese ravioli *30*
    crispy wontons with piquant
        dipping sauce *22*
    fish soup with wontons *65*
    sweet fruit wontons *242*
    wonton soup *60*
wood (cloud) ears *13*
    fish-flavoured shredded
        pork *152*

Y

yellow bean sauce:
    chicken with celery & cashew
        nuts *125*
    chicken with yellow bean
        sauce *113*
    Szechuan chilli chicken *121*
    transparent (cellophane) noodles
        with yellow bean sauce *225*
Yunnan cooking *10*

Z

zucchini *see* courgettes